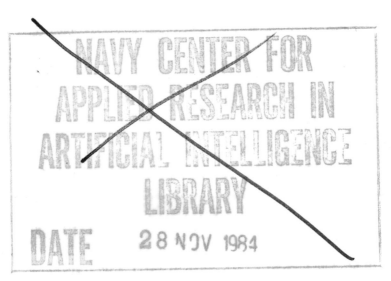

The AI Business

The AI Business

The Commercial Uses of Artificial Intelligence

edited by

Patrick H. Winston

Karen A. Prendergast

The MIT Press

Cambridge, Massachusetts

London, England

The fonts in this book are Almost Computer Modern, set using Donald E. Knuth's TEX, with help from Daniel C. Brotsky.

Library of Congress Cataloging in Publication Data
Main entry under title:
The AI business.
  Bibliography: p.
  Includes index.
    1. Artificial intelligence—Congresses. 2. Robots, Industrial—Congresses. 3. Expert systems (Computer science)—Congresses. I. Winston, Patrick Henry. II. Prendergast, Karen A. III. Title: A.I. business
Q334.A45 1984   338.4'700153'5   83-25572
ISBN 0-262-23117-4

Contents

Preface

Some people believe Artificial Intelligence is the most exciting scientific and commercial enterprise of the century. Others raise distress flags, fearing eventual misuse. Still others scoff, arguing that the technology will come to nothing. One thing is clear, however: Artificial Intelligence generates passion, and passion stimulates hyperbole-riddled rhetoric, and that rhetoric dangerously obfuscates. It is hard to tell if the field's promoters are pied pipers leading us to the disappointment of excessive expectations or missionaries beckoning us to almost inconceivable opportunity.

Wishing to clear the air, Howard Austin, the field's Wall Street ambassador, proposed an unusual colloquium. His idea was that MIT's Industrial Liaison Program would work with F. Eberstadt & Company, a prominent investment banking firm, to bring together four groups of people: one group to supply the academic perspective, another group to represent the hard core, financially oriented people, a third to represent the industrial research and development people who can look at the questions from both sides, and a fourth to represent solutions-oriented people, who use Artificial Intelligence, sometimes without admitting it, because there is a job to be done.

Everyone agreed that the proposed mix of views made sense. Dr. Austin, J. Peter Bartl and Constance A. Marino of MIT's Industrial Liaison Program, Loretta Kulak and Philip K. Meyer of F. Eberstadt & Company, and Karen A. Prendergast of MIT's Artificial Intelligence Laboratory proceeded to make the Colloquium happen.

The result was a spectacular success. The colloquium attracted twice as many attendees as the previous record-holding colloquium hosted by the Industrial Liaison Program (on genetic engineering). More important, however, the colloquium exposed exciting views, together with heated differences of opinion. Frank P. Satlow of the MIT Press realized that both the views and the opinions should be recorded and made widely available. This book, consisting of edited transcripts of the colloquium talks, is the result.

The illustrations were done by Elizabeth B. Heepe. Daniel C. Brotsky, Priscilla M. Cobb, Boris Katz, Dikran Karagueuzian, Helen I. Osborne, and Carol A. Roberts also helped enormously in the development of the book.

P. H. W.
K. A. P.

The AI Business

1
Perspective

Patrick H. Winston
Professor of Computer Science
Director, Artificial Intelligence Laboratory
Massachusetts Institute of Technology

Professor Winston is involved in the study of learning by analogy, commonsense problem solving, expert systems, and robotics. He received the B.S., M.S., and Ph.D. from the Massachusetts Institute of Technology.

The primary goal of Artificial Intelligence is to make machines smarter. The secondary goals of Artificial Intelligence are to understand what intelligence is (the Nobel laureate purpose) and to make machines more useful (the entrepreneurial purpose). Defining intelligence usually takes a semester-long struggle, and even after that I am not sure we ever get a definition really nailed down. But operationally speaking, we want to make machines smart.

The typical big-league, artificial-intelligence laboratory, and there are many of them now, will be involved in work like that shown in figure 1. We at the MIT Artificial Intelligence Laboratory work in robotics, a field spanning manipulation, reasoning, and sensing. We do research in learning, language, and what some people call expert systems, something that I often prefer to call design and analysis systems, by virtue of the common misuse of the term *expert systems*. We are also involved in issues basic to Computer Science, such as programming and computer architecture.

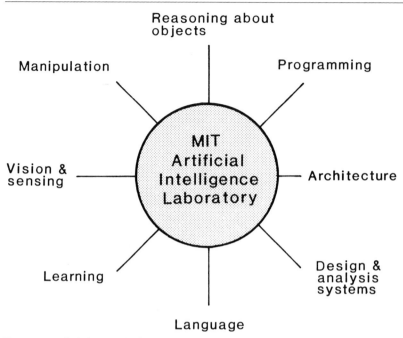

Figure 1. Subfields of Artificial Intelligence.

The Past: Six Ages

The history of Artificial Intelligence can be divided into a variety of ages, as shown in figure 2. First is the prehistoric time, starting in 1842 when Charles Babbage first tinkered with his machines. Lady Lovelace, for whom the ADA programming language is named, was Babbage's main sponsor. She was besieged by the press, wondering if Babbage's machines would ever be as smart as people. At that time, she intelligently denied it would ever be possible. After all, if you have to wait for a hundred years or so for it to happen, it is best not to get involved.

The prehistoric times extended to about 1960 because the people who wanted to work on the computational approach to understanding intelligence had no computers. Still, people like Claude Shannon and John von Neumann made many speculations.

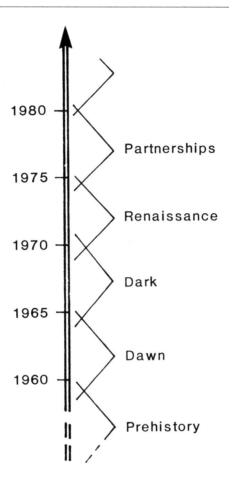

Figure 2. Ages of Artificial Intelligence.

Around 1960 we start to speak of the Dawn Age, a period in which some said, "In ten years, they will be as smart as we are." That turned out to be a hopelessly romantic prediction. It was romantic for interesting reasons, however. If we look carefully at the early predictions about Artificial Intelligence, we discover that the people making the predictions were not lunatics but conscientious scientists talking about real possibilities. They were simply trying to fulfill their public duty to prepare people for something that seemed quite plausible at the time.

The Dawn Age was sparked by certain successes. A program for solving geometric analogy problems like those that appear on intelligence tests was developed. Another was a program that did symbolic integration, spawning today's MACSYMA and other mathematics manipulation systems. These two examples, integration and analogy, are particularly worth noting because they introduced ideas that have become extraordinarily popular in the creation of expert systems. Retrospectively, the analogy program was based on the paradigm of describe-and-match, and the integration program was based on the paradigm of if-then rules.

I call the next period the Dark Age because little happened. There was a dry spell because the tremendous enthusiasm generated by the Dawn Age made everyone think that the enterprise of creating intelligent computers would be too simple. Everyone searched for a kind of philosopher's stone, a mechanism that when placed in a computer would require only data to become truly intelligent. The Dark Age was largely fueled by overexpectation.

Then we had a Renaissance. During this Renaissance Artificial Intelligence began to make systems that caught people's eyes. Elsewhere in this book Randall Davis describes MYCIN and other systems developed during this period. Such systems are the harbingers of today's excitement.

The Renaissance was followed by the Age of Partnerships, a period when researchers in Artificial Intelligence began to admit that there were other researchers, particularly linguists and psychologists, with whom people working in Artificial Intelligence can form important liaisons.

I like to call our present age the Age of the Entrepreneur.

If there were substantial ideas about how to do impressive things as early as 1960, why have we waited until 1983 to have a conference about how Artificial Intelligence might be commercialized?

The Successes

Let us agree that something has to be well known and in daily use to be successful. By this definition, there are only a handful of successful systems clearly containing artificial-intelligence technology.

One of the most conspicuous successes is the XCON system (also known as R1) developed by Digital Equipment Corporation and Carnegie-Mellon University for doing computer configuration. Others are DENDRAL and PUFF, products of Stanford University, developed for analyzing mass spectrograms and for dealing with certain lung problems. Still others include General Motors's CONSIGHT system and Automatix's AUTOVISION[R] II, both of which endow increasingly intelligent robots with a limited but important ability to see.

Other successes are less domain specific. One, a product of Artificial Intelligence Corporation, is INTELLECT, a natural language interface system. Another is MACSYMA, a giant system for symbolic mathematics developed at the Massachusetts Institute of Technology and marketed by Symbolics, Incorporated.

As I recently went over this list of successes with some friends, one pointed out that I had left out some of the most dramatic developments of Artificial Intelligence. One is the LISP programming language, a serious by-product of Artificial Intelligence. It is not surprising that the first major spinoffs of the MIT Artificial Intelligence Laboratory have been two LISP Machine companies, Symbolics, Incorporated and LISP Machine, Incorporated. If we go even further back, there are those who would argue that time-sharing was a major development that came out of Artificial Intelligence. Time-sharing is not Artificial Intelligence, but Artificial Intelligence demanded it.

Part I: Expert Systems

Human experts specialize in relatively narrow problem-solving tasks. Typically, but not always, human experts have characteristics such as the following: Human experts solve simple problems easily. They explain what they do. They judge the reliability of their own conclusions. They know when they are stumped. They communicate smoothly with other experts. They learn from experience. They change their points of view to suit a problem. They transfer knowledge from one domain to another. They reason on many levels, using tools such as rules of thumb, mathematical models, and detailed simulations.

An expert system is a computer program that behaves like a human expert in some useful ways. Today's state of the art is such that expert systems solve simple problems easily, occasionally explain their work, and say something about reliability.

Some expert systems do synthesis. XCON configures computers, for example. Other rule-based expert systems do analysis. MYCIN diagnoses infectious diseases, and the DIPMETER ADVISOR interprets oil well logs.

Currently, there are a dozen or two serious expert systems whose authors have commercial aspirations. By dropping the qualifier *serious*, the number grows to a few thousand. The reason is that creating a simple, illustrative expert system is now a classroom exercise in advanced artificial-intelligence subjects. Soon expert systems will be created in elementary courses in computing at the early undergraduate level.

All of this activity has attracted top-management interest, aroused the entrepreneurial spirit, and stimulated investor curiosity. Are the interest, the spirit, and the curiosity misadvised? It is too soon to be sure since few projects have had time to succeed and none has had time to fail.

Nevertheless there are some questions that can be answered, or at least debated. The contributors to this book address this list:

- Can today's technology revolutionize whole industries, or can it just deal with isolated, albeit important, targets of opportunity?
- Where are the most susceptible problems: engineering design, equipment maintenance, medicine, oil, finance?
- What are the obstacles to introducing expert systems: finding the right people, working with the existing human experts, getting snared by technically exciting but off-the-mark ideas?
- How hard will it be to build systems that exhibit more of the talents of real human experts?

Part II: Work and Play

A work station is a computer system that can be an exciting, productive partner in work or play. To be a good work station, a computer system must offer many features. First, we must be able to talk to the computer system in our own language. For some systems the language must be English or another natural language; for other systems the language must be that of transistors and gates, or procedures and algorithms, or notes and scales. Second, we must be able to work with the computer system the way we want to, not necessarily the way dogma dictates. In engineering design, for example, some people work bottom up; others prefer to work top down; still others work middle out or back and forth. All should be accommodated. Third, the computer system must constitute a total environment. Everything we need should be smoothly accessible through the system, including all the necessary computational tools, historical records, and system documentation. And fourth, the computer-systems hardware must be muscular and the graphics excellent.

Some existing work station products, like Daisy Systems Corporation's LOGICIAN and GATE MASTER, are extraordinarily important in the design of extremely complicated integrated circuits, often containing tens of thousands of transistors. Another work-station-oriented product, Artificial Intelligence Corporation's INTELLECT, is not so domain oriented. INTELLECT is designed to be a powerful interface between decision makers and whatever data bases they need to work with. While INTELLECT began as a natural language interface, it is becoming the hub of a multitool, multifile information system, with much of the power residing in the parts having no direct concern with English input and output.

Daisy Systems Corporation and Artificial Intelligence Corporation may be merely among the first flow of a potential cornucopia. People are developing work stations for such diverse activities as tax planning, chemical synthesis, robot assembly, musical composition, expository writing, and entertainment.

Where are the likely early successes? The contributors to this book, all experienced in creating sophisticated work stations or work station components, share their views with us in addressing questions like the following:

- How important is natural language interaction? What does it take to get natural language interaction?

- What constitutes a minimally muscular computer and minimally excellent graphics?

- How important is it for work station modules to be able to explain what they do? How important is it for users to be able to intervene whenever they want?

- Who can design and build work stations with human-like intelligence? A dozen people? Any computer engineer willing to learn?

Part III: Robotics

An intelligent robot is a system that flexibly connects perception to action. Humans are examples of intelligent robots for the following reasons. First, we can see and feel forces. Consequently we can cope with uncertain positions and changing environments. Second, we have graceful arms capable of fast, accurate motion, together with fantastic hands capable of grasping all sorts of objects. Third, we think about what we do. We note and avoid unexpected obstacles. We select tools, design jigs, and place sensors. We plan how to fit things together, succeeding even when the geometries are awkward and the fits tight. We recover from errors and accidents.

In contrast, most of today's industrial robots are clumsy and stupid. For the most part they cannot see, feel, move gracefully or grasp flexibly, and they cannot think at all. Most of today's industrial robots move repetitively through boring sequences, gripping, welding, or spraying paint at predetermined times, almost completely uninformed by what is going on in the factory. Of course practical robots need not necessarily resemble people. After all, they are built of different, often superior materials, and they need not perform such a wide range of tasks. Nevertheless many industrialists believe there are many tasks that defy automation with anything short of sensing, reasoning, dextrous, closed-loop robots, with human-like abilities if not human-like appearance.

Consequently an increasing number of major corporations are making bold moves. For a while the general pace was slow in the robot-using industries, and outside of Japan there was little rush to accept and exploit the technology produced by Artificial Intelligence. Now the picture is changing. Small companies like Automatix are growing rapidly by supplying industry with turnkey products in which vision is a productivity-multiplying component. Large companies like IBM are established supplicrs with intensive development

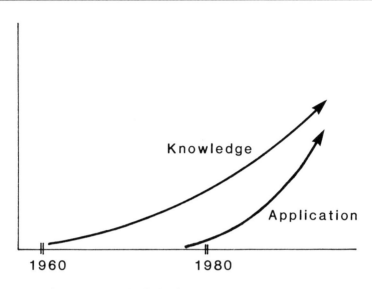

Figure 3. Stiction model of the future.

efforts underway. Where will this new wave of automation go? How far? How fast? While there is little agreement among the contributors to this book, questions like these are addressed:

- Why is it relatively easy to build humanless parts-fabrication factories and relatively hard to build humanless device-assembly factories?

- What are the industrial tasks that require human-like sensing, reasoning, and dexterity? Is it better to eliminate those tasks by redesigning factories from scratch?

- What can be done by exploiting special lighting arrangements? How far have we gone with the simple vision systems that count each visual point as totally black or totally white, with no shades of gray?

- Is the robot itself important? Can we improve productivity with robots alone, or must we think instead about improving whole manufacturing systems?

Part IV: Today and Tomorrow

Finally there is the question of money. Are the venture capitalists ready for Artificial Intelligence? If so, how long will their readiness last? Is current interest just a passing fad?

Will the commercialization of Artificial Intelligence be driven by need-pull or technology-push? Is Artificial Intelligence becoming commercialized because there are problems that desperately need new solutions, or is it because there is neglected technology lying around waiting for eager entrepreneurs to make use of it? What sort of progress will there be?

One theory of progress is a kind of mechanical-engineering model, a stiction model, as shown in figure 3. During the stiction period, the gap between the work in the university research laboratories and the first signs of life in the marketplace constantly grows. Once you get through this stiction period, you move into the period of friction, where the time delay grows smaller, and commercialization marches together with basic research at a steady rate. There are other models of progress. The balloon theory, shown in figure 4, is one I sometimes believe in when I read the advertising of some of the artificial-intelligence companies. I have a fear that this field has been hyped beyond all belief, and there is a serious danger that it might be oversold.

Figure 5 shows the staircase model of progress. In this model the relationship between the amount of accumulated knowledge and the application of that knowledge is not a linear phenomenon. Knowledge has to accumulate for a long time before there is a sudden burst of entrepreneurial activity that exploits all of the accumulated knowledge. This model says that accumulated knowledge can go only so far and that more knowledge has to accumulate over a period of years before there is another leap forward on the applications curve.

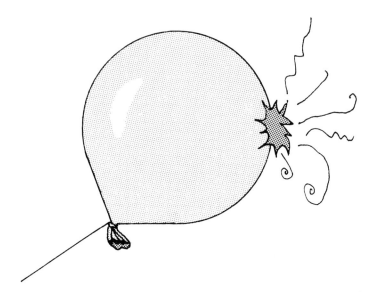

Figure 4. Balloon model.

Application

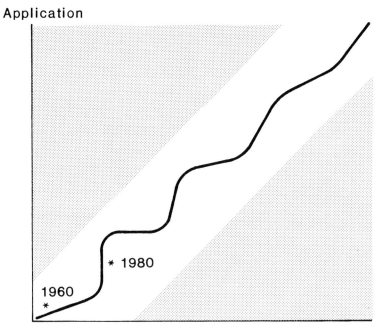

* 1980

1960
*

Knowledge

Figure 5. Staircase model.

We must ask, Which is the correct model for how Artificial Intelligence will develop? At this point, are we merely skimming off the easy problems? Are we repeating in the commercial world what happened in the early days of Artificial Intelligence? If this is a correct model, then we must worry about a Dark Age for the applications of Artificial Intelligence, just as we had one in the basic research area. I do not think there will be a new Dark Age. Too much is happening, as the contributors to this book demonstrate. I believe that the correct attitude about Artificial Intelligence is one of restrained exuberance. In the chapters that follow it is clear that there are hard-core dissenters on both sides of my position.

For More Information

Feigenbaum, Edward A., and Pamela McCorduck, *The Fifth Generation*, Addison-Wesley, Reading, MA, 1983.

Winston, Patrick Henry, *Artificial Intelligence, Second Edition*, Addison-Wesley, Reading, MA, 1984.

Part I

Expert Systems

2
Amplifying Expertise
with Expert Systems

Randall Davis
Associate Professor of Computer Science
Artificial Intelligence Laboratory
Massachusetts Institute of Technology

While he was at Stanford University, Professor Davis was an early contributor to the MYCIN project and developed TEIRESIAS, a tool for knowledge acquisition. His current research focuses on systems that work from descriptions of structure and function and that are capable of reasoning from first principles to support a wider range of robust problem-solving performance. Professor Davis serves on the editorial board of Artificial Intelligence *and is the coauthor of* Knowledge-Based Systems in Artificial Intelligence. *He is a consultant to several major organizations in the area of Artificial Intelligence and expert systems, and he is a founding consultant of Teknowledge and Applied Expert Systems. He received the BA from Dartmouth College and the PhD in Artificial Intelligence from Stanford University.*

Work on expert systems has received extensive attention recently, prompting growing interest in a range of environments. Much has been made of the basic concept and of the rule-based system approach typically used to construct the programs. My purpose is to review what we know, assess the current prospects, and suggest directions appropriate for basic research.

To build expert systems is to attempt to capture rare or important expertise and embody it in computer programs. It is done by talking to the people who have that expertise. In one sense building expert systems is a form of intellectual cloning. Expert-system builders, the knowledge engineers, find out from experts what they know and how they use their knowledge to solve problems. Once this debriefing is done, the expert-system builders incorporate the knowledge and expertise in computer programs, making the knowledge and expertise easily replicated, readily distributed, and essentially immortal.

The potential of expert systems is exciting and significant. But building expert systems is an art, and the artists are few and far between. To be sure, some kinds of expert systems are turned out as classroom exercises, but like all other classroom exercises, there is a long distance between an exercise and a commercial product. Turning out commercial products is currently a significant undertaking.

Evolution of Expert Systems

Our perception of expert systems today is analogous to our perception of computers fifteen years ago. Back then the data-processing prima donnas in the back room were the only people who claimed to understand the new beast with all the blinking lights. Not many other people used computers. Now personal computers are as common as typewriters and soon will be no more mysterious than telephones.

Expert systems will follow the same evolutionary path. There will be a new set of prima donnas in the back room— the knowledge engineers. The technology will be remote, inaccessible, and awkward to work with at first. Eventually the tools will improve, the technology will become accessible, and personal expert systems are likely to be commonplace in the corporate environment and in society at large.

Searching for the Philosopher's Stone

Expert systems is an area of Artificial Intelligence characterized by an intense focus on knowledge. The stores of
knowledge in expert systems must be large because experience shows that a lot of knowledge is needed to solve
interesting problems. The knowledge must be task specific
because experience also shows that we need to know specific
things about particular problems in order to solve them.
There seems to be no philosopher's stone, no single clever
trick that will solve problems for us across all problem
domains.

In the early 1960s workers in the field thought if they
could find one or two powerful ideas, they would be able to
solve the problem of Artificial Intelligence. Since generality
seemed to be a key aspect of human intelligence, research
on generality followed. We tried to find one or two very
powerful methods that would provide human-like generality.

The approach, unfortunately, did not produce the progress
we expected. Although a person can do something with
almost every problem, he will do terribly on almost every
problem, except the ones he truly understands. A person
who is not familiar with a problem can get somewhere but
not very far. In fact people solve problems well only when
they know a great deal about the problem domain.

Expertise is knowing what to do. That means that our
programs will have to know what they are doing. (This
sounds obvious today, but it was an insight that took a
substantial effort to establish firmly.) Expertise includes a
constellation of behaviors (figure 1). Problem solving is the
most obvious and though necessary, it is insufficient. Would
we be willing to call someone an expert if he could solve
a problem but was unable to explain the result, unable
to learn anything new about the domain, and unable to
determine whether his expertise was relevant? I think not.

☐ **Solve the problem**

☐ **Explain the result**

☐ **Learn**

☐ **Restructure knowledge**

☐ **Break rules**

☐ **Determine relevance**

☐ **Degrade gracefully**

Figure 1. Nature of expertise.

Work in expert systems to date has explored only the first three of these behaviors in any depth. First-generation systems like DENDRAL and MACSYMA focused solely on performance. Second-generation systems began to explore explanation (MYCIN and DIGITALIS ADVISOR) and knowledge acquisition (TEIRESIAS). Of these behaviors performance is still the best understood. Our efforts at explanation and knowledge acquisition have only scratched the surface.

By and large, other topics have been almost totally unexplored. What would it mean, for example, to restructure knowledge? One example comes out of the so-called procedural versus declarative controversy. We as experts on knowledge representation went to work structuring and restructuring knowledge so that procedural became declarative, got turned back into procedural again, and so forth. I think it became clear after we went around that loop a couple of times that the problem is at least in part in the eye of the interpreter, but nevertheless, there we were, restructuring and reorganizing knowledge.

What about breaking rules? One of the most frustrating things for an apprentice to learn is that there are almost as many exceptions as there are rules. Experts clearly understand the spirit as well as the letter of the rule. Experts also know when a problem is outside their spheres of expertise and when to suggest asking someone else for an answer. Clearly none of the present expert systems can do this yet. Experts also degrade gracefully; that is, as they get close to the boundaries of their knowledge, they become less proficient at solving problems. Their skill decreases smoothly rather than precipitously as do most of today's programs.

Development of a Field

The first stage of development of any field is traditionally case studies. Ideally we test one single dimension of a design—one idea on knowledge representation, or control, or system architecture. Each of these is, in effect, an isolated point in the design space.

As the set of such experiments grows, a collection of architectural principles may emerge. By examining many case studies, we may begin to understand the shape and character of the design space. This allows us to make empirical observations about which parts of the space make sense for which kinds of problems. Note that these are simply empirical observations—we do not really understand why they hold; we can only say that, with our experience, this design looks like the right one to use.

Eventually we get to something worthy of being labeled a science. For our purposes that stage is characterized by an understanding that goes beyond a set of empirical observations. There is instead an understanding of why a particular design is appropriate for a particular task and perhaps a much better understanding of the character and shape of the design space.

Work on expert systems is currently somewhere between the stage of case studies and the stage of architectural principles. As is traditional for fields at that stage of development and as is particularly appropriate for expert systems, the existing knowledge is well captured as a collection of informal rules of thumb.

Observations about Building Expert Systems

We can make several general observations about the art of building expert systems:

- In the knowledge lies the power.
- The knowledge is often inexact and incomplete.
- The knowledge is often ill specified.
- Amateurs become experts incrementally.
- Expert systems need to be flexible.
- Expert systems need to be transparent.

The most fundamental observation—that in the knowledge lies the power—suggests that problem-solving performance often arises from extensive stores of knowledge about the task, not from a large collection of domain-independent methods.

The knowledge is inexact and incomplete because the kinds of problems attacked in Artificial Intelligence rarely have complete laws or theories. Artificial Intelligence often deals with inexact and informal knowledge. The knowledge is often ill specified because experts cannot always express exactly what it is they know about their domains. As a result knowledge explication becomes an important task. Builders of expert systems need to help the experts make precise what it is they know and how they apply it to the problem at hand.

People and programs become experts incrementally. One direct consequence is the importance of flexibility and transparency. Our systems will spend most of their lives being changed, updated, and improved. If it is too difficult to change them, the whole process will come to a halt.

Transparency is similarly motivated. To improve the system, we have to know what it did in order to determine what it is we ought to change. Programs must be able to explain why they do what they do. If the system is a black box, it becomes impossible to make that determination, and system evolution will cease.

□ **Separate the inference engine and knowledge base**

□ **Use as uniform a representation as possible**

□ **Keep the inference engine simple**

□ **Exploit redundancy**

Figure 2. Some architectural principles.

Architectural Principles

Some architectural principles have also begun to emerge (figure 2). One suggestion is to separate knowledge of how to use rules from the rules themselves, dividing the expert system into an inference engine and a knowledge base. In this way, the knowledge in the knowledge base becomes more easily identified, more explicit, and more accessible. If the two are intermixed, domain knowledge will get spread out through the inference engine, and it becomes less clear what we ought to change to improve the system. The result is a less flexible system.

A second architectural principle is uniformity of representation. This cuts down the number of mechanisms required, keeping system design simpler and more transparent. Each time a new representation is added to the system, something else in the system has to be able to handle it, has to know its syntax or semantics to be able to use it. Hence fewer representations mean a simpler, more transparent system.

Keeping the inference engine simple helps in several ways. Since explanations are generated by replaying the actions of the system, keeping those actions simple means that little work is necessary to produce comprehensible explanations. Knowledge acquisition is similarly easier. When the inference engine is less complicated, less work

☐ **Narrow domain of expertise**

☐ **Fragile behavior at the boundaries**

☐ **Limited knowledge representation language**

☐ **Limited input/output**

☐ **Limited explanation**

☐ **One expert as knowledge base "czar"**

Figure 3. State of the art of expert systems.

is needed to determine exactly what knowledge to add to improve system performance.

A fourth principle—exploiting redundancy—is illustrated by work on HEARSAY that showed how redundancy can be a remedy for incomplete and inexact knowledge. The trick is to find multiple overlapping sources of knowledge with different areas of strength and different shortcomings. Properly used, the entire collection of knowledge sources can be a good deal more robust than any one of them taken alone.

State of the Art

Figure 3 characterizes the current state of the art. Because expert systems deal with very narrow domains of expertise, we have to constrain sharply what it is we hope to achieve with them. As we get closer to the boundaries, their behavior becomes fragile and, rather than degrading gracefully, tends to fall apart precipitously.

Since the effort in building these systems lies in accumulating large knowledge bases, the knowledge representation typically used is one of the simpler ones, like attribute-object-value triples, production rules, and so forth. And since the natural language problem has yet to be solved, we are stuck with limited interaction languages, usually keyword-based parsing of input and template-generated production of text on the output.

Our model of explanation is useful but limited at the moment to recapitulation of the system's actions. In many cases, however, explaining the system's behavior is sufficiently informative.

Finally, we do not yet know very much about dealing with multiple experts. How do you reconcile differing and perhaps conflicting views among acknowledged experts? At the moment we do not know, so we appoint one expert knowledge-base czar and attempt to build the system in that person's image.

Calibrating the Technology

Now that Artificial Intelligence has become a focus of strong attention, there is concern about the growing collaboration between industry and people doing basic artificial-intelligence research. There are issues of manpower spread thin over a wide range of sites and concern about manpower available to train the next generation. Equally important are the expectations industry has about what Artificial Intelligence and expert systems can accomplish and how quickly the promise can be fulfilled. It is important to calibrate the distance between research results and commercial products. Figure 4 shows the time required to create various expert systems, as of 1981.

The systems shown in figure 4 vary enormously with respect to the scale of the problems they attempt to solve. For example, MACSYMA is probably two orders of magnitude larger than PUFF. Others differ greatly in the amount of knowledge they need and in the amount of effort required to build the knowledge base. The systems also vary with respect to the level of performance achieved. Some of these systems solve real-world problems routinely, and others are research vehicles that never made it past the laboratory stage.

Man–years

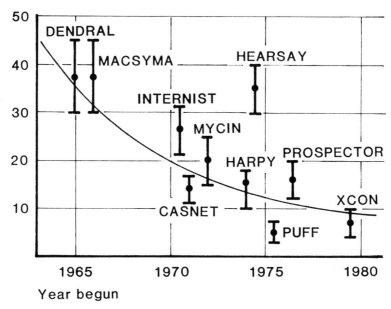

Year begun

Figure 4. Time required to create various expert systems.

One clear point emerges: developing a substantial expert system with real performance takes at least five man-years of effort, assuming the team already has some background in artificial-intelligence problem-solving techniques. If the team is starting from scratch with this technology, then developing a high-performance expert system can take considerably longer.

The graph also shows a decrease in the time required to build a system. One reason for the decrease is history: the older programs started first. All other things being equal, the younger programs would have accumulated fewer man-years. But this would predict only a linear reduction. A second, more interesting reason is the accumulation of ideas, code, and experience over the past fifteen years. The genealogy is as follows: DENDRAL begat MYCIN, which begat PUFF; HEARSAY provided an important foundation for HARPY and then profited by its experience. As a result we get a form of the iceberg phenomenon: a great deal of work goes into the first of these in each line of succession, and then the next can be built on that foundation.

The matching of tools to tasks is a third phenomenon that helps to account for the decrease in time required to build a system. The early attempts to solve problems in Chemistry with DENDRAL and in Mathematics with MACSYMA led to the development of new technologies for building expert systems. As the technology matured, a feeling developed for appropriate applications. In a sense the positions reversed: now the tools are helping us to choose appropriate tasks. The two become more closely matched—hence the shorter development time for more recent systems. The creation of knowledge base development tools has also accelerated the process of system construction.

Another way to gauge the state of the art is to look at the range of systems that have been developed. On a scale from a gleam in somebody's eye to wide commercial use, five systems have reached the stage of commercial use, as shown in figure 5. But a larger number of programs are somewhere between the stage of debugged program and experimental use.

Of the systems built to date, R1 has by far the most clearly defined development process, evolving through a sequence of stages similar to those listed here (figure 6). In its first formal evaluation the system was tested on approximately twenty cases. The results suggested that R1 would soon solve problems correctly 90 percent of the time. This was very encouraging and indicated that the program was ready to be distributed to its user community for more extended testing. But when it was placed in that setting, users criticized system performance 40 percent of the time.

Performance suddenly plummeted to the 60 percent level. What happened? Some of those problems were mistakes on the part of the users resulting from incorrect data or a

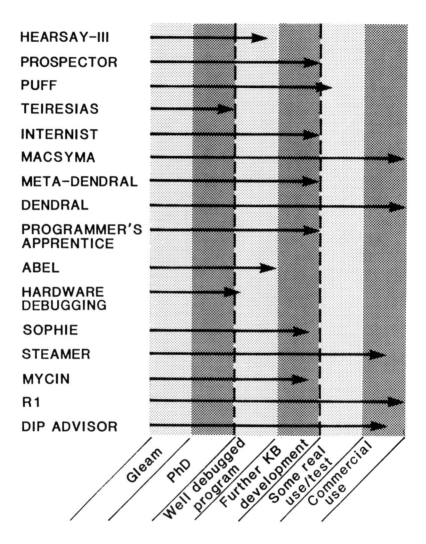

Figure 5. State of some well-known expert systems.

misunderstanding of program operation. But there was a
more basic lesson: research environments, no matter how
carefully tailored, are not identical to user environments.
They differ with respect to the problem mix, how familiar
users are with the program, and a range of other factors. As
a result evaluations in the research environment can be at

☐ **System design**

☐ **System development**

☐ **Formal evaluation of performance**

☐ **Formal evaluation of acceptance**

☐ **Extended use in prototype environment**

☐ **Development of maintenance plans**

☐ **System release**

Figure 6. Stages of development of an expert system.

---

best only rough approximations of the results expected when the program is placed in the user community. And many expert systems developed in the laboratories never reach the stage of formal evaluation in the research environment.

John McDermott, one of the developers of R1, has said that R1's knowledge base grew at least as much during the final stage of its development as it did in any of the previous stages of its development. It is important to understand that expert systems like this one are not built, polished, and then distributed. The process of developing an expert system is one of constant, incremental growth and improvement that will continue during the entire useful life of the system. It is a substantial investment of time and manpower.

MYCIN: A Case Study

MYCIN is an expert system developed at Stanford University in the early 1970s to do infectious disease diagnosis and therapy selection. Expert systems like MYCIN work because of what they know about the domain. The mechanism that uses knowledge can be trivial.

One of the problems of doing medical diagnosis is that there is not always enough information available about symptoms. Test results are not always available when the physician needs to make diagnostic decisions. Since some infectious diseases are life threatening, the physician must make a decision quickly. Another problem is that there are few hard and fast laws in Medicine. Much medical diagnosis is of a form of simple associations between symptoms and diseases. Being able to capture judgmental, inexact knowledge is an important part of how experts do their jobs.

The domain of medical diagnosis was chosen for three important reasons. First, the overuse and misuse of antibiotics are serious problems. Antibiotics are extremely powerful medicines with toxic side effects. Physicians must be careful when prescribing them individually and must be especially careful when prescribing them in combination. Two drugs together can have a much more toxic effect than either one has individually.

Second, there is the problem of the maldistribution of expertise. If you are in New York, or Chicago, or Los Angeles when you develop a rare disease, there are experts who can help because they have seen that disease before. But if you happen to be in a remote village, you may be out of luck. It is unlikely that someone in the remote village will have had the disease, and it is unlikely that the local physician will have seen a case similar to it. Experts in almost any field tend to congregate with the other experts, which often means they migrate toward urban areas.

Third, MYCIN works in a relatively small domain. The program does not have to know all of medicine to diagnose infectious disease. Such self-containment goes hand in hand with tractability. Proper problem solving is a key to building successful expert systems.

MYCIN in Action

Here is an example of MYCIN in operation. The program interviews the physician, asking questions about the patient and collecting information:

```
----------PATIENT-248----------
1)   Patient's name:  (first-last)
**   Dick H.
2)   Sex:
**   MALE
3)   Age:
**   52
4)   Have you been able to obtain positive microbiological
     information about a possible infection of Dick H.?
**   YES
-----------INFECTION-1---------
5)   What is the infection?
**   ENDARTERITIS
```

This style of interaction is similar to what goes on in hospitals. There are specialists on hospital staffs available for consultation whenever a less-specialized physician wants expert advice. MYCIN's authors designed the program to fit into the existing pattern of seeking and providing consultative help.

The interview continues:

```
The first significant organism from this blood culture
(CULTURE-1) will be referred to as:

----------ORGANISM-1----------

9)   Enter the identity of ORGANISM-1:
**   Unknown
10)  Is ORGANISM-1 a rod or coccus (etc.):
**   ROD
11)  The gram stain of ORGANISM-1:
**   GRAMNEG
12)  Have there been POSITIVE cultures yielding organisms
     about which you will NOT be seeking advice?
**   YES
```

Note that the physician can answer that he does not know or that the information is not available yet. The program will then do the best it can with the available information.

After between thirty and as many as eighty or ninety questions in a consultation, the physician sees a diagnosis similar to this:

```
INFECTION-1 is ENDARTERITIS with BACTEREMIA
<Item 1>   E. COLI [ORGANISM-1]
<Item 2>   SALMONELLA (species unknown)
                      [ORGANISM-1]
<Item 3>   KLEBSIELLA-PNEUMONIAE [ORGANISM-1]
<Item 4>   PSEUDOMONAS-AERUGINOSA [ORGANISM-1]
<Item 5>   ENTEROBACTER [ORGANISM-1]
<Item 6>   PROTEUS-NON-MIRABILIS [ORGANISM-1]
```

This case is ambiguous. Even with the best medical expertise available and all of the known facts, it is difficult to tell which of the six listed possibilities the patient has.

One approach to helping the patient is to give medicine for each problem: one pill for *E. coli*, another for salmonella, and so on. But if a physician gives a patient six different antibiotics, there is a good chance the patient will die. Consequently an important second phase of MYCIN does therapy selection, selecting one or two drugs to take care of all the problems.

MYCIN prints out these comments:

```
[Rec 1] My preferred therapy recommendation is as follows:
        In order to cover for Items <1 3 4 5 6>:
              Give:  GENTAMICIN
              Dose:  128 mg (1.7 mg/kg) q8h IV (or IM)
                     for 10 days
              Comments:  Modify dose in renal failure
        In order to cover for Item <2>
              Give:  CHLORAMPHENICOL
              Dose:  563 mg (7.5 mg/kg) q6h for 14 days
              Comments:  Monitor patient's white count

Do you wish to see the next choice therapy?
**   NO
```

In this case MYCIN recommended two medicines to treat all the possibilities.

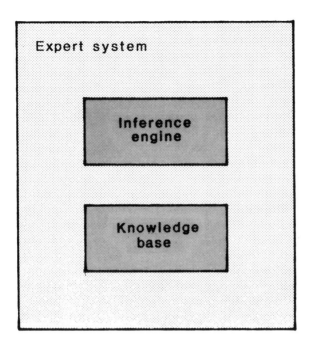

Figure 7. Structure of MYCIN.

MYCIN asks the physician if the conclusion is good enough. Clearly the machine has not taken over. It provides advice, but the physician remains responsible for making decisions about treatment. The physician can ask MYCIN to provide another recommendation.

One Inference Engine, 500 Rules

MYCIN's architecture is simple (figure 7). The knowledge base contains everything we know about infectious disease diagnosis and therapy. The inference engine does the computation, taking knowledge from the knowledge base and putting it to work.

It is important to think about the knowledge base and the inference engine separately. One of the things that distinguishes building expert systems from doing traditional programming is that this separation is maintained because we plan to keep the same inference engine even when a new domain requires a new knowledge base. By unplugging one collection of knowledge and plugging in another, we have a new consultation system for yet another problem, leveraging all of the work that goes into building the inference engine.

MYCIN's knowledge base contains between 400 and 500 rules, each of which looks like this:

```
Rule 27

If      1)  the gram stain of the organism is gram negative,
            and
        2)  the morphology of the organism is rod, and
        3)  the aerobicity of the organism is anaerobic,

Then        There is suggestive evidence (.7) that the
            identity of the organism is Bacteroides.
```

This is a simple if-then inferential rule. If we know that certain conditions have been met, then we can make a certain conclusion. Note also that the rules are inexact. This particular rule says that if three things are known, there is suggestive evidence, measuring 0.7 on a scale of 0 to 1 that the organism is a Bacteroides.

The rule is a comprehensible chunk of knowledge. To understand why this is good, think of extracting four lines of code from a random piece of software. There is little chance the four-line chunk would make sense by itself. But this one five-hundredth of the MYCIN knowledge is self-contained and understandable. In evaluating a potential application for MYCIN-like technology, it makes sense to ask if this kind of dicing is possible. Successful applications

require a domain that can be chopped into a few hundred
or a few thousand rule-sized chunks, which are separate,
distinct, and comprehensible by themselves.

Let us turn to the inference engine. We begin by asking for
the name of the organism bothering the patient. MYCIN's
inference engine reaches into the knowledge base to pull out
all the rules that make conclusions about identity. In fact,
there are many such rules, one of which is rule 27.

Rule 27 is relevant in this case only if each of its
preconditions has been met: if the gram stain of the organism
is gram negative, the shape is rod, and it is anaerobic. How
is it possible to find out if the gram stain is negative? By
starting all over again, retrieving all of the rules that have
anything to say about negative gram stain and trying each
in turn. This is known as backward chaining. The inference
engine starts with the thing it is trying to accomplish and
moves backward through the set of knowledge-base rules.
When it finally runs out of rules, it asks the physician a
question.

Answering How and Why Questions

Another feature of MYCIN-type expert systems is that
their behavior is transparent. A physician can ask why the
question the program asks is relevant. The response will be
something like this:

```
14)   Is the patient's illness with ORGANISM-1 a
      hospital-acquired infection?
**    Why
```

[Why is it important to determine whether the infection
with ORGANISM-1 was acquired while the patient was
hospitalized?]

```
[2.0]  This will aid in determining the identity of
       ORGANISM-1.
       It has already been established that
          [2.1]  the morphology of ORGANISM-1 is rod
          [2.2]  the gram stain of ORGANISM-1 is gramneg
          [2.3]  the aerobicity of ORGANISM-1 is facul

       Therefore, if
          [2.4]  the infection with ORGANISM-1 was
          acquired while the patient was hospitalized
       then
                    there is weakly suggestive evidence (.2)
                    that the identity of ORGANISM-1 is
                    pseudomonas [RULE050]
```

MYCIN was using rule 50 and already had certain information about the patient. If the physician adds this fact, then
MYCIN will know whether this rule will fire. If it does fire,
MYCIN will have more information about the topic that it
is dealing with.

In addition to interrupting a consultation, the physician
can wait until the end and ask MYCIN how it reached its
conclusion:

```
**HOW DID YOU DECIDE THAT ORGANISM-1 WAS AN E.COLI?
I used rule 084 to conclude that the identity of
        ORGANISM-1 is e.coli.  This gave a cumulative
        c.f. of (.51).
I used rule 003 to conclude that the identity of
        ORGANISM-1 is e.coli.  This gave a cumulative
        c.f. of (.43).
```

The explanation technology produces an audit trail, review-
ing its own logic. By keeping track of the rules that were
used, MYCIN can describe how it reached its conclusion.

MYCIN's power lies in its knowledge. In simple tests
MYCIN compared favorably with some of the experts in the
field, yet the inference engine is trivial. MYCIN achieves
its credible record because of the 500 rules stored in the
knowledge base. These rules were not found in a manual

of infectious disease diagnosis. They were extracted slowly from the experts. One reason it took five or six years to develop the MYCIN system was that the knowledge had never been expressed that way before. Part of the difficulty, part of the excitement, and part of the fun in expert-system building is to make sense out of jumbled concepts.

Economic Impact

It is not difficult to find real problems where an expert performs slightly better than the average person doing the same job and where the disparity is extremely costly. At times the benefit of simply narrowing this gap can range into the tens of millions of dollars per year. Clearly the economic consequences of the technology are substantial.

Picking the Right Problem

Here are some characteristics of good problems:

- There are recognized experts.
- The experts are provably better than amateurs.
- The task takes an expert a few minutes to a few hours.
- The task is primarily cognitive.
- The skill is routinely taught to neophytes.
- The task domain has high payoff.
- The task requires no common sense.

The first two tend to rule out astrology; one might argue that they rule out choosing stock portfolios as well.

The task should take somewhere between a few minutes and a few hours. If it is something an expert takes only a few seconds to do, then there is little to be gained. If it takes an expert more than a few hours, it is probably too big given the current state of expert-systems technology.

The task should be primarily cognitive. Medicine and physics qualify; tennis, juggling, and bicycle riding do not. It is good if the skill is routinely taught to people who do not know it because it means the experts are accustomed to explaining themselves.

The task domain must have a high payoff because the investment to get useful performance will be great. In the academic environment, we talk about the intellectual payoff—that is, we attack problems because we think they will teach us something interesting. In the commercial environment, it is the economic payoff that matters. Make sure the payoff is likely to be substantial because the effort certainly will be.

A good problem involves no common sense. Paradoxically we understand some of the intellectual processes of professional chemists better than we understand any of the intellectual processes of children. A five-year-old child can reason about what happens when he turns over a glass of water, but we do not yet know how to build programs that can do that simple kind of commonsense reasoning. Expert systems based on an established, taught body of knowledge rather than on common sense are more likely to be built successfully.

Getting Started Requires Skilled Artists

Many companies want to move expert-systems technology out of university research laboratories into real-world applications. The potential benefits are exciting intellectually and significant economically.

At first everything looks easy since there are now several vendors of expert-system shells. The difficulty lies in fleshing out those shell systems, building the required knowledge bases. Of approximately 2,500 people actively working on Artificial Intelligence in the United States, fewer than 250 are experienced and actively working in the area of expert systems. Although the number is growing, there will be a critical shortage for some time. To build a knowledge base, it is necessary to lure capable people with a state-of-the-art computing environment, the right location, and competitive financial compensation.

Summary

Expert systems are an attempt to identify, formalize, encode, and use the knowledge of human experts as the basis for a high-performance program. These systems often have significant economic impact because they can replicate and distribute expertise.

In surveying the state of the art of expert systems, two important calibration points are provided by the magnitude of investment necessary to build a robust system and the stage of development reached to date by most expert systems. Data from existing efforts, though meager, seem to suggest that even in the best of cases, at least five man-years of effort are necessary before an expert system begins to perform reliably. It is also revealing to note that most expert systems to date have been developed only through the stage of construction of the basic knowledge base. Relatively few so far have progressed to the stage of extended testing, further development, and documentation.

Expert-systems technology is still relatively new, and the accomplished practitioners are few. But as some recent systems have made clear, the promise and the value of the technology is substantial. We look to the future with considerable excitement.

For More Information

Buchanan, Bruce G., and Edward H. Shortliffe, *Rule-Based Expert Programs: The MYCIN Experiments of the Stanford Heuristic Programming Project*, Addison-Wesley, Reading, MA, 1984.

Campbell, A. N., V. F. Hollister, Richard O. Duda, and Peter E. Hart, "Recognition of a Hidden Mineral Deposit by an Artificial Intelligence Program," *Science*, vol. 217, no. 3, 1982.

Davis, Randall, "Expert Systems: Where Are We? And Where Do We Go from Here," Report AIM-665, Artificial Intelligence Laboratory, Massachusetts Institute of Technology, Cambridge, MA, 1982.

Davis, Randall, and Jonathan King, "An Overview of Production Systems," in *Machine Intelligence 8*, edited by Edward W. Elcock and Donald Michie, John Wiley and Sons, New York, 1977.

Davis, Randall, and Douglas B. Lenat, *Knowledge-Based Systems in Artificial Intelligence*, McGraw-Hill Book Company, New York, 1982.

Davis, Randall, Bruce G. Buchanan, and Edward H. Shortliffe, "Production Rules as a Representation for a Knowledge-Based Consultation Program," *Artificial Intelligence*, vol. 8, no. 1, 1977.

Davis, Randall, Howard Austin, Ingrid Carlbom, Bud Frawley, Paul Pruchnik, Rich Sneiderman, and Al Gilreath, "The Dipmeter Advisor: Interpretation of Geological Signals," *Seventh International Joint Conference on Artificial Intelligence*, Vancouver, British Columbia, Canada, 1981.

3
XCON: An Expert Configuration System at Digital Equipment Corporation

Arnold Kraft
Manager, External Relations
Intelligent Systems Technologies Group
Digital Equipment Corporation

Mr. Kraft, who has been with Digital Equipment Corporation for six years, is a member of the group of people who develop artificial intelligence-based applications for use within the corporation. Prior to joining Digital, Mr. Kraft was manager of information systems at a division of ADT and worked in the marketing and research group at Wang Laboratories. Mr. Kraft received the Bachelor of Business Administration from the University of Massachusetts at Amherst and the Master of Business Administration from the Amos Tuck School, Dartmouth College.

Our primary objective in starting expert-systems work at Digital Equipment Corporation (DEC) was to increase our own internal asset utilization. We needed tools to solve complex problems in complex environments. XCON (short for expert configurer) is one of the tools we developed to help us configure VAX computer systems.[1]

VAX system orders sent to Digital reflect the company's broad á la carte product offering. This breadth and depth of products causes complexity when configuring VAX system orders since each customer's order is usually unique.

[1] XCON, is also known as R1. John McDermott from Carnegie-Mellon University, who developed the original program, named the system R1, reportedly saying, "Three years ago I wanted to be a knowledge engineer, and today I are one."

The manual process for technically editing orders did not bring to bear all the available expertise needed to configure an order optimally and was showing signs of stress relative to coping with the increasing order volume and product complexity.

Digital developed XCON to help configure VAX computer systems more efficiently and to have the task performed in an optimal manner.

XCON's job is to locate components in sensible physical locations and to connect everything together properly. For example, one of XCON's tasks is to decide if an order specifies something that makes sense. XCON asks itself if the specified VAX system can be built and if it is supportable. If not, XCON tells us what is wrong, documents how to correct the problem, and then produces detailed output for use by manufacturing and field service personnel.

A Star Performer

We have used XCON daily in our plants since 1980. So far XCON has analyzed nearly 20,000 unique orders and is running now with 95 to 98 percent accuracy. It has become an indispensable and effective business tool.

How much money has XCON saved? Exact numbers are confidential, but it is well known that the saving has been substantial enough to make people at Digital believers in a bright future for expert systems in particular and Artificial Intelligence in general.

XCON began in 1978 as a joint development effort between Digital Equipment Corporation and Carnegie-Mellon University. Digital took the prototype out of the university environment and into the real world of day-to-day manufacturing. All development work and day-to-day operation are on VAX 11/780 computers. XCON was first installed in a systems manufacturing plant in Salem, New Hampshire.

XCON has over 2,000 rules. Here is a a sample rule (translated into English):

```
Rule R88

If      The current subtask is assigning devices
           to unibus modules
        and there is an unassigned dual port disk drive
        and the type of controller it requires is known
        and there are two such controllers,
           neither of which has any devices assigned to it
        and the number of devices which
           these controllers can support is known
Then    Assign the disk drive to each controller
        and note that each controller supports one device
```

While complicated looking, the rule's content is simple: To put a disk on a particular bus, match up all the components to be sure that they are the right ones, and if they are, assign the bus, the controller, and the disk simultaneously.

In developing XCON, it was important to measure benefits along the way. As with anything radically new, there were skeptics who worried how Digital would get a return on the substantial resources invested. Consequently we were careful to measure certain characteristics of the technicians who did configuration manually, concentrating on how well they performed, where they were located, and what the costs were, particularly in allowance losses. In Digital vernacular, an allowance is something we have to give away. We also tracked the installation time required since the detailed output of XCON is used by field service staff as well.

Since XCON ensures a complete and workable system, not only could it be verified, built, and installed better and more quickly, but it helps to avoid scenarios like the following. If a $500,000$ VAX system arrived at the customer's site without a $10 cable, we would give the customer that cable for free more often than not. Although allowance losses like this add up over time, there is a more significant cost in terms of lost time and goodwill when the customer must wait for something as minor as a missing cable. XCON performs the tasks of consistently ensuring correctness and completeness much better than human technicians.

Another experimentally proved benefit is that there are fewer changes in orders configured by XCON than in orders configured manually. XCON gets it right the first time, so the cycles are dampened out. Today, when the field service person gets the box marked, "Open me first," he finds a reliable road map for putting together everything in the system – the same road map used by the factory technicians.

Inside XCON

Prior to our joint XCON effort done in collaboration with Carnegie-Mellon University (CMU), two major efforts were not completely successful, both using conventional technology rooted in FORTRAN or BASIC. These learning experiments helped us because they assured that the XCON project was labeled research, not development. Consequently careers did not depend on quick results. It is important that first efforts in expert systems be arranged so that a critical business function is not dependent on immediate and complete success. Allowances must be made for the learning curves of the expert system's authors, the experts, and the users of these systems.

The two prior efforts taught us a great deal more about the nature of the configuration problem. Each effort helped to accumulate, in one place, more concrete data about our systems. The most tangible and immediate benefit was the creation of a series of manual configuration sheets and guides for use by salespeople and customers. These configuration guides were practical and immediately useful. Some of the methods of graphically portraying information about our hardware are still in use today in the current sales literature.

CMU and Digital developed the first prototype and put it into initial use in Digital in December 1979 despite some people who worried that it would never work and others who worried that it would work and threaten their jobs. In 1980 we began to use it to configure all VAX orders. In 1981 Digital became self-sufficient, and we weaned ourselves from Carnegie-Mellon help by hiring and training our own people to support the continuing work and languages.

Much of the work developing XCON had to be done in the factory because we had to capture the knowledge we needed from practicing experts. It is necessary to find an expert who can help chart the problem space and describe what really happens as problems are solved.

Missionary Work

As Digital worked on and used XCON, XSEL was in the back of our minds. Just as XCON is for getting machines built and installed, XSEL is for assisting customers in properly configuring their systems. The goal of XSEL is to be able to help a salesperson, using a portable terminal in the customer's office, prepare quotes for Digital computer systems. Compared to XCON, XSEL has to be much more interactive. XSEL will have all the knowledge of XCON and more. XSEL is now in the field-test stage and works with VAXes and with PDP11/23s. Shortly we will ramp the field test up to daily use by the U.S. sales force. Our goal is to keep up with all future hardware and software announcements for use by both XCON and XSEL.

Naturally, salespeople could be very threatened by this type of expert system. Imagine the plight of a computer-systems salesperson with ten or twelve years experience, who could go to a customer or prospect and using his or her wealth of accumulated knowledge prepare the framework of a quotation with only minimal reference to technical documentation. Now, all of a sudden, a portable terminal and a remote computer are part of the salesperson's tool kit. The salesperson is now, potentially, portrayed as having to rely on the computer and expert system, thus appearing less self-sufficient. We have spent a lot of time with sales users, dealing with the psychological aspects of these work pattern changes as they affect each user, as well as with the changes themselves.

XSITE exists because we need to know where customers are going to put our computer systems. Everyone has heard stories about computers that could not be made operable because the power or air-conditioning was insufficient or because the equipment would not fit through the door or into the elevator. XSITE tries to deal with some of those problems by taking into account the environment in which the delivered system will be placed. XSITE hands that information over to XCON, which then checks things like cable-length restrictions. XCON, for example, will not let disks be 300 meters from the processor if that is not the proper configuration.

XSITE can be thought of as a module of XSEL. When everything is done, the customer knows things like how many Btu's of cooling are needed, together with power requirements in terms of voltage, frequency, and phasing, right down to the part number for the receptacle the electrician has to install.

Digital Equipment Corporation has immersed itself in expert systems technology for many reasons. First, rule-based expert systems are good when a large amount of human expertise is required to solve the problem. Second, there is a large amount of knowledge, and that knowledge may appear to be unstructured. Third, the knowledge is represented as rules or heuristics. Fourth, this is a problem that people do well. Fifth, the problem is not algorithmic (or you think there is an algorithm and do not know it). Sixth, it may not be possible to write a full, formal specification. Last, they help us to manage change within Digital Equipment Corporation's fast-moving world.

A rule-based system is not subject to the same degree of collapse as a conventional system when there is a need to change the original function. We need systems that we can prototype quickly and then make the decision to proceed or stop based on that prototype's demonstrated characteristics. We have already changed course rapidly on several projects.

Whenever possible, we try to make our expert systems work together. XCON, XSEL, and XSITE relate as a team to business problems. After we got XCON working, we branched off into related areas, leveraging from our previous experience. Our success with XCON, XSEL, and XSITE has led us to explore artificial-intelligence technology in a number of areas, mostly in manufacturing, corporate business order distribution, and diagnosis.

There are, of course, some perceived shortcomings to becoming involved in expert systems. For example, expert systems tend to be memory intensive. However, hardware is relatively inexpensive. It is the expert-systems experts who are expensive – put the hardware against the problem. By this, we mean that you must take maximum advantage of your knowledge engineer and your domain expert, and enhance the development of the expert systems by supplying enough capital equipment of the proper kind. Another potential problem is that the end users and programmers may resist accepting and using expert systems. Our solution is to deal with the psychological aspects of the change to new technology and to train them meticulously.

What are the maintenance and support requirements? Maintenance requires knowledgeable experts in the problem domain, as well as rule writers. Expert systems are never correct all the time, just as humans never are. At first, we were not sure how many people would be needed to support XCON. As the system matured we saw that a relatively stable set of metrics evolved around things like how much effort is required to add a new type of disk to XCON.

How do you test an expert system? Testing is done by constantly trying out many tough orders that an expert feels are tricky and convoluted. The programmers test each new rule as they write it. Expert systems are not going to solve all the world's problems, but they can be used in conjunction with conventional information systems to attack new classes of problems that may have seemed intractable.

We know the systems that we build are not going to have 100 percent success records. Consequently, we aim to provide some level of result explanation. In Professor Davis's examples, the systems provided interactive explanation. XCON's explanations are at the end, explaining why a component was used or changed. The important thing is that the explanation is somewhere.

A lot of missionary work is still needed. Since Artificial Intelligence is not yet part of management culture, there is a lot of selling to management to be done.

Sitting at the Masters' Feet

It is important to have a mature expert, capable of describing how he does the job. A large amount of human expertise must be captured in a typical effort. When Digital developed XCON, the knowledge engineers listened for hours to an expert telling us about his knowledge, until we thought we knew everything. Then, at the point of exhaustion, perhaps over lunch or a midnight break, someone would say, "What about...?" One short question would start a four-hour lecture about a new avenue of thought that the expert had not remembered to tell us about before. Consequently it is important to have a methodology that captures information when you get it, where you get it, and how you get it.

Development must be user driven. If the users think that this system will help them to alleviate a problem or provide a better solution or be more cost-effective than the current methodology, they will use it. If they think it is being foisted off on them, they will not use it. Expert systems cannot be forced into place; they must be carefully woven into the fabric of an organization.

Proliferation

Some of the other systems we are developing are IMACS and ILOG, in the manufacturing area. Digital does a lot of manufacturing all over the world. IMACS is a system of several cooperative expert systems within a manufacturing plant. Its goal is to manage the flow of work better within that plant in cooperation with conventional systems. ILOG is exploring the problem of coordinating the shipment of material from many plants to the customer's site.

Many problems that have resisted conventional software solutions lend themselves to the emerging technology of expert systems. We expect knowledge engineering to become an important tool in Digital's software repertoire.

For More Information

McDermott, John, "R1: A Rule-Based Configurer of Computer Systems", *Artificial Intelligence*, vol. 19, no. 1, 1982.

McDermott, John, "R1's Formative Years," *AI Magazine*, vol. 2, no. 2, 1982.

McDermott, John, "Domain Knowledge and the Design Process," Proceedings of 18th Design Automation Conference, Nashville, TN, 1981, *Design Studies*, vol. 3, no. 1, 1982.

McDermott, John, "XSEL: A Computer Salesperson's Assistant," in Machine Intelligence, edited by J. Hayes and D. Michie, 1982.

McDermott, John and Barbara Steel, "Extending a Knowledge-Based System to Deal with Ad Hoc Constraints," *Seventh International Joint Conference on Artificial Intelligence*, Vancouver, British Columbia, Canada, 1981.

4

DIPMETER ADVISOR:
An Expert Log Analysis System
at Schlumberger[1]

James D. Baker
Austin Engineering Center
Schlumberger

Dr. Baker has worked in operations research, pattern recognition, image processing, mathematical and statistical modeling, mathematical representation of systems, and methodologies for developing complex systems. He has directed the development of artificial-intelligence techniques and their application to industrial problems at Schlumberger Doll Research. These efforts include the DIPMETER AD-VISOR, an expert system for oil field log interpretation. He is currently manager of the Schlumberger Austin Engineering Center. Prior to working for Schlumberger, Dr. Baker worked at Honeywell, Texas Instruments, and the Johns Hopkins University Applied Physics Laboratory. He holds the BA, the MA, and the PhD in Mathematics.

The people who interpret data expertly are a small but critical group in Schlumberger. One person who has worked himself well up into the company comes to mind. He became famous by leading an oil company across the panhandle of Texas, helping it decide where to drill wells. He started by looking at the data from the well under consideration. Going through an analysis, he might have reasoned as follows: "At the time of deposition, which was several

[1]The results discussed here represent the efforts of several individuals in the artificial-intelligence groups at Schlumberger-Doll Research Center and at Fairchild Artificial Intelligence Laboratory.

million years ago, this area represented a channel, now 10,000 feet underground. I can determine the direction from the well to the center of the channel, and I can determine the direction of the flow. By bringing in my knowledge of geology, I can know how sands were deposited, and I can determine where I should go to maximize my likelihood of having a successful well on the next effort."

It is difficult to do decide where to drill wells. Our business problem is that we do not have enough of these valuable people. Schumberger's solution is to embody the skill of its valuable people in computer-based expert systems.

To Drill or Not to Drill

The principal business of Schlumberger is gathering and interpreting data. Sensors are lowered into the bore hole, and, measurements are made as the sensors are raised. Some measurements are taken every tenth of an inch and some are taken only every six inches. There are as many as twenty different kinds of sensors, but two or three can be used at once. The fact that there are many kinds of sensors adds to the complexity of the problem.

The key question is, Is there hydrocarbon under the ground? If so, what kind is it? Oil? Gas? How much is there? Can it be removed? Depth is also important because in completing a well, making it a producer, we need to know the exact location of the hydrocarbon. Finally, we need to know where to move the rig to drill the next hole. In oil field explanations, we have a large variety of problems with many possible answers.

DIPMETER ADVISOR

Data from the sensors dropped into bore holes are plotted on logs, which are sheets of paper six to ten feet long, folded up like an accordion (figure 1). These data indicate

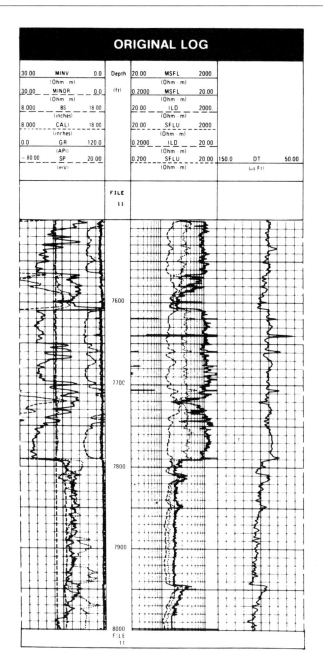

Figure 1. Data from bore-hole sensors are plotted on logs.

W   E

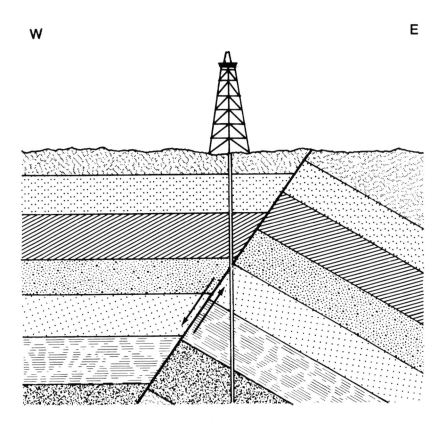

Figure 2. Dipmeter is dropped down the bore hole to measure the tilt of underground formations.

how different kinds of energy (sonic, electrical, and nuclear) interact with the formation. Understanding these data is the intellectual challenge. The DIPMETER ADVISOR, Schlumberger's first expert system, attempts to emulate a special type of expert in this interpretation, starting with measurements from the dipmeter tool. The dipmeter measures the tilt of the underground formations (figure 2). In one place the layers are basically flat. In another the layers start to incline at a substantial degree.

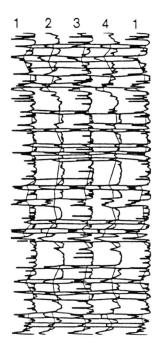

Figure 3. Plot of data obtained from dipmeter.

A sensor on each of the dipmeter tool's four arms measures the conductivity of the formation as the tool is pulled out of the hole. This results in four curves that look approximately the same. As the sensor comes out of a hole bored into a tilted formation, not all of the arms will measure the movement into the new formation at the same time (figure 3). By observing the differences in the measurements, we can determine the magnitude of the inclination, as well as the direction.

This data may be represented in another way, as shown in figure 4. The vertical lines represent degrees of inclination, starting with 0° and going to 90°. The horizontal dot placement indicates the magnitude of the tilt. The tail on

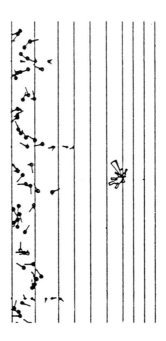

Figure 4. Another representation of data obtained from the dipmeter.

the end of each dot, sometimes called a tadpole, indicates the direction of the tilt.

It is possible to associate certain types of patterns with these data (figure 5). One of the patterns indicates roughly constant magnitude with increasing depth. Another pattern indicates increasing magnitude with increasing depth. Still another pattern indicates decreasing magnitude with increasing depth. These patterns can be detected by part of the DIPMETER ADVISOR system. From relationships among these patterns, combined with other data, we can deduce the geology.

This information appears on the screen of a work station, in this case a Xerox 1100 Dolphin. The screen is divided into several areas, one area displaying the basic dip data, another displaying a summary of the whole log, and another

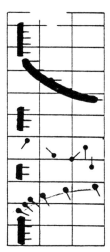

Figure 5. The relationships among the patterns associated with data from the dipmeter logs, combined with other data, describes the geology of the area.

displaying log data from other sensors that are combined with dip information to help in the analysis. Areas of special interest can be marked for re-examination.

A rule in the DIPMETER ADVISOR for interpreting this dipmeter data might be:

```
Rule NFR9

If        there exists a normal fault, and
          there exists a red pattern
             with bottom above the top of the fault,
             with length greater than 200 ft.,
             with azimuth perpendicular to the strike
                of the fault
Then      the fault is a growth fault
             with direction to downthrown block
             opposite to the azimuth of the red pattern
```

This type of rule deals with a large number of ideas: a normal fault, a red pattern, and some of the geometry. The goal of this kind of rule is to identify, to the greatest degree possible, what type of fault is involved.

Currently, there are 90 such rules in the DIPMETER ADVISOR system. We started out two years ago with 30 rules and increased to 150. After redesigning part of the system, we dropped back to 90 rules with basically the same functionality as the larger system. As many as 5 or 6 of these rules work together to reach a particular conclusion.

The DIPMETER ADVISOR goes through many steps before reaching conclusions, as shown in figure 6.

First, the system verifies that the data are correct. The validity check is needed because several things can go wrong. For example, if the bore hole collapses, the sensors will be unable to measure anything. Another possible problem is that a correlation cannot be made between the four sensors, producing a void in the data.

After the DIPMETER ADVISOR verifies that the data are correct, it begins the structural dip analysis. Structural dip refers to large tilts in the formation that have occurred after deposition. These tilts are important for two reasons: they are likely indicators that there is a fault in the area, and the tilts must be removed (that is, the structure must be retilted by the system in order for the analysis to continue).

In the third step the DIPMETER ADVISOR tries to identify the geometry and the characteristics of the faults that are present.

The last step is a stratigraphy analysis. We want to know what is there, how was it deposited, and what other geological structures were involved.

Figure 7 is a summary of one of the wells that we analyzed. The DIPMETER ADVISOR determined that there are three areas of structural dip. One is 25°, which is substantial. In the structural analysis two faults have been identified: a growth fault and a late fault. There are two unconformities—fault-like events that we cannot further classify.

The big discovery in the stratigraphy analysis was a distributary front. On top of the distributary front are two

Validity check

Washout zones
Blank zones
Mirror image zones

Structural dip analysis

Green pattern detection
Structural dip zone determination
Structural dip removal

Structural feature analysis

Structural interruption detection
Structural pattern detection
Structural feature description

Stratigraphic feature analysis

Lithology determination
Depositional environment analysis
Stratigraphic pattern detection
Stratigraphic feature description

Figure 6. DIPMETER ADVISOR System: Interpretation steps.

channels flowing in substantially different directions. There are three distributary fans. Sometimes we can even tell the shape of these particular fans.

Both experts and nonexperts use the system. The system interprets well, especially in the area of structural dip and structural analysis. We do not have as much experience with stratigraphy, which is harder to deal with and more difficult to verify.

Interestingly we have not accurately modeled what the experts do. Instead we have found that experts glance

Structural DIP zones	Structural analysis	Stratigraphy analysis
	Normal fault	**Distributary channel**
3.63° Magnitude 13141 Ft. Top depth 331° Azimuth 13809 Ft. Bottom depth	13753 Ft. Top depth 148° Strike 238° Dir-to-down Growth Class 13753 Ft. Bottom depth	15106 Ft. Top depth 79° Dir-to-axis 180° Flow 15112 Ft. Bottom depth
	Unconformity	**Distributary channel**
6.69° Magnitude 13809 Ft. Top depth 214° Azimuth 14435 Ft. Bottom depth	13681 Ft. Top depth 13809 Ft. Bottom depth	15114 Ft. Top depth 175° Dir-to-axis 70° Flow 15124 Ft. Bottom depth
	Normal fault	**Distributary front**
25.47° Magnitude 14435 Ft. Top depth 243° Azimuth 15500 Ft. Bottom depth	14375 Ft. Top depth 26° Strike 116° Dir-to-down Late Class 14435 Ft. Bottom depth	15114 Ft. Top depth 70° Flow 15168 Ft. Bottom depth
	Unconformity	**Distributary fan**
	14351 Ft. Top depth 14335 Ft. Bottom depth	15124 Ft. Top depth 180° Flow Fan or crescent Shape 15134 Ft. Bottom depth
		Distributary fan
		15138 Ft. Top depth 70° Flow Elongated Shape 15168 Ft. Bottom depth
		Distributary fan
		15178 Ft. Top depth 218° Flow Fan or crescent Shape 15186 Ft. Bottom depth

Figure 7. DIPMETER ADVISOR: Interpretation results.

at the data and very quickly reach a conclusion. They make conjectures, and the rest of the interpretation process is either the verification or the alteration of the initial conjectures. While this idea has been around some time, it would have been much more difficult to substantiate without the experience of having experts work with this prototype system.

Painless Software

Automatic programming is a label that means different things to different people. What I mean is the automatic generation of software. If we can build an expert system that will interpret logs and do many other kinds of analysis we should be able to build an expert system that can write software because writing software is another activity involving human expertise.

The problem is to relate rock models to log data through equations. The interpretation problem is to compute the relative constituents of the parts. For example, if we decompose porosity, we can determine how much water is present and how much hydrocarbon is present.

The input to our system, which we call ΦNIX, is the following: a rock model, specified by the user; log data; equations; and a specification of the variables we want to compute, plus any necessary parameters. The output is a program, written in FORTRAN, that computes the desired variables.

We have a mechanism for equation manipulation, a program-synthesis function that maps the design into the target language. The user interface is powerful enough to communicate in the language of interpretation.

We would like to embed ΦNIX in a large system of interpretation, one in which log data can be analyzed through interactive graphics, models of geology are suggested, programs (using ΦNIX) written for the desired output, and a computation system can perform the required calculations.

Signal Correlation

Until now we have been concerned primarily with analysis of single wells. How do we do interpretation in a field made up of many wells? The problem is to put together all of the data representing different wells to come up with an interpretation of very large geological structures. The amount of data can be vast because there may be many wells, there may be many logs associated with each well, and the depth of the wells can be 15,000 feet or more.

One of the biggest problems is to correlate the signals from different wells. The goal is to be able to integrate signal processing, visual perception, and geological knowledge for the multiwell correlation problem. One of the reasons exploiting geological knowledge is so difficult is that we have even fewer experts in this domain than for dipmeter analysis, and these experts do not always agree on how they do their work. In the beginning, our colleagues at the Fairchild artificial-intelligence center emphasized the signal processing and visual processing part of this problem.

First, let us discuss the matching of logs. The logs in figure 8 represent two different wells. The hypothesis is that we can mark an interval, AB, on both of the logs and then correlate all of the points in the intervals. The people at Fairchild have developed an algorithm based on dynamic programming that will match these interior points, shown in figure 8).

At the top and the bottom of the correlation in figure 9 are the original logs. Between is a smoothed version. In the middle are the lines indicating what the program has said is the optimal matching. The interesting point is that the program has suggested that there is a missing section—that is, there is an interval on this log that is mapped into a point on the other. Part of the geology in one well does not exist in the other. This is a common feature and one that makes interpretation even more difficult.

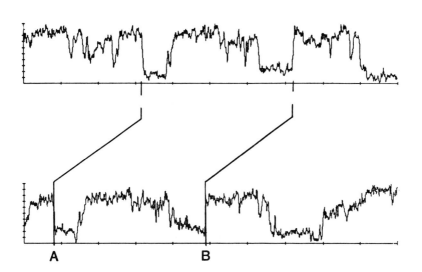

Figure 8. Matching two logs.

Leveraging Experience

A question we have been asked a number of times is why Schlumberger is using Artificial Intelligence. We believe we can do a better job at log interpretation using Artificial Intelligence than we could if we did not. We think artificial-intelligence problem-solving techniques are useful and expert-systems technology is improving rapidly. Moreover we think that the tools of Artificial Intelligence are important. Building software environments for rapid prototyping is a way to test new systems. Environments for developing software and the LISP computer systems themselves are important contributions from Artificial Intelligence.

Artificial-intelligence systems in the 1980s will be embedded in larger systems. An important ingredient of these larger systems will be the user interface, which will be graphical and highly interactive. Artificial Intelligence will be only one part of many problem-solving components, among them numeric computation, pattern recognition, and signal processing.

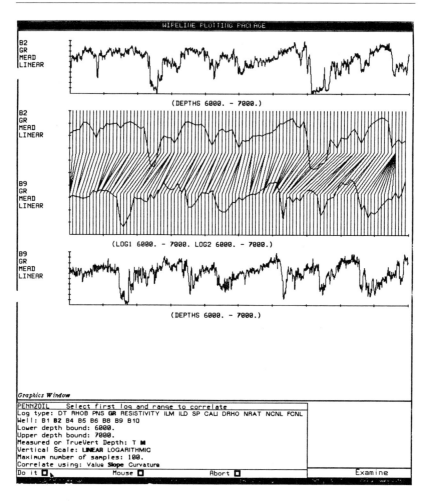

Figure 9. Logs from two different wells, as shown on the screen of a Symbolics LISP Machine.

One of the most important future contributions Artificial Intelligence will make will be in the area of software development. Much of our work at Schlumberger has been done using the INTERLISP-D environment. If we look at the resources generally required to build our software, our improvement was about an order of magnitude better than we expected. In software development a 20 to 30 percent improvement is often considered a reasonable goal. In our research on software at our research laboratory in Ridgefield, Connecticut, we have desired productivity improvement factors of three or four. In the future, I believe we can expect productivity gains of as much as a factor of ten or more.

For More Information

Davis, Randall, Howard Austin, Ingrid Carlbom, Bud Frawley, Paul Pruchnik, Rich Sneiderman, and Al Gilreath, "The DIPMETER ADVISOR: Interpretation of Geological Signals," *Seventh International Joint Conference on Artificial Intelligence*, Vancouver, British Columbia, Canada, 1981.

Dipmeter Interpretation: Volume I—Fundamentals, Schlumberger, 1981.

Gershman, A., "Building a Geological Expert System for Dipmeter Interpretation," *Proceedings of the European Conference on Artificial Intelligence*, July, 1982.

Smith, Reid, G. and James D. Baker, "The DIPMETER ADVISOR System, A Case Study in Commerical Expert System Development," *Schlumberger Doll Research Technical Report.*

5
CADUCEUS: An Experimental Expert System for Medical Diagnosis

Harry E. Pople, Jr.
Professor
Graduate School of Business
University of Pittsburgh

Professor Pople develops methods of hypothesis formation, problem solving, and decision making in medical diagnosis. In collaboration with Jack D. Myers, MD, he developed a succession of systems, collectively referred to as CADUCEUS, generally regarded as the most comprehensive, most successful artificial-intelligence-based decision support system in Medicine. He recently began to apply medical decision-making techniques to the problems of decision making in business and to the design of intelligent management systems. Professor Pople received the BS in Electrical Engineering from MIT and the doctorate in interdisciplinary systems and communications from Carnegie-Mellon University.

Dr. Jack Myers, my principal collaborator, and I have worked on a system for expert consultation in internal medicine for about twelve years. Dr. Myers, a professor of Medicine at the University of Pittsburgh, learned Medicine in the 1930s, at a time when a specialist in internal medicine could learn all there was to know. He has been able to keep up ever since by being a top-notch person and by holding an academic position.

When Dr. Myers decided that he wanted to do research, he came to me and asked whether we could develop a computer system that could do what he does. He expressed considerable concern about fragmentation in medical teaching. Everyone is a specialist in something; we do not produce generalists any more. Not only have the generalists become specialists, but the specialists have become subspecialists and subsubspecialists. Dr. Myers is concerned about that because it is common knowledge that a patient who goes to a lung specialist undoubtedly will come away with a lung diagnosis, no matter what is really wrong.

Critical Partnership

How can we use computers to make up for this deficiency in medical training? Can we build a generalist? From the beginning of our work, Dr. Myers set the standards high because he feels that there is no point building a general practitioner. They do not see the more interesting diseases often enough to recognize them when they come along. Our generalist was to operate at a high level, that of an expert consultant. We wanted to build a program to which someone might come with difficult problems.

We spent two or three afternoons a week for six months going over case studies. He taught me Medicine, to the extent that he could, illustrating what he thought he wanted our program to deal with. We tried to understand what skilled physicians do as they go through the process of coming to grips with a challenging medical problem.

Deciding What to Decide

It was obvious from the beginning that the physician, and hence our program, deals with multiple diagnoses, ruling out traditional approaches to decision analysis. There are a lot of programs around, based primarily on Bayesian statistical schemes or pattern-recognition schemes, that could find one diagnosis, coming up with a probability spectrum across

a decision set. But in internal medicine the one-diagnosis
assumption is inappropriate.

It also was clear that physicians piece together solutions
to complicated problems step by step. Diagnosis is not a
matter of fetching the whole picture from memory, with
multiple pieces. Instead it is like solving a crossword puzzle.

Physicians have to be able to proceed no matter in what
order the data are provided. In general it is not reasonable
to fill out a whole vector of data values before commencing
treatment. One reason is that a patient may come into a
hospital comatose, eliminating the possibility of getting a
history. Another reason is that time pressure may prevent
the physician from running to the laboratory. Finally there
is cost. Some clinics do not make interpretations until
hundreds of tests are run. Dr. Myers objects to that practice
because of the tremendous expense. We decided our program
must be prepared to proceed on the basis of whatever data
it might have.

From our discussions, it also became clear that a physician
thinks first in very general terms, becoming more and more
specific. There is a refinement with respect to an initial
hypothesis.

Finally, it is very important that the physician be able to
disregard irrelevant data. The first system we built worked
beautifully as long as we dealt only with textbook cases. But
as soon as we brought in real patient data, everything fell
apart. The data from real patients are full of noise. There
are red herrings and errors. Even worse, some patients will
misrepresent things, lie, or forget, and laboratories make
mistakes. And even the good data can be irrelevant because
there are a lot of things we do not know about Medicine,
leaving many parts of the record forever unexplained.

Perhaps the most mysterious part of what a physician does
is to decide what the decision problem is. He has to choose
from among thousands and thousands of possible diagnoses
where to focus his attention. The physician does not proceed

by systematically considering all possibilities in turn, but moves very quickly into a focused set of possibilities known as a differential diagnosis.

After a year I understood enough of what I needed to do as a computer scientist to make progress.

A Paradox

Once a physician has a differential diagnosis in mind, the enterprise of going through the set of possible explanations systematically is straightforward. But formulating that differential diagnosis in the first place is difficult since the physician cannot make the assumption that only one thing is wrong with the patient. Many different decision problems must be formulated and solved.

Let me stress one thing that we understand now that we did not know in the beginning. There are a number of pragmatic, commonsense rules that the physician uses. One important rule is that physicians try to account for all the significant data that they see. Given that a physician observes an abnormal finding ordinarily associated with a significant pathology, he must find out what causes that finding. The rule applies across all findings, and the physician is unhappy if there is anything that cannot be accounted for.

Another important rule is that physicians try to explain everything under one umbrella. They do not like to give the patient two diseases if one will do. A corollary is that physicians try to find a total diagnosis that can account for the preponderance of the data with the fewest diseases.

Once a decision problem is correctly formulated, powerful strategies for solving that problem can be invoked. One such strategy is that physicians try to solve problems using elimination. Having ruled out several possibilities, perhaps the only thing left is, say, a pneumoccocal pneumonia. I have seen physicians make judgments using elimination that otherwise would seem to go against some of the evidence.

They will say a particular disease is the only one possible because all else has been ruled out.

Note the paradox. I am suggesting that the process of formulating a differential diagnosis is itself heuristic. I am also suggesting that decisions are often made by elimination, a technique that is valid only if there is a complete set of plausible hypotheses in the first place. This is the commonsense explanation for what goes wrong in the diagnostic process on those occasions when something does go wrong.

INTERNIST I

We defined a medical knowledge base for the system we call Internist I. That knowledge base contains knowledge about diseases and a set of things we call manifestations. In addition there are intermediate diagnosable conditions that are not really diseases. All are tied together in a causal network. For example, it is known that hepatitis can cause a problem in the blood called hyperbilirubinemia, and that in turn is manifested by jaundice. Physicians know a lot about such causal chains.

Figure 1 shows the data base for pallor and jaundice. On the right side is pallor associated with anemia, one cause of pallor. But pallor is also associated with fibrotic hepatocellular involvement, which can cause bleeding, which in turn can cause pallor.

Here we have jaundice associated with a type of anemia called hemolytic anemia. Under hepatobiliary involvement, we have a number of kinds of liver disease, with jaundice associated with most of them, including hepatic vein obstruction, biliary tract involvement, and hepatocellular involvement.

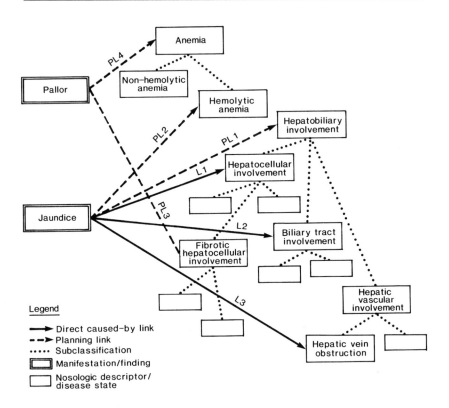

Figure 1. Example of the INTERNIST I data base.

The basic algorithm in INTERNIST I exploits this data base as follows. Suppose we observe pallor and jaundice. INTERNIST I asks what set of diseases can account for those findings. To pick the most likely, it could simply do a tally, counting one point for every finding explained by the disease. The actual scoring is somewhat more complex (Pople 1982), but the principle is the same. Then INTERNIST I sorts that list and comes up with a leading contender. It constructs a differential diagnosis consisting of the disease that is the most highly ranked and its competitors. Given that differential diagnosis, we invoke a problem-solving strategy and repeat. Let me illustrate how with a case run several years ago.

A Very Sick Woman

Here we have positive initial findings:

*SEX FEMALE

*AGE GTR THAN 55

*URINE SEDIMENT RBC

*JAUNDICE

*PROTHROMBIN TIME INCREASED

*SKIN ECCHYMOSES

*OBESITY

*EDEMA SUBCUTANEOUS

*FECES GUAIAC TEST POSITIVE

*HEMATOCRIT BLOOD LESS THAN 35

*UREA NITROGEN BLOOD LESS THAN 35

*SGOT 40 TO 120

*ALKALINE PHOSPHATASE INCREASED NOT OVER 2 TIMES NORMAL

*ELECTROPHORESIS SERUM ALBUMIN DECREASED

*BILIRUBIN CONJUGATED BLOOD INCREASED

*BILIRUBIN INDIRECT TO DIRECT RATIO BLOOD INCREASED

*ABDOMEN XRAY FLUID PERITONEAL CAVITY

*ASCITIC FLUID OBTAINED BY PARACENTESIS

*ASCITIC FLUID SPECIFIC GRAVITY LESS THAN 1:013

*ASCITIC FLUID PROTEIN LESS THAN 3 GRAM (S) PERCENT

*LIVER SMALL

*VOMITING COFFEE GROUND

*STUPOR

*REFLEX (ES) DEEP TENDON INCREASED GENERALIZED

*RBC RETICULOCYTE (S) GTR THAN 5 PERCENT

*PLATELET (S) LESS THAN 50,000

*POTASSIUM BLOOD INCREASED

*CHLORIDE BLOOD INCREASED

*UREA NITROGEN BLOOD GTR THAN 60

*CREATININE BLOOD INCREASED

*CSF XANTHOCHROMIA

*CSF GLUTAMINE INCREASED

*RBC TARGET (S)

*RBC SCHIZOCYTE (S)

```
*IRON BINDING CAPACITY TOTAL LESS THAN 240
*HAPTOGLOBIN DECREASED
*SODIUM URINE LESS THAN 20 MEQ PER DAY
```

The patient is a woman older than fifty-five, with many medical problems. She has jaundice, so she may be anemic or have a liver problem. INTERNIST I finds many things. There is subcutaneous edema and retained fluid. The woman not only has anemia and jaundice but other problems having to do with liver enzymes. Consequently INTERNIST I is going to look at the liver.

"Ascitic fluid obtained" means she has fluid in the abdomen. The liver, by percussion test, is seen to be small, and that is a bad sign, probably meaning it is nearly wiped out. Vomiting coffee grounds indicates digested blood, meaning that she is bleeding. We also have some initial negative findings:

```
-JAUNDICE FAMILY HX
-JAUNDICE PERSISTENT HX
-JAUNDICE REMOTE HX
-JAUNDICE INTERMITTENT HX
-HEPATITIS ACUTE HX
-ALCOHOLISM HX
-FEVER
-URINE DARK HX
-FECES LIGHT COLORED
-WBC 14,000 TO 30,000
-WBC 4,000 TO 14,000 PERCENT NEUTROPHIL (S) INCREASED
-WBC LESS THAN 4,000
-GLUCOSE BLOOD INCREASED
-GLUCOSE BLOOD LESS THAN 50
-ANTIBODY HEPATITIS B
-HEPATITIS B SURFACE ANTIGEN
-ANA POSITIVE
-ANTIBODY MITOCHONDRIAL
-ANTIBODY SMOOTH MUSCLE
-ALPHA FETOGLOBULIN INCREASED
```

```
-COPPER BLOOD DECREASED
-CERULOPLASMIN BLOOD DECREASED
-SODIUM BLOOD DECREASED
-BICARBONATE BLOOD LESS THAN 20
-IRON SERUM LESS THAN 45
```

The value of negative data is that they can downgrade a hypothesis. The scoring mechanism lowers a disease's score if certain findings are expected but not found.

A transcript of part of an actual dialog between the physician and INTERNIST I follows:

```
*GO
DISREGARDING: EDEMA SUBCUTANEOUS, LIVER SMALL, OBESITY,
STUPOR, VOMITING COFFEE GROUND, ABDOMEN XRAY FLUID
PERITONEAL CAVITY, ALKALINE PHOSPHATASE INCREASED
NOT OVER 2 TIMES NORMAL, ASCITIC FLUID SPECIFIC GRAVITY
LESS THAN 1:013, BILIRUBIN INDIRECT TO DIRECT RATIO
BLOOD INCREASED, CHLORIDE BLOOD INCREASED, POTASSIUM
BLOOD INCREASED, RBS SCHIZOCYTE (S), RBC TARGET (S),
SGOT 40 TO 120, ASCITIC FLUID OBTAINED BY PARACENTESIS,
ASCITIC FLUID PROTEIN LESS THAN 3 GRAM (S) PERCENT,
CSF GLUTAMINE INCREASED, HAPTOGLOBIN DECREASED, IRON
BINDING CAPACITY TOTAL LESS THAN 240, PARTIAL
THROMBOPLASTIN TIME INCREASED, PROTHROMBIN TIME
INCREASED, SODIUM URINE LESS THAN 20 MEQ PER DAY

DISCRIMINATE: ACUTE MONOCYTIC OR MYELOMONOCYTIC LEUKEMIA,
ACUTE MYELOBLASTIC LEUKEMIA
```

At this point the set of findings that are being ignored is printed. Dozens and dozens of facts are set aside in the beginning. Internist I has focused on a subset of the data and has formulated its first differential diagnosis, with a view toward discriminating between acute monocytic or myelomonocytic leukemia versus acute myeloblastic leukemia.

Now the program asks the right questions, weighing those two possibilities, accumulating evidence for or against each.

```
*GO
WBC MYELOMONOCYTE (S) GTR THAN 20 PERCENT?
NO
```

WBC MONOBLAST (S) AND PROMONOCYTE (S) GTR THAN 20 PERCENT?
NO
PLEASE ENTER FINDINGS OF URINALYSIS ROUTINE AND MICROSCOPIC

It asks for findings about blood count. It asks about the morphology of some of the white blood cells: myelomonocytes, monoblasts, promonocytes, and the rest. In this example it gets negative evidence from all.

*GO
URINE HEMATURIA GROSS WITH MICROSCOPIC CONFIRMATION?
NO
WBC MYELOBLAST (S) AND PROMYELOCYTE (S) GTR THAN
20 PERCENT?
NO

DISREGARDING: FECES GUAIAC TEST POSITIVE, OBESITY, SKIN
ECCHYMOSES, STUPOR, VOMITING COFFEE GROUND, ABDOMEN XRAY
FLUID PERITONEAL CAVITY, ASCITIC FLUID INCREASED,
CHLORIDE BLOOD INCREASED, CREATININE BLOOD INCREASED,
POTASSIUM BLOOD INCREASED, RBC SCHIZOCYTE (S), UREA
NITROGEN BLOOD 30 TO 60, UREA NITROGEN BLOOD BTR THAN
60, URINE SEDIMENT RBS, ASCITIC FLUID OBTAINED BY
PARACENTESIS, ASCITIC FLUID PROTEIN LESS THAN 3 GRAM (S)
PERCENT, CSF GLUTAMINE INCREASED, HAPTOGLOBIN DECREASED,
IRON BINDING CAPACITY TOTAL LESS THAN 240, PARTIAL
THROMBOPLASTIN TIME INCREASED, PLATELET (S) LESS THAN
50,000, SODIUM URINE LESS THAN 20 MEQ PER DAY

PURSUING: MICRONODAL CIRRHOSIS (LAENNECS)

For a while it continues to look for evidence to support one or the other of those leukemias, but eventually it reconsiders, coming to a totally different view of the problem. Instead of trying to discriminate between two kinds of leukemia, it pursues micronodal cirrhosis, which turns out to be the correct diagnosis. It shifted gears, reformulating its decision problem.

*GO
LIVER FINE NODULE (S)?
N/A
CONCLUDE: MICRONODAL CIRRHOSIS (LANNECS)

DISRGARDING: FECES GUAIAC TEST POSITIVE, OBESITY, SKIN
ECCHYMOSES, STUPOR, VOMITING COFFEE GROUND, BILIRUGIN

INDIRECT TO DIRECT RATIO BLOOD INCREASED, CHLORIDE BLOOD
INCREASED, CREATININE BLOOD INCREASED, POTASSIUM BLOOD
INCREASED, RBC SCHIZOCYTE (S), UREA NITROGEN BLOOD 30
TO 60, UREA NITROGEN BLOOD GTR THAN 60, URINE SEDIMENT
RBC, CSF GLUTAMINE INCREASED, HAPTOGLOBIN DECREASED,
IRON BINDING CAPACITY TOTAL LESS THAN 240, PARTIAL
THROMBOPLASTIN TIME INCREASED, PLATELET (S) LESS THAN
50,000, SODIUM URINE LESS THAN 20 MEQ PER DAY

CONCLUDE: TRANSUDATIVE ASCITES

DISREGARDING: FECES GUAIAC TEST POSITIVE, OBESITY, SKIN
ECCHYMOSES, STUPOR, VOMITING COFFEE GROUND, BILIRUBIN
INDIRECT TO DIRECT RATIO BLOOD INCREASED, CHLORIDE BLOOD
INCREASED, RBC SCHIZOCYTE (S), URINE SEDIMENT RBC, CSF
GLUTAMINE INCREASED, HAPTOGLOBIN DECREASED, IRON BINDING
CAPACITY TOTAL LESS THAN 240, PARTIAL THROMBOPLASTIN TIME
INCREASED, PLATELET (S) LESS THAN 50,000

PURSUING: RENAL FAILURE SECONDARY TO LIVER DISEASE
(HEPATORENAL SYNDROME)
CONCLUDE: RENAL FAILURE SECONDARY TO LIVER DISEASE
(HEPATORENAL SYNDROME)

DISREGARDING: FECES GUAIAC TEST POSITIVE, OBESITY, SKIN
ECCHYMOSES, VOMITING COFFEE GROUND, BILIRUBIN INDIRECT
TO DIRECT RATIO BLOOD INCREASED, CHLORIDE BLOOD INCREASED,
RBC SCHIZOCYTE (S), URINE SEDIMENT RBC, HAPTOGLOBIN
DECREASED, IRON BINDING CAPACITY TOTAL LESS THAN 240,
PARTIAL THROMBOPLASTIN TIME INCREASED, PLATELET (S) LESS
THAN 50,000

PURSUING: HEPATIC ENCEPHALOPATHY

*GO
ASTERIXIS?
NO

DISREGARDING: OBESITY, SKIN ECCHYMOSES, STUPOR, VOMITING
COFFEE GROUND, BILIRUBIN INDIRECT TO DIRECT RATIO BLOOD
INCREASED, CHLORIDE BLOOD INCREASED, RBC SCHIZOCYTE (S),
URINE SEDIMENT RBC, CSF CLUTAMINE INCREASED, HAPTOGLOBIN
DECREASED, IRON BINDING CAPACITY TOTAL LESS THAN 240,
PARTIAL THROMBOPLASTIN TIME INCREASED, PLATELET (S) LESS
THAN 50,000

PURSUING: SINUSOIDAL OR POSTSINUSOIDAL PORTAL HYPERTENSION

PLEASE ENTER FINDINGS OF AUSCULTATION ABDOMEN
*GO

ABDOMEN BRUIT CONTINUOUS PERIUMBILICAL?
NO
PLEASE ENTER FINDINGS OF INSPECTION ABDOMEN
*GO
ABDOMEN VENOUS PATTERN CENTRIFUGAL FLOW?
N/A
CAPUT MEDUSAE?
NO

DISREGARDING: OBESITY, SKIN ECCHYMOSES, STUPOR, VOMITING
COFFEE GROUND, BILIRUGIN INDIRECT TO DIRECT RATIO BLOOD
INCREASED, CHLORIDE BLOOD INCREASED, RBC SCHIZOCYTE (S),
URINE SEDIMENT RBC, CSF GLUTAMINE INCREASED, HAPTOGLOBIN
DECREASED, IRON BINDING CAPACITY TOTAL LESS THAN 240,
PARTIAL THROMBOPLASTIN TIME INCREASED, PLATELET (S) LESS
THAN 50,000

DISCRIMINATE: SINUSOIDAL OR POSTSINUSOIDAL PORTAL
HYPERTENSION, PLASMA CELL MYELOMA

HEMATEMESIS?
NO
SPLENOMEGALY MODERATE?
YES
PLEASE ENTER FINDINGS OF XRAY LUNG FIELD (S)
*GO
CHEST XRAY PLEURAL EFFUSION (S)?
NO
PLEASE ENTER FINDINGS OF NEUROLOGIC EXAM MUSCULOSKELETAL
*GO
PARAPLEGIA?
NO
RBC ROULEAUX INCREASED?
NO

DISREGARDING: OBESITY, SKIN ECCHYMOSES, STUPOR, VOMITING
COFFEE GROUND, BILIRUBIN INDIRECT TO DIRECT RATIO BLOOD
INCREASED, CHLORIDE BLOOD INCREASED, RBC SCHIZOCYTE (S),
URINE SEDIMENT RBC, CSF GLUTAMINE INCREASED, HAPTOGLOBIN
DECREASED, IRON BINDING CAPACITY TOTAL LESS THAN 240,
PARTIAL THROMBOPLASTIN TIME INCREASED PLATELET (S) LESS
THAN 50,000

PURSUING: SINUSOIDAL OR POSTSINUSOIDAL PORTAL
HYPERTENSION

Here it asks a few more questions about fine nodules
in the liver. These nodules cannot be felt in a patient

with a lot of fluid, so it is told the information is not available. Nevertheless it concludes the micronodal cirrhosis. Then it decides that the acites is transcudative without asking any more questions. It concludes immediately that the renal failure constitutes the so-called hepatal-renal syndrome because of causal links tying cirrhosis to real-hepatal syndrome. At this point it really should have been able to deal with the encephalopathy—the neurological problem is clearly hepatic. But it asks a key question and gets a negative response, so it asks about photohypertension. Eventually, however, it solves the encephalopathy and the other problems in the case.

Iterating toward Answers

As a result of building this system, we have discovered a great deal about medical reasoning. But despite the successes of this system, there are some glaring deficiencies. We never would have learned about those deficiencies had we not experimented seriously with a system. By building a system that is close to what we wanted, we were in a position to learn how to go to the next level. If there is any message that runs through all of the systems work that I know about, it is just this: the business of building expert systems in a tough area, where there are problems people care about, is a process of progressive deepening. You build a theory, you build a program to test that theory, and as you go through the process, your understanding about what is going on progressively grows.

For More Information

Pople, Harry E., Jr., "On the Mechanization of Abductive Logic," *Third International Joint Conference on Artificial Intelligence*, Stanford, CA, 1973.

Pople, Harry E., Jr., "Heuristic Methods for Imposing Structure on Ill-Structured Problems: The Structuring of Medical Diagnostics," in *Artificial Intelligence in Medicine*, edited by Peter Szolovits, Westview Press, Boulder, CO, 1982.

Shortliffe, Edward H., *MYCIN: Computer-based Medical Consultations*, Elsevier, New York, 1976. Based on a PhD thesis, Stanford University, Stanford, CA, 1974.

6
The Low Road
the Middle Road
and the High Road

John Seely Brown
Head
Cognitive and Instructional Sciences
Xerox Corporation

At Xerox Dr. Brown started a basic research group in Cognitive Sciences primarily concerned with understanding how people understand and construct mental models of complex systems. His group was responsible for creating INTERLISP-D and the associated Xerox 1100 line of LISP machines. More recently he investigated how process models gain explanatory power and developed methodologies aimed at constructing more principled process models of cognition. His research continues to be interdisciplinary, involving Artificial Intelligence and psychological and educational issues. Prior to joining Xerox Dr. Brown headed the Intelligent Computer Assisted Instruction Group at Bolt Beranek and Newman. From 1969 to 1973 Dr. Brown held joint faculty appointments in the Department of Information and Computer Science and the Department of Psychology at the University of California at Irvine. Dr. Brown received the BA and MS in Mathematics and the PhD in Computer and Communication Sciences from the University of Michigan.

One can hardly pick up a magazine these days without reading a new story about Artificial Intelligence and the wonders of expert systems. Given all this hype, one cannot help but wonder what the great intellectual breakthroughs in Artificial Intelligence must have been to warrant all this attention. The answer is simple: basically there have been no major intellectual breakthroughs in the last few years. Progress, yes; revolutionary breakthroughs, no. One of the great fathers of knowledge engineering is pleased to tell his audiences that his systems use techniques that have been around for at least ten years. What, then, can explain why Artificial Intelligence has suddenly taken off?

The answer rests not in the intellectual arena but in the recent dramatic advances in hardware, particularly hardware that can effectively execute LISP—the *lingua franca* of Artificial Intelligence. Artificial-intelligence systems that required dedicated, million-dollar mainframes five years ago now can run on machines that cost only $25,000. For the first time we have cost-effective delivery engines for expert systems, a major change. This fact alone is possibly enough to explain why Artificial Intelligence is now catching on. But there is another reason, more subtle, that is worth understanding because the real payoff in Artificial Intelligence during the next few years may not be in expert systems but rather in commercially exploiting the artificial-intelligence mentality (a mentality for coping with ill-defined, constantly changing problems) and the intelligent programming environments that have emerged to enable artificial-intelligence researcher to cope with immensely complex programs. In order to understand this nonstandard position, let us consider some of the properties of Artificial Intelligence.

Ignoring Yesterday's Constraints

Artificial Intelligence is possibly the only discipline that has consistently ignored the realities of yesterday's computer environments, relieving itself of the then dominant concern with conserving CPU cycles and memory and focusing on what was possible rather than what was realistic. By ignoring yesterday's realities, the way was paved to a new culture, a new paradigm, and a new point of view, one that is now ideally situated to take advantage of nearly limitless computrons that are now becoming available.

In order to pursue the barely possible, the Artificial Intelligentsia have been forced to develop a powerful arsenal of programming tools that help manage the complexity of writing and experimenting with gigantic programs, programs constantly undergoing radical change as the programmer zeros in on a crisper understanding of the problem he or she is trying to solve. Gradually these tools became integrated, creating programming environments that facilitate exploratory programming—a programming methodology or style crucial to Artificial Intelligence. Why? Because intelligence is a moving target. One of the founders of Artificial Intelligence once defined intelligence as being that attribute of human behavior that we admire but do not understand. In some ways Artificial Intelligence can be characterized as the study of inherently ill-defined problems where research efforts try to transform complex, ill-defined problems into defined ones.

Power Tools for Programmers

One result of the ill-defined nature of artificial-intelligence problems is that we cannot write logical specifications of what we want. This means only a few people, not a programming hoard, can work together on writing a system. Thus an artificial-intelligence team consists of a couple of people at most. It is not at all surprising that Artificial Intelligence has developed power tools for the wizard programmer. One or two wizards work on an ill-defined problem, write a gigantic system, explore the issues, and move on.

Power tools fall into two categories. One type helps us engage in rapid cost-effective experimentation and debugging. These tools, for example, facilitate both local and global program change. By local program change I mean that we can stop computation when a bug occurs, save the entire program state, use very fancy window systems and browsers to find where things went wrong, make a change, start the computation up again from where it left off, and see if the change fixed the problem. If it did not, fold back the computation to where the change was made and make another patch. Tools like that are very powerful.

Global change comes from what might be called the pancake philosophy: always throw the first one away. This philosophy applied to programming holds that we throw away the first program we write, even if it is a hundred thousand lines long. Of course we do not throw away everything. After we figure out why the program loses, we use power tools to browse over it and radically transform it. The tools must help keep track of what happens when changes are made, they must understand the ramifications of the changes, they must know where everything is in the files, and they must update the data bases concerning who calls whom in the program when the change is made. Such tools border on being intelligent in their own right.

The other class of power tools is aimed at making a program arbitrarily efficient once its definition has settled down. For example, these tools provide methods to instrument programs in order to probe where time is being spent and then to provide means to craft highly efficient data structures and accessing methods in order to improve the efficiency of the final system.

One of the greatest myths is that LISP is good only for exploratory programming and that once one settles on the final prototype, everything must be rewritten in a traditional system programming language. I believe that with the tools that now exist, we can move from the ill defined to the defined and then continuously turn down the screws until we have code that is as efficient as it would have been if it had been written in a traditional systems programming language. Indeed in our own LISP machines, the entire operating system, including the real-time tasks of handling Ethernet traffic, is written in LISP.

Exploratory programming may be crucial to Artificial Intelligence, but so what? The thesis being put forth here is that in the short run, it is precisely the exploratory programming tools (and methodologies) that have emerged from artificial-intelligence research that can be applied to a whole host of traditional problems, problems that barely require Artificial Intelligence but nonetheless do involve uncertainty and change. Indeed it is amazing to realize how many of the problem arenas tackled in classical computer science defy explicit problem specifications at the outset, such as user interfaces.

For example, it is nearly impossible to specify ahead of time exactly how an electronic, personal calendar system should appear. No matter how carefully we think through all the options that it should have and how the interface should be shaped, within the first five minutes of using it we will discover that it is not what we meant or wanted. Woe if the system is cast in concrete and has taken months to implement. Instead we need to be able to construct a prototype rapidly of our best guess and from there experiment and evolve until we converge on what we really need and can use. This is where artificial-intelligence technology, in the short run, can make a major difference. It can provide the tools and programming environment to make this kind of exploration cost effective.

Three Roads to Success

People learning Artificial Intelligence are often confused because at one place they hear that heuristic rules are everything. When they go to another place, they hear that knowledge representation is where the action is. Then they go somewhere else and find that the secret lies in causal models. And here you hear that it is not Artificial Intelligence where the short-term leverage lies, but rather it is in the powerful programming tools that have emerged over the last ten years. How can we make sense of all these different viewpoints? The answer lies in thinking about what I call low-, medium-, and high-road approaches to Artificial Intelligence.

The low-road approach has to do with putting the intelligence into the programming environment itself—that is, to provide the programmer tools that understand the structure of the language he or she is programming in and the systems he or she is crafting (for example, structural editors, data base query systems for answering questions about the programs).

The medium-road approach covers two kinds of systems. The first are the traditional knowledge engineering systems that use if-then rules to encode their knowledge. The use of if-then rules, however, is not the important characteristic of these systems; rather it is the kind of knowledge they encode. These systems encode experiential knowledge, or empirical associations, that an expert has accumulated after seeing many similar situations—for example, seeing time and again that some given symptom could be successfully treated by invoking a given therapy. In brief this kind of knowledge can be best thought of as being the shallow or the surface knowledge of a domain of expertise. This kind of knowledge underlies the handling of typical cases or standard problems. It is woefully inadequate, however, in handling the novel situation. For such cases the high road is needed.

The other kind of middle-road approach is one that combines intelligent interfaces with a powerful, but opaque, domain-specific (mathematical) tool. In such a scheme the intelligent interface knows about the tool and how best to use it. The tool itself encodes a great deal of domain expertise but where the expertise is implicitly rather than explicitly encoded. For example, DENDRAL gets much of its power from this kind of scheme. At its core is a brilliant mathematical algorithm for generating non-isomorphic subgraphs. Another example is the SOPHIE system that obtained its leverage from its use of SPICE, an electronic circuit simulator. SOPHIE was, among other things, a smart electronic troubleshooter. The basic idea was to build a system that could determine the consequences of hypothetical changes to a circuit. For example, what would happen if the value of a resistor were changed or a transistor shorted?

Our first approach was to axiomatize all of the required knowledge in order to put it into a theorem prover. What a dumb idea! Instead a winning idea was to use an extraordinarily powerful circuit simulator surrounded with some intelligent sugar coating. The sugar coating consisted of a collection of intelligent agents that knew all about the idiosyncrasies of the simulator, knew how to communicate with it, knew how to set up, run, and analyze experiments with it, and then how to abstract an answer from the simulation data. These agents also had to know how to propose (using heuristics) experiments or boundary conditions, experiments whose answers would help answer the current question or problem.

We can argue about how much action is in the sugar coating and how much is in the deep mathematical algorithms comprising the core knowledge. My position is that there is action in both; it pays to get leverage out of opaque tools by covering them with semi-intelligent agents. The catch is to establish a synergy between current artificial-intelligence techniques and powerful engineering tools that already exist and that already contain true expertise.

The high-road approach goes beneath the surface models of the experiential knowledge to codify the deep conceptual models. An example of a deep conceptual model would be having a good understanding of the physiological mechanisms of the body for working in the domain of Medicine. It is sometimes necessary to fall back on an understanding of physiological mechanisms when the unusual presents itself. Currently we have few systems that can reason from first principles or causal models in order to infer how to handle the unanticipated or novel situation. Such approaches will become commercially important when the demand for robustness increases.

Real Experts Use More Than Rules

Real experts handle the unanticipated; in fact their ability to handle the unexpected is often what causes them to be judged an expert. To handle the unusual or novel problem, they cannot use just experiential knowledge. Instead they must use deeper causal models of the domain. They draw on causal models to make sense out of conflicting data and to decide what to throw away, what to keep, what to modify, what to believe in, and what to reject.

It is often possible to judge if someone is pursuing primarily the middle-road versus the high-road approach by noting if the primary emphasis is on encoding large collections of rules coupled with relatively simple inference mechanisms or on constructing powerful inference schemes, schemes that operate on a few well-crafted conceptual models.

Once a visitor to our laboratory looked at a system we have for constructing causal explanations of how circuits work. We offered to analyze a circuit of our visitor's choice, and our system satisfactorily explained his circuit. Then he asked, "How many rules do you have in this system?" We said, "Maybe seventy-five." "Seventy-five rules," he said, "that is ridiculous, trivial. I just came from a place that had one thousand rules in its system." His remark stunned us. We were proud that we had only seventy-five rules because we were trying to show how to get maximum distance from the minimum number of rules. One thing that characterizes the high-road approach is the aim to improve the inferential machinery so that more work is done with fewer rules. By having fewer rules, we can more easily characterize what the system can and cannot do, a requisite task for good engineering.

The low-road systems are inherently brittle. They cannot handle anything that was not explicitly put into them. Although the middle-road systems have some ability to handle situations they have not been explicitly told about, they are still confined to the situations their designers had in mind. To get real robustness, we must go to deep, underlying causal models. Without those causal models, systems are likely to collapse when they encounter something slightly beyond their narrow expertise.

Conceptual models provide a backdrop that helps us probe experts. It is difficult to penetrate the rationalizations that experts often have about how they solve a problem. We must set up questions that push experts beyond surface-structure knowledge down to deep-structure knowledge. But without explicit models of a domain's conceptual underpinnings, it is hard to know what types of questions will push them and how to make sense out of what they say because at this deeper level, people are hopelessly inarticulate.

Proceed with Caution But Be Catholic

I do not advocate using just one of these three approaches. I suggest we adopt a research strategy that travels the low, medium, and high roads simultaneously.

Some of our most far-out high-road research has come back, with surprising speed, to affect the low road directly. We want to understand more about the notions of introspection so that we can learn how to create systems that know about themselves. In order to make headway on that problem, one of the researchers in our laboratory built a purely reflective language, a language that at any moment can stop, go up one level, and look at itself. It can even look at how it is looking at itself, generating an infinite hierarchy of reflections. That work has not only helped us make sense out of introspection and reflection in human thinking, but it is having a major impact on the next generation of debugging tools—tools that can suspend a computation and step back and look at its current state without stepping all over itself. The majority of current debugging tools use all kinds of techniques to protect the state of computation so that the debugging programs themselves do not seriously alter that state when they themselves are run. A theory of this procedural reflection is providing an elegant, practical mechanism for solving this problem.

Artificial Intelligence is beginning to grow up. Basic research in Artificial Intelligence is no longer just the mere spinning of hypotheses. Nor does it involve just the building of complex systems, systems that are often as opaque as the phenomena they are purporting to explain.

For More Information

Brown, John S., Richard R. Burton, and Johan de Kleer, "Pedagogical, Natural Language and Knowledge Engineering Techniques in SOPHIE I, II, and III," in *Intelligent Tutoring Systems*, edited by D. Sleeman and J. S. Brown, Academic Press, London, England, 1982.

de Kleer, Johan, and John S. Brown, "Assumptions and Ambiguities in Mechanistic Mental Models," in *Mental Models*, edited by D. Gentner and A. S. Stevens, Lawrence Erlbaum Associates, Hillsdale, NJ, 1983.

Sheil, Beau, "Power Tools for Programmers," *Datamation*, February, 1983.

Smith, Brian C. "Reflection and Semantics in LISP," *Proceedings of the 1984 Principles of Programming Languages Conference of the ACM (POPL)*, February, 1984.

Williams, Michael D., James Hollan, and Albert L. Stevens, "An Overview of STEAMER: An Advanced Computer Assisted Instructional System for Propulsion Engineering," *Behavior Research Methods and Instrumentation*, vol. 2, no. 13, 1981.

7
Expert Systems:
A Discussion

Winston

Before we rush home to build expert systems of our own, we should consider the difficulties of starting such an effort. I would like to ask Dr. Baker about his experiences recruiting people at Schlumberger. My guess is that Schlumberger had some misconceptions about how to recruit people in Artificial Intelligence and what it takes to set up a group. Now that it has had several years of experience, I would like to ask Dr. Baker if he has advice about setting up a group and what he would do differently if he were starting all over again.

Baker

The acquisition of good people is one of our largest problems. Not building up our artificial-intelligence staff beyond what we considered a critical level has been our largest mistake. We tended to have too few people and too many problems. To recruit good people in Artificial Intelligence has been one of our most difficult problems simply because there are not enough good people to go around.

I am not sure how we would do things differently. A good problem and a good computing environment are the best tools for recruiting people. For a while we lagged in our computing environment. Now we think that things are a little better. At least we do not hear nearly as many complaints from our employees now, and sometimes the people even have nice things to say about us.

The two major variables, again, are the good computing environment and the good problem to work on. Success in some area will also attract people who are not willing to make that initial step into your organization.

Winston

Dr. Baker, could you quantify that a little bit? In particular could you say something about what you consider to be an adequate computing environment in terms of what kinds of machines per person? Could you also say something about what you consider to be a minimal group to reach critical mass?

Baker

First, let me tell you a bit about the history of our computing environment. Five or six people formed the original project. All of these people shared a DEC 2020 at the time, which certainly was not adequate. We considered going to either a larger DEC 20 system or a VAX system, but we could not get the kind of environment we wanted for LISP. We ended up going the route of personal work stations.

It is difficult to give the numbers of the people that we have in our artificial-intelligence group today. There are about forty-five people in the department, of whom about twenty-five are researchers. At least half have some inclination toward Artificial Intelligence. Many have PhDs in Artificial Intelligence; some have master's degrees in Artificial Intelligence; others are trained in other backgrounds and work on artificial-intelligence problems.

We now use personal work stations. We set a goal about eighteen months ago that all senior scientists in the group would have personal work stations, which would be networked into a larger computer system. We are about two-thirds there at the present time. A number of our work stations are in a public area. Although all of the work stations are constantly in use, we are not suffering from lack of computing power.

In terms of how many people are needed for a critical mass in Artificial Intelligence, I think it is in the neighborhood of ten professionals. These people would be augmented by support from programmers and technicians.

Winston

I would like to ask Mr. Kraft a related question. I know that Schlumberger's approach, at least in the beginning, was to hire people with degrees in Artificial Intelligence or those who were established in the field. Perhaps as a consequence, Schlumberger's acceleration into the field was somewhat slower than it might have been. Digital's approach seems to be different. Is it the case that you have taken a lot of current employees and put them into your Artificial Intelligence effort at Digital?

Kraft

We have used two approaches. We went to the universities for help with prototypes. We also hired some PhD-level people from the outside. The majority of the people working on artificial-intelligence projects at Digital were other kinds of programmers we already employed, whom we retrained. Not all are capable of starting completely new projects or using all the techniques, but we realized we could not get the staff we needed to grow as fast as we wanted. Internal training courses we have developed for these people have been very successful.

Davis

I was interested in the atmosphere of your talk in the sense that it sounds like an enthusiastic endorsement of the field. When I present that kind of enthusiasm to industrial audiences, I get the reaction that this is nigh unto heresy. Leaving aside your own personal conversion for the moment, how has that attitude been received? Did Digital change its mind all of a sudden? What happened?

Kraft

It was a slow progression. As people began to see that this might work and they got positive feedback from people in the factories, they started to feel that XCON was a useful tool. Then the salespeople got wind of it and wanted to use it but complained that it was just too unfriendly. They demanded something better, so we launched off into XSEL. Once again Digital was willing to put up seed money for a research-level effort.

Winston

I believe almost all of the projects you are working on at Digital now are intended for internal use. Can you say anything about Digital's plans, if any, to become a knowledge-engineering company, as opposed to a consumer of knowledge engineering?

Davis

To what extent is Digital's image of itself changing? Has it begun to stop thinking of itself as a hardware vendor? Has it augmented that image?

Kraft

We have thought about the continuum of everything from delivering artificial-intelligence languages in a VMS environment all the way out to turnkey custom systems. We are trying to understand what it takes to deliver those things. There is no commitment to do that yet, but there is a commitment to understand what the problem is and what it takes to solve the problem.

Internally we are developing that expertise. Whether we will bring it to the marketplace is an open question. Are we getting more into software and applications? While our revenues come mostly from hardware, we are paying increasing attention to software.

Winston

Perhaps for symmetry we should ask Dr. Baker similar questions with respect to Schlumberger's interest in Artificial Intelligence. Schlumberger branched out from the oil-exploration business to a serious commitment to electronics. There must be some interest at Schlumberger in creating expert systems for these other areas as well. Can you say something about that?

Davis

Let me read you a quote: "Coal and oil have made the industrial revolution because they brought abundant and cheap physical power. Microprocessors and memory will make another revolution because they bring abundant and cheap intellectual power. A simple, almost obvious statement, and yet difficult to fully grasp in its finality. The scientists call it the new era of Artificial Intelligence." Jean Riboud, the president of Schlumberger, said it in 1980. He went on to say, "This technical revolution, Artificial Intelligence, is as important for our future as the surge in oil exploration."

There is a certain irony there. The surge in oil exploration has fizzled. One would hope the commitment to Artificial Intelligence has not quite. Are you planning any bold moves?

Baker

In the wireline or oil-field services part of Schlumberger, we are basically a service company. When we talk about a commercial system, we mean one that we would use to give answers to our clients. It would be commercial in the sense that all of our software tends to remain with us when we give the answer to our clients.

In the beginning there was some skepticism about Artificial Intelligence at Schlumberger. Our demonstrations of the DIPMETER ADVISOR and of what we could do with some of the artificial-intelligence computer systems tended to overcome that skepticism. I do not know about plans for building things that will be sold outside. I think there are some activities at Fairchild that are basic research in nature. There are also some things being developed to help other parts of the company very much the way the work at Digital is going now.

Winston

On one side, Professor Pople, you have a fellow whose company has saved substantial amounts of money because of Artificial Intelligence, and on the other side you have a fellow from a company that will make unthinkable amounts of money from Artificial Intelligence. Yet you have been rather reticent about when you think medical diagnosis systems will be practical. When do you intend to form your company, and where can I buy stock?

Pople

We often have people come through looking for opportunities to invest in this new technology. It is very hard to steel oneself and to say, No we don't want your money. We are a long way from the point that we can begin to think of deploying the kind of systems that we have.

We probably have a fifty man-year investment in the project. I do not know how many dollars have been invested, but if we count direct investment and indirect investment, such as free computer services, it is probably something of the order of magnitude that Mr. Kraft saves yearly. I estimate we have about seven million dollars invested now in the INTERNIST/CADUCEUS activity. The payoff is quite a way down the road.

I have tried to figure out what distinguishes our situation from the ones described by my copanelists here. Part of the difference is in the nature of the expertise. Jack Myers happens to be a super-pro in the medical reasoning process. He set his sights at the beginning on a very tough problem. While we have made tremendous inroads in that problem, we certainly have not solved it. I would like to put this in the context of my interpretation of what Artificial Intelligence is all about.

A paradigm from the beginning of artificial-intelligence investigations that has proved to be very helpful has been this. People interested in understanding reasoning and modeling reasoning should tackle tough problems – not with the goal of making money by solving those problems but because by working with tough problems we may develop insights that will have some kind of fundamental import.

There will be new ideas. I think that is why chess has been so helpful. Toy problems have led to insights that we could not have had any other way. The value of those insights has been considerable, although hard to quantify precisely, since the contribution is indirect. I think that the kind of work we are doing falls into that general paradigm. I think that we are doing basic research in Artificial Intelligence.

Winston
I think parachute packers still have to jump once in a while. To draw an analogy, would you be more comfortable being diagnosed by CADUCEUS than by a dart throw at the medical listings in the telephone book?

Pople
I would be much happier with Jack Myers running CADU-CEUS. CADUCEUS is a beautiful tool in Jack Myers's hands. I don't trust it with anybody else at this point.

Davis
That brings up a question I am sure you must have heard hundreds of times. A mistake made when configuring a VAX is going to cost only a few thousand dollars. If you misinterpret an oil-well log, it might cost you a million or so, but nobody dies. What are your thoughts about the social, ethical, and legal issues involved with using medical tools based on Artificial Intelligence?

Pople
There will probably be a period where those of us who build these systems are at considerable risk. Should we be covered by some sort of comprehensive insurance like workmen's compensation? No individual program should bear the whole risk of the major lawsuits as we learn about this. At some point, clearly, the tide will turn. Physicians will be at risk if they fail to consult these programs.

Davis

Medical malpractice is defined as doing as well as an established colleague. Essentially it is defined by peer review. A physician who does not look in a textbook now is guilty of negligence. The day may come when a physician who does use the new technology and makes a mistake will be in trouble; a physician who does not use it and makes a mistake will be negligent.

Pople

In terms of the questions of social issues and acceptance by the medical community, I am not concerned that physicians are as conservative as some people think. They are quick adopters of new technologies that can be demonstrated to be of value to them. Our experience is that there are a lot of good physicians waiting in the wings for us to bail out, to use Professor Winston's analogy. We have very positive reactions from people who have seen the system at work.

Davis

One of the things that all of our panelists share is geographic location. Have you found that your recruiting has been more difficult because of your East Coast location?

Baker

People do like the West Coast, and once they are situated there, they tend to like to stay there. The larger problem for Schlumberger has been that we are not in a major metropolitan area.

Kraft

Digital has had some success recruiting people because it is a growing, nurturing environment. But there are not a lot of people out there, and there is a lot of competition for scarce top-level resources. That is why we have turned more to training our own people as well as trying to recruit from the outside. It is difficult to compete with someone who likes the West Coast life-style.

Winston
Many of us who have visited electronics firms in the Palo
Alto area have been astonished at the turbulence of the
personnel. Do you perceive similar turbulence with artificial-
intelligence workers as more companies enter the field? If
so, do you have any thoughts about whether the scarcity of
artificial-intelligence workers will require you to do anything
special with respect to trying to keep them? To be more
precise, do you have any fears that all of the people who
are getting good at this are going to go off and form their
own companies?

Kraft
That is always a possibility. The only thing you can do is give
them all the tools they need and the management support
and flexibility to do the things they want. For instance,
being a vendor, we have enough hardware for everyone to
work with. It is important to have computer power, the right
terminals, and a management structure that appreciates the
fact that they are walking on the leading edge of technology,
not a gangplank.

Winston
I would like to talk a little bit about university and industry
interaction. From my perspective, I would like Digital and
Schlumberger to give us space, people, and money, in roughly
that order. I wonder what you feel you would like to see the
universities do. In particular, would you like us to do things
in ways different from what we are doing now?

Kraft
I like to see university people who want to work with
industry on problems that may have practical application.
I would like to see more university people visit industry and
more industry people visit the universities.

Pople
I have been extraordinarily lucky to have someone with the
expertise of Jack Myers willing to work with me all this

time. That is one of the things that industry can provide for people who are interested from the academic side. Industry can also provide interesting, tough problems. Joint research at this level has the potential to be extremely rewarding.

Baker

The relationship between industry and the university in Artificial Intelligence is vital. Our core research group does most of our artificial-intelligence work. But we also use people in the universities, we send money, and we have outside contracts with consulting organizations. To do our job requires a combination of these resources. As long as resources are short, this type of interaction is going to have to continue.

Winston

There is an alternative view, having to do with the issue of whether we as a country are eating our seed corn in this area. It is an issue we must all face soon if the universities are to continue to provide industries with new ideas.

Part II

Work and Play

8
Inventing the Future

Alan Kay
Chief Scientist and Vice-President
Atari Corporation

Dr. Kay is responsible for advanced research activities at Atari. Prior to joining Atari, Dr. Kay was a cofounder of the Xerox Palo Alto Research Center and head of its Learning Research Group. Dr. Kay designed SMALLTALK, a programming language for the nonprogrammer, conceived the Dynabook personal computer idea, and codesigned several Xerox PARC personal computers. Dr. Kay received the BS in Mathematics and Molecular Biology from the University of Colorado at Boulder and both the MS in Computer Science and Physiology and the PhD in Computer Science from the University of Utah.

Businesspeople always ask what is going to happen in the future. At Xerox Palo Alto Research Center executives constantly badgered us. Finally I said that the best way to predict the future is to invent it. The future is not laid out on a track. It is something that we can decide, and to the extent that we do not violate any known laws of the universe, we can probably make it work the way that we want to.

Natural Problems, Natural Enemies

Scientists and businesspeople should be allies, but they often are natural enemies much of the time, probably because of their contrasting or conflicting styles. Both believe that they might be able to make money on technology, but they often do not understand the combination of risk and recognition that is required.

I told an executive at Xerox about the great system we were building and I topped off the discussion by saying that the project was risky and had only a 20 percent chance of success, "We're taking risks, just like you wanted." The executive looked at me and said, "Boy, that's great; just make sure it works."

This is why the gambling houses make a lot of money. Most people are willing to accept the idea of 20 percent something or other, but they want to be in that 20 percent, 100 percent of the time. They do not ever want to be in the other 80 percent. But if something is really risky, it means you will lose four out of five times.

Recognition of the new and valuable goes with risk. The tragedy of the Xerox situation from my standpoint was that Xerox did take the risk. They funded us for ten years *blank check*, and we produced things that were ten years ahead of their time, but Xerox did not have the faintest idea what it was when we turned it out.

Unwillingness in the academic community to take risks has led to what I call NSFitis, the problem with funding done on congressional cycles. The NSF funding process almost requires researchers to write up the results of research done the year before as their proposals for new research, thus guaranteeing that they will have those results at the end of the actual funding year. This process leads at best to creative mendacity. The golden age of DARPA funding in the 1960s got better results with a different strategy: fund people rather than projects; no meddling for some years, then swift justice.

Here is something another group of Xerox executives wondered about. (The poor Xerox executive is of course a place holder for all such folk.) Some executives visited the Palo Alto Research Center once so we could explain to them why we wanted to spend more money for VLSI development

tools than the cost of a VLSI fabrication center that they
wanted to build. They could understand the fabrication
center. It would cost considerable millions of dollars, and it
occupied lots of square feet. There were wonderful machines
that cost hundreds of thousands of dollars each, clean rooms,
people, strange-looking lights, air compressors, and filters.
They could make lists and rate things by cubic feet and how
long the shipping would be.

We explained to them that if they did not spend three
times as much on software development tools for doing
VLSI design, then they would have a fabrication center that
would rarely build anything. Chips are getting larger and
larger. Communications problems between different parts of
the chips now dominate logic design. These executives were
uncomfortable because software is insubstantial. It takes
three times as long to do a software system as it does to do
a comparable hardware system. They thought that the way
you got software is that the software fairy sprinkled system
dust on the hardware.

At the time I could not understand how we both could be
living in the same century. Since then I have realized that
although executives dealing with technology are not stupid,
they are not in the same world as the technical person. It is
the difference of point of view that leads to problems: point
of view is worth 80 IQ points.

Not of This World

What does it mean to represent something from our world
in a world that is not of our world? What does it mean to
do things in that world that are not like the things in this
world? How can we translate back into our world in such a
fashion to get a message that actually means something to
us? I think that is mysterious to everyone. Most people in
Artificial Intelligence who have had a glass of wine will tell
you they do not actually understand it much either. The
reason for the mystery is that the correspondences between

what we think is going on in the world and the kinds of
symbols that we use in communication are very fragile. The
nature of much of the fragility is not understood. Every
time we make a model of some kind, we leave out lots of
things, and we base what we do on guesses about causal
relationships rather than on firm understanding.

Intelligence is a difficult concept. School teaches us that
we are not intelligent. The main problem we have with
educating children is that by the time they are ten, they have
been convinced that they are stupid. Our major difficulty
with the kids at the Atari computer camps is not to teach
them programming, which everybody can learn, but to
break them loose from the notion that they cannot solve
problems. In fact kids are natural-born problem solvers.
They just do not apply things that they have learned for
ten years to things that schools have convinced them they
cannot do.

The Personal Computer: A Ten-Year Gestation

It takes at least ten years for an idea to go from first
appearance in the laboratory through translation into the
commercial and, especially, the consumer world. Around
1962 some students at MIT made up a game called Spacewar
on a PDP1 computer. That game was played throughout
the research community for a decade. Nolan Bushnell, the
founder of Atari, brought Spacewar out as a commercial
video game in 1972. To take another example, the first
personal computer was developed around 1965. The LINC
was a little, stand-alone computer with its own virtual
memory and a display screen. But it cost only $18,000 in the
days before cheap computers were known. Several thousand
were built as biomedical research computers. It took ten
years before a machine of roughly the same configuration
came to be sold for the home.

At Xerox this ten-year-lag phenomenon is particularly
poignant because it was about ten years ago that the Alto,

the first powerful personal computer, started working. I will give you a little of the history behind the Alto because it illuminates the way scientists and businesspeople interact.

Research often starts off with a noble failure. The Flex Machine of 1967-1969 was mine. It was probably the second personal computer ever done and the first to run a higher-level language directly, but it was a flop. The problem with the machine was that we had aimed it at noncomputer professionals, such as doctors and lawyers who could not understand the somewhat arcane programming language I had devised. This was a great shock to me, because as a graduate student, I thought all things were possible. For the first time I realized that nobody is going to use a tool, no matter how powerful, unless there is a meaningful communications interface.

Ten years ago we built the Alto at Xerox PARC. It had a high-resolution display with twice as many dots as the Apple Lisa. The Alto had an early version of the mouse to move a pointer on the screen. The display was a bit-map display not because we liked bit maps but because we thought the eventual 1980s notebook-sized Dynabook computer would have a liquid crystal display, which would be only on or off, and we wanted to see what that was like. We did not want to constrain the graphics in any particular way so we allowed the users to customize their own character fonts. Interestingly the Alto was partially designed by concentrating on features that are the very opposite of those in the FLEX machine, which I had designed earlier. The principle is that if some set of features does not work, maybe the opposite of those features will! Hardware is just crystallized software. The Alto first came alive as a piece of hardware in 1973 and was well understood by 1974 and 1975. In 1976 Xerox, for three months, had planned to bring it out as a product. That probably would have changed the face of computing in the United States if that had happened, but the management of the company could not tell the difference between it and the 850 word processor that had been done in Dallas and it decided to bring out the word processor instead.

Disappearance of Computers

Computers as boxes are not long for this world. Computers are too important to put on people's desks. We do not have our desks everywhere. We often go to the beach and on planes. The first time I ever saw a flat screen display, in 1968, I realized that computer mobility was only a matter of time. Thank goodness, I had no idea how much time. I thought it would take five years to build computers whose physical dimensions are the size of the display we want to see.

We call that idea the Dynabook. When I went to Xerox, that is what we worked on. It was a ten-year-long project that gave rise to many of the work station ideas that we have today. The idea was that Dynabook would be so portable that we could carry other things too. In other words, if we were going to carry anything, we would probably carry the Dynabook. We now have a more sophisticated notion of portability and just what that should mean. Computers are going to disappear as physical objects. They will disappear into the wiring of our houses and into the clothes that we wear.

The Dynabook project is not an example of management by objectives. Management by objectives does not work in research. Management by objectives is a strategy that ensures that all the good research people will leave. The people who are willing to stay are what you deserved in the first place.

Consider the analogy of the computer industry with publishing. After the industrial revolution the profit margins on paper went down to almost zero. Up until that time the economics of selling books mostly centered on selling the paper rather than the biblical messages that were often written on it. The novel was then an isolated art form. But after the industrial revolution the novel became extremely popular because it was the discardable piece of content that the publishers needed. The publishing industry settled into a situation in which there was no profit margin on the hardware and the software could not be controlled by a single publisher. The publishing business became a business of distributing information in the most efficient way possible.

That is happening in the computer industry now. Profit margins on chips are abysmally low. Captive software has not been a reality for several years. Even companies like IBM and AT&T say they will make open systems and will not risk developing software for their products anymore.

String Pullers

Perhaps the most difficult thing for people to grasp is that it takes almost fifteen years to accept a new programming language. This is unbelievable. A generation in Computer Science is about three years; that is the length of time it takes to write an operating system. So we are talking about five generations for the acceptance of a programming language.

Most programming languages bring the following image to my mind: there is a demented but incredibly powerful Greek god pulling the strings on all of the puppets in the universe. There are an awful lot of strings that have to be pulled. String-pulling languages, such as PASCAL, BASIC, ALGOL, and ADA, comprise about 90 to 95 percent of all the languages. Imagine a bearded programmer who whispers in the Greek god's ear what the god should do next.

Negotiating Diplomats

A second model that came out of the 1960s led to the work on SMALLTALK that I did and the work on Actors that Carl E. Hewitt of the MIT Artificial Intelligence Laboratory did. Instead of a Greek god there are a lot of ambassadors who have to negotiate with each other to get anything done. They cannot tell each other what to do since that would start a war. But what one ambassador can say is, "Will you do this?" And the other says, "Yeah, I'll probably do this, if I get around to it." He gets around to it eventually, and things work out. This ambassador model works better because each ambassador has a great deal of autonomy and protection. Whatever the ambassador can do can be done at any time, without worrying about what the other ambassadors are able to do because the ambassadors are protected from each other by protocols.

Hardy Frontiersmen

There is a third model, the hardy frontiersman model, that is just starting to gain support. Instead of wheedling and negotiating, the hardy frontiersman model calls up the image of a frontier barn raising where people are naturally attracted to the parts of the job that they are best at.

The problem attracts the problem solver rather than there being a problem solver that tries to solve the problem. This shows a great deal of promise. It fits in very neatly with Professor Winston's analogy and metaphor ideas, since analogy and metaphor are among the strongest ways of discovering whether the experts can find the right parts of a problem to work on.

Market Analysis

The computer industry is moving from a box-selling industry to a service industry. If the leaders in the industry have any sense, the computer industry will become a way-of-life industry. The computer should be noticeable only when it is not around, like the telephone.

Do not use market analysis to predict the future. Market analysis has failed to predict all of the interesting and high-impact technological innovations of the twentieth century because it tends to look at trends. But there is no trend that led from the railroad to the airplane. There is no trend that led from the horse and buggy to the car; no trend that led from the desk calculator to the pocket calculator; no trend that led from the ditto machine to the Xerox machine; no trend that led from the mainframe computer to the personal computer.

Amplifying Communication and Fantasy

I suggested to our Xerox executives that there are certain themes deep inside humanity, without which we cannot be human.

Two of those themes are communication and fantasy. I consider the airplane a communications device. I consider the photocopier a communications device. The railroads thought they were in the railroading business, and IBM thought they were in the computer business, but both were really in the communications business. History shows clearly that anytime anybody makes a communications amplifier, even if it costs more than what it is displacing, it is still going to do well if it is an improvement.

I characterize fantasy as that collection of worlds where things are simpler and more controllable. It is not just displacing ourselves from the real world when we go to the theater, or the movies, or watch television. It is also things like mathematics and science. They are all simpler and more controllable than real life. Fantasy becomes much more powerful when we can control it. Video games are the triumph of control over detail. It is actually a way of enfranchising a disenfranchised society as far as being able to control things.

These things are so important because building complex things is hard. The control of complexity is the problem. Most things that people discover are fairly simple. The problem is that there are so many wrong ways of doing things, and there are so few signposts marking the wrong directions that it is a tremendous intellectual feat to do significant work at all.

The signposts in Artificial Intelligence hardly exist, so usually when we find something, it is greeted with curious reactions: "Well, why didn't I think of that before?" Or, "Gee, anybody could do that." That is true; anybody could if they happen on the right way. But getting to that right way requires a strong combination of powerful tools and a kind of intuition only a few people possess. The amount of leverage that a person has depends greatly on the kinds of systems that he uses.

In 1970, I was the co-head of the Robot Group in the Stanford University Artificial Intelligence Project. In those days the key problem was to look at a table with a TV camera and to have a robot arm stack blocks. We could never get the TV camera and the computer to locate the blocks so the arm could do its part of the job. We finally came up with a great solution—intelligent blocks. The blocks would see where the arm was and waddle over to it.

For More Information

Abelson, Harold, and Andrea diSessa, *Turtle Geometry*, MIT Press, Cambridge, MA, 1981.

Clocksin, William F., and Christopher S. Mellish, *Programming in Prolog*, Springer-Verlag, New York, 1981.

Hewitt, Carl E., and Peter de Jong, "Open Systems," Report AIM-691, Artificial Intelligence Laboratory, Massachusetts Institute of Technology, Cambridge, MA, 1982.

Kornfeld, William A., and Carl E. Hewitt, "The Scientific Community Metaphor," *IEEE Transactions on Systems, Man, and Cybernetics*, vol. SMC-11, no. 1, 1981.

Papert, Seymour, *Mindstorms*, Basic Books, New York, 1981.

Winston, Patrick Henry, and Berthold K. P. Horn, *LISP*, Addison-Wesley, Reading, MA, 1981.

9
The Engineer's Apprentice

Aryeh Finegold
President
Daisy Systems Corporation

In 1980 Mr. Finegold cofounded Daisy Systems Corporation in order to design the LOGICIAN, a computer work station for VLSI design. Prior to 1980 Mr. Finegold worked at Intel, where he was responsible for input-output architecture within the product line architecture department. In addition he directed logic design and prototyping of the 8089 input-output processor and developed an application system for the 8089. Mr. Finegold received the BS in Electrical Engineering from Technion-Israel Institute of Technology and has done graduate work in Computer Science.

It would be nice to assert that Daisy Systems is an artificial-intelligence company. Unfortunately, I cannot. I have never found two artificial-intelligence scholars who agree on what Artificial Intelligence is, so I have to be content with explaining what we do. At Daisy we create intelligent work stations that increase the productivity of electronic design engineers.

A Babel of Tools

How do electronic engineers design products today? What are the problems they face? One problem is similar to the problem that programmers face: programmers want to speak English to their machines. While hardware design engineers do not necessary want to speak English to their machines, they do want to do their design work using high-level descriptions.

Consider this analogy. If architects were to design houses the way electronic design engineers design microprocessors, they would not begin by describing a house with three bedrooms, one kitchen, and two bathrooms. Instead they would start by describing the individual tiles on the floors and the individual bricks in the walls. This is not to say that design-automation tools are not available to electronic design engineers. There are plenty of tools. The problem is getting them to talk to each other.

When I designed microprocessors at Intel Corporation, a microprocessor was only 15,000 transistors, and it typically took a PhD graduate five months to do a logic simulation. It took that long because he had to start by explaining the schematic in a language that the logic simulation package could understand. Today people are introducing microprocessors with 150,000 transistors and working on the next generation, with still another zero involved.

Reinventing the Wheel

Another problem is reinventing the wheel. People are converting design today from printed circuit board technology to gate-array technology. To do that conversion, sophisticated design engineers scan the schematics of the printed circuit board. Every time they find a counter, they have to design a combination of gates that a gate array can use to do the same function.

Why is it necessary to do that over and over? Why not simply write a program that automatically translates counters into the appropriate translation for the gate array? If we asked a design engineer that question, he would say it is impossible because the translation is content dependent. He would have to look at where the counter is used in order to decide how to translate it into a particular technology.

If we consider programs that do things like printed circuit board routing or gate-array layout, one of the big problems is the tendency to dominate the human, even though the tool is basically good. Consequently a design engineer who has spent many years doing integrated circuit layout is forced to make an unfortunate choice: let the machine do all the work or do all the work himself. If he lets the machine do it, the machine will tell him to keep out of things, that it is doing the whole job. But when the machine ends up with five wires undone, the engineer is supposed to fix it. He does not know why the program placed what it did or why the remainder could not be handled. He must rethink the entire problem from the beginning.

Another problem is that tools that are available today tend to dictate policy rather than supply mechanisms. A good example is that most layout systems are for bottom-up design. The designer who prefers to do a top-down design is out of luck.

Engineers' Natural Language

Because of these problems Daisy designed a work station that basically lets the design engineer sit in front of a high-performance graphics terminal that speaks in his own engineering language, with nands, nors, and other symbols.

Everything that the engineer enters on the keyboard or the tablet goes into a common database, from which it is automatically translated into a form suited to any available design automation program. The engineer, sitting at the terminal, can do a simulation that enables him to see how the new computer or new controller will behave. Similarly he can go down to a level where he can do logic simulation and actually probe nodes in the future machine. He can even go down to the physics and do circuit simulation at the transistor level. Moveover, he can analyze the testability of his product, generating interfaces to test equipment. With our latest product, the GATE MASTER, he can work back and forth between the logic design and the layout design.

This type of design environment has solved the traditional design problems.

The design engineer speaks his natural language with our
LOGICIAN or GATE MASTER. This natural language is
not English but a language tailored to the profession. While
I was at Intel, responsible for putting together an IC family,
my group consisted of a Japanese design team, an Israeli
design team, and a marketing group from California. It was
impossible to communicate with each other; we almost gave
up trying. Then I started drawing on a whiteboard, using
nand and nor gates and waveforms. Suddenly everyone's
eyes opened up. In five minutes we had everything done. The
Japanese and the Israelis went home and built the right chips
because they spoke the same language as do electronic design
engineers everywhere. This natural language of nand and
nor gates is the convenient language to describe engineering
thinking to programs.

Our work station enables design engineers to sit in front
of terminals and enter information in their kind of language.

Inventing the Wheel Once

At Daisy we have an integrated knowledge base system
that carries the engineer's thought all the way from a
concept down to the point where a design is ready to
go to manufacturing. Our system understands what nand
gates are and what nor gates are. Rather than just pushing
polygons around, our system knows as things are drawn
that doing certain things with nands does not make sense.
Often the system knows that the intention must have been
to do something else, perhaps with a nor. Our system
recognizes logic symbols for what they are rather than as a
semantic-free combination of pixels on a screen.

Daisy uses a modeling language that translates automatically from the graphics to the design automation tools. Once
the design engineer shows the system how to do something,
the system will do the right thing forever. If the design
engineer invents a new kind of logic, all he has to do is
describe that new logic to the LOGICIAN work station

or to the GATE MASTER work station. Similarly he can describe how to translate a counter from printed circuit board technology to gate-array technology, and the system will know how to do it from then on.

Working Hand in Hand

Daisy's approach from the start has been to supply mechanisms rather than to enforce policy. I believe strongly in working hierarchically, in breaking big problems into smaller problems. Nevertheless our machines also support the bottom-up approach because there are people who prefer to think that way. If that is the way they like it, that is the way they will get it from us. We will not force our way of thinking on their ways of working.

I have mentioned the issue of the machine dominating the man. The better mode, obviously, is to work hand-in-hand through an interactive process. One good example is in the GATE MASTER product. The LOGICIAN, our original product, addressed the electronic design phase, generating input to a physical layout system. Our newer GATE MASTER product integrated both systems. The design engineer using the GATE MASTER can design a semi-custom IC by designing the logic, jumping into the layout, looking at how much area his logic is going to take. If he likes what he sees, he can carry on with the logic, and if he does not like what he sees, he can go back to the logic he has done and change things around.

Previous systems for automatic placement and routing were such that you submitted runs and prayed that when you came back in the morning there would be only five lines to route. The cost? Two days in an industry where two days is a long time. With our system you can start manually, drop into an interactive placement and routing, and watch the machine work in front of you. You see things happen on the screen so you can stop the system at any time to go back to a manual mode for a while. After making your suggestions, you can let the machine continue. You have control. You understand what the machine has done because you interacted with it all the time.

Virtual Probes into Virtual Machines

Another example of interactiveness is our logic simulation. The traditional logic simulation tools are batch process tools. You submit your simulation request to the machine to be run in the evening when the computer is not busy, and you return in the morning, greeted by an enormous stack of printout. You scan it, looking for what has gone wrong. Most of the time you are looking for a snowball in a blizzard. With our logic simulation tool, you sit in front of an image of the machine to be simulated. You connect virtual probes to that machine, one that does not exist yet, as if you were in your laboratory using a regular oscilloscope. The probes then produce waveforms that the machine would produce if it were running in real time in front of you. You can insert signals, disconnect things, and connect things, all at the terminal interactively, in almost real time. Bug fixing takes minutes, not days.

Solutions and Dreams

Are we an artificial-intelligence company? I think Daisy is a solution company. We provide solutions to the problem of increasing the productivity of electronic design engineers. In order to do that we have transferred technology. One of the sources of that technology is the field of Artificial Intelligence. For that transferred technology, we thank the universities, including MIT.

Daisy is one place in which investors have not regretted their support. But rather than telling you how successful Daisy is myself, let me tell you what President Ronald Reagan said in his March 4, 1983, policy speech on the world economy, delivered to the Commonweal Club in San

Francisco. His speech ended this way: "I began today by saying that if we believe in our ability to work together, we can make America the mightiest trading nation on earth. Here in this room, and not far from this building, are people in companies with a burning commitment that we need to make our country great. One of those companies, the Daisy Systems Corporation, is a computer firm in Sunnyvale, California. It was formed in August, 1980, and it made $7 million in sales in its first shipping year. This year it expects to see $25 million and by 1986, $300 million. Daisy Corporation is already selling its products in the markets of France, Norway, Belgium, Great Britain, Germany, Israel, and Japan. Its work force has nearly quadrupled in the last year."

My dream for America is to take that kind of success and multiply it by a million.

For More Information

Stallman, Richard M., and Gerald J. Sussman, "Forward Reasoning and Dependency-directed Backtracking in a System for Computer-aided Circuit Analysis," *Artificial Intelligence*, vol. 9, no. 2, 1977.

Sussman, Gerald J., and Richard M. Stallman, "Heuristic Techniques in Computer Aided Circuit Analysis," *IEEE Transactions on Circuits and Systems*, vol. CAS-22, no. 11, 1975.

10
The Programmer's Apprentice

Charles Rich
Research Scientist
Artificial Intelligence Laboratory
Massachusetts Institute of Technology

Dr. Rich codirects the Programmer's Apprentice project. The project's goals are to create an artificial-intelligence theory of the design and construction of large software systems and to apply this theory to automated tools that increase programmer productivity and reliability. Dr. Rich has worked most recently on new techniques for representing the knowledge of expert programmers. He is tutorial chairman for the American Association for Artificial Intelligence and a member of the ACM (SIGART, SIGPLAN and SIGSOFT) and the IEEE Computer Society. He received the BS in Engineering Science from the University of Toronto and the MS and PhD in Artificial Intelligence from MIT.

A dark cloud is hanging over much of the computer industry. Its properties are well known to all of us: software is chronically late and notoriously unreliable. A way to disperse this cloud is to introduce programming apprentices. To see why, let us begin by looking at the history of software technology (figure 1).

Figure 1 is an example of what Professor Winston calls the Staircase Theory. The first major jump in programming technology was the invention of high-level languages, such as FORTRAN. These languages led to an order of magnitude improvement in productivity and reliability over using assembly languages. Following that there was a period of little innovation. Then there was a smaller jump, which can

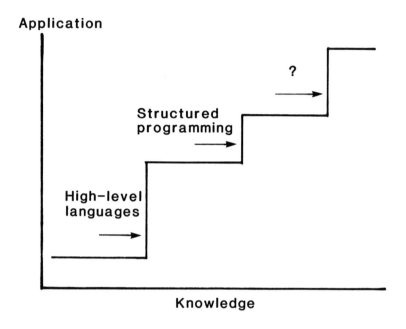

Figure 1. History of software technology.

be credited to the introduction of structured programming and other related methodologies.

We are now in another flat period of small improvements and diminishing returns. Unfortunately the appetite for new software is growing so fast that it threatens to overtake our ability to satisfy that appetite with available software producing tools. Where are the ideas going to come from for the next major order-of-magnitude improvement in software productivity?

Suppose you have a programming shop with ten programmers who share one VAX computer. You can improve productivity by giving each programmer a personal VAX. Now suppose you want to give each programmer the equivalent of ten VAX computers, a reasonable capital investment relative to the programmer's salary, given that hardware costs are going down and salaries are going up. What will you do with the rest of that computing power? How are you going to bring it to bear on the productivity problem?

Everyone a Chief Programmer

Artificial Intelligence has an answer: you can give each programmer the equivalent of a personal helper. In the early 1970s Harlan Mills of IBM popularized the idea of the chief programmer team. His idea was to surround each expert programmer with a support team of assistant programmers, documentation writers, and program librarians. The effect is to increase the expert programmer's productivity because the expert programmer spends less time trapped in mundane details and trivial bugs. Instead he concentrates on the parts of the software development process that can be done alone, those parts that have the greatest effect on the profitability and reliability of the software in the long term.

We propose to provide every programmer with a support team consisting of intelligent computer programs. The distinction between this view and the traditional software development paradigm is that we take seriously the idea of adding another agent to the programming picture (figure 2). We call this agent the Programmer's Apprentice.

Our goal is to make it possible for the programmer to interact with the apprentice in much the same way that he interacts with another, though less talented, human programmer. This metaphor has several important features. The first is that it provides a familiar framework for the delivery to the programmer of artificial-intelligence-based facilities, such as automatic documentation, automatic error detection, and ultimately automatic programming.

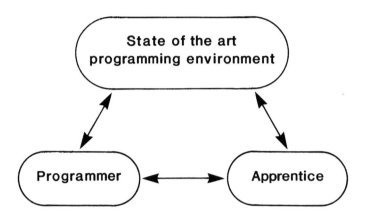

Figure 2. Adding a new agent to the programming picture.

The goal of totally automatic programming over a wide spectrum of applications is far in the future. But that need not deter us from present success through the apprentice metaphor.

An Incremental Approach

The importance of the apprentice metaphor is that it allows us to take an incremental approach to the problem of automating a programming task. We start with the programmer's delegating to the apprentice the simplest and most routine parts of the programming task because that is all we know how to do right now. As techniques improve, we will transfer more of the programming load from the programmer to the apprentice.

The apprentice paradigm has several other important features. We start with a state-of-the-art programming environment, which is important for two reasons. First, we do not want to reinvent everything already developed in state-of-the-art programming environments. Second, it is important not to take away from the programmer anything he can already do. For the audience that we are targeting, expert professional programmers, it is important to avoid the mistake of trying to help programmers by preventing them from doing things. Programmers must always have full access to the existing tools in the programming environment.

To provide the kinds of assistant services we have in mind, the apprentice itself also has to have access to the existing programming environment. For example, it needs to be able to find a file the programmer wants to edit, to run a compilation, and to look for compilation errors.

Knowledge-Based Editing

Let us look at a limited demonstration of an apprentice-like system that we currently run on LISP Machines at the MIT Artificial Intelligence Laboratory. The scenario in the demonstration illustrates the differences between what the programmer can do with the help of the apprentice compared to what he would do without an apprentice. The scenario involves what we call knowledge-based editing. In the scenario the programmer makes low-level design decisions but he delegates the coding work to the apprentice. This delegation depends on the apprentice's understanding the vocabulary of programming design.

To begin the scenario, the programmer asks the apprentice to implement a program as a search, a standard programming concept.

```
<KBE>Define a program DELETE with a parameter SYMBOL.
<KBE>Implement it as a search.
```

```
DELETE:  PROCEDURE(SYMBOL) RETURNS  (...);
             DCL SYMBOL ...,
                 AGGREGATE ...,
                 BOOL ...,
                 ITEM ....;
             AGGREGATE = *arg*:
         LP:  *enumerator*(AGGREGATE, BOOL, ITEM);
             If BOOL THEN RETURN (NULL());
             If *test*(ITEM) THEN RETURN (*action*());
             GOTO LP;
           END DELETE;
```

It is our job as apprentice developers to make sure that the apprentice has an adequate model of search in its knowledge base. Based on that model the apprentice can write the code as shown. Without the apprentice the programmer would have had to type in all the code manually, with the associated risk of errors.

Easy Intervention

In the following interaction, the programmer has invoked another standard programming design cliché, Trailing Pointer List Enumeration. This additional choice does not correspond to any filling in of blanks. Instead what is happening is that the apprentice, in order to preserve the quality of the code, has reorganized and recoded it. This is crucial. It is important for the programmer to be able to intervene in the partially automated process at any point.

Just as in VLSI routing the programmer has to be able to deal with the few things that the automated system cannot do. He must be able to understand what the automated system has done. The code must be readable at all points. Taking a fill-in-the-blanks methodology literally leads to incomprehensible code, just like the output of an old-style automatic router.

```
<KBE>Implement the enumerator as a trailing pointer
list enumeration of "HASH(SYMBOL)".
```

```
DELETE:  PROCEDURE(SYMBOL) RETURNS (...);
            DCL SYMBOL ...,
                CURRENT POINTER,
                PREV POINTER,
                HASH EXTERNAL ENTRY(...) RETURNS (...),
                NODEPTR POINTER,
                1 NODE BASED (NODEPTR),
                  2 VALUE ...,
                  2 NEXT POINTER;
            PREV = HASH(SYMBOL);
            CURRENT = PREV->NEXT;
     LP:    IF CURRENT=NULL() THEN RETURN (NULL());
            IF *test*(CURRENT) THEN RETURN
              (*action*());
            PREV = CURRENT;
            CURRENT = CURRENT->NEXT;
            GOTO LP;
          END DELETE:
```

Next we see that the programmer can choose the level at which he wants to instruct the apprentice—in this case by typing in a piece of PL/1 code.

Note, however, that the programmer describes the place
where the code is supposed to go in terms of its role in the
overall design rather than specifying exactly which line it
goes in:

```
<KBE>Implement the test as "CURRENT->VALUE=SYMBOL".


DELETE:  PROCEDURE(SYMBOL) RETURNS (...);
             DCL SYMBOL...,
                 CURRENT POINTER,
                 PREV POINTER,
                 HASH EXTERNAL ENTRY (...) RETURNS (...),
                 NODEPTR POINTER,
                 1 NODE BASED (NODEPTR),
                   2 VALUE...,
                   2 NEXT POINTER;
             PREV = HASH(SYMBOL);
             CURRENT = PREV->NEXT;
       LP:   IF CURRENT=NULL() THEN RETURN (NULL());
             IF CURRENT->VALUE=SYMBOL
                THEN RETURN (*action*()):
             PREV = CURRENT;
             CURRENT = CURRENT->NEXT;
             GOTO LP;
           END DELETE:
```

The apprentice can also remember what remains to be done,
keeping track of which design decisions have not yet been
made:

```
<KBE>What needs to be done?
Implement the action of the program.
Use the previous value of the enumerator.



<KBE>Implement the action as a splice-out of "PREV".



DELETE:   PROCEDURE(SYMBOL);
              DCL SYMBOL ...,
                  CURRENT POINTER,
                  PREV POINTER,
                  HASH EXTERNAL ENTRY (...)RETURNS (...),
                  NODEPTR POINTER,
                  1 NODE BASED (NODEPTR),
                    2 VALUE...,
                    2 NEXT POINTER;
              PREV = HASH(SYMBOL);
              CURRENT = PREV->NEXT;
        LP:   IF CURRENT=NULL() THEN RETURN;
              IF CURRENT->VALUE=SYMBOL
                  THEN DO; PREV->NEXT = PREV->NEXT->NEXT;
                  RETURN; END:
              PREV = CURRENT;
              CURRENT = CURRENT->NEXT;
              GOTO LP;
            END DELETE:
```

The next interaction illustrates some rudimentary automatic documentation. The apprentice answers a specific query from the programmer interactively. The answer the query requires is not obvious from the code and demands a certain amount of program analysis, automatically invoked by the apprentice:

```
<KBE>Describe the ports of DELETE.
The SYMBOL parameter.
The TBL free variable input.
The TBLSIZE free variable input.
The TBL side-effect output.


<KBE>Display the source of the TBL output.


DELETE:  PROCEDURE(SYMBOL);
             DCL SYMBOL ...,
                 CURRENT POINTER,
                 PREV POINTER,
                 HASH EXTERNAL ENTRY (...) RETURNS (...),
                 NODEPTR POINTER
                 1 NODE BASED (NODEPTR),
                   2 VALUE ...,
                   2 NEXT POINTER;
             PREV = HASH(SYMBOL);
             CURRENT = PREV->NEXT;
        LP:  IF CURRENT NULL() THEN RETURN;
             IF CURRENT->VALUE=SYMBOL
                 THEN DO PREV->NEXT = PREV->NEXT->NEXT;
                 RETURN; END;
             PREV = CURRENT;
             CURRENT = CURRENT->NEXT;
             GOTO LP;
         END DELETE:
```

We recently extended this part of our demonstration in the direction of generating permanent documentation as distinguished from answering interactive queries.

When Can I Have One?

Figure 3 dramatizes the various stages and corresponding orders of effort required to move an idea like knowledge-based editing from the laboratory out into the real world. The areas of these rectangles are scaled by orders of magnitude from the smallest to the middle to the largest. The tiny innermost

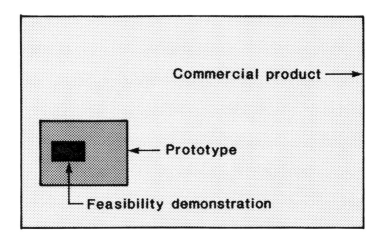

Figure 3. From the laboratory to the cold world: Orders of effort.

rectangle is the first stage, the feasibility demonstration. This usually takes place in the laboratory and produces a rickety, wired-together system. The poor engineering quality of these demonstration systems is the result of concentrating all resources on those aspects of the system that inquire into the theoretically important issues. Efficiency, robustness, and user friendliness are sacrificed.

Once feasibility has been demonstrated, the next step is to produce a prototype. The fundamental goal of the prototype is to get feedback from a group of users different from the group of people who wrote it. To develop a usable prototype, it is necessary to pay attention to all those things that were ignored in the feasibility stage, such as efficiency, modularity, and the user interface. In our experience if the feasibility demonstration is of nontrivial size, then the prototype is a major software project. Much of that prototype work is not as important theoretically as the initial feasibility demonstration.

We have no experience bringing things to the level of a commercial product. That step is probably also an order of magnitude jump in effort, just like the step from the feasibility demonstration to the prototype.

There are two key points to emphasize. The first is the notion of incremental automation. Programming is an example of a task that it will not be possible to automate totally for a long time. In all such tasks there are significant gains to be had by incremental, partial automation. The key to carrying out the incremental automation successfully is a careful analysis of the task in order to identify an important division of labor between the person and the intelligent assistant program. The Programmer's Apprentice is one example of this division of labor. The second point to emphasize is the length of time required to move from feasibility demonstration through prototype to commercial product. In our project we have learned the hard way about the amount of effort and time required to move between these stages.

Significant improvements in programmer productivity and software reliability have been frustratingly hard to achieve. Of the many different software production technologies currently in the laboratory stage, programming apprentices based on artificial-intelligence techniques promise to yield the most dramatic improvements.

For More Information

Rich, Charles, and Howard E. Shrobe, "Initial Report on a LISP Programmer's Apprentice," *IEEE Transactions on Software Engineering*, vol. SE-4, no. 6, 1978.

Waters, Richard C., "The Programmer's Apprentice: Knowledge Based Program Editing," *IEEE Transactions on Software Engineering*, vol. SE-8, no. 1, 1982.

11
Intelligent Advisory Systems

Roger Schank
President, Cognitive Systems, Incorporated
and
Chairman, Department of Computer Science
Director, Artificial Intelligence Department
Yale University

Professor Schank, a member of the Yale University faculty since 1974, founded Cognitive Systems, Incorporated, in 1979. He is a member of the governing board and a founder of the Cognitive Science Society, as well as a founder and member of the board of editors of the Cognitive Science Journal. *He has published several books on computers and understanding. Professor Schank received the MA and PhD in Linguistics from the University of Texas.*

I am trying to be two things at once. I persist in being a professor despite the fact people who are involved in financing my business think that giving it up would be a good idea, and I persist in being president of a company despite the fact that the president of my university thinks that giving *that* up would be a good idea. Perhaps that is why I have a schizophrenic view of what it is I am trying to do. I want to build practical artificial-intelligence systems, but my major preoccupation in life is exploring how people work. I believe these two goals are related.

I began my work in the field of Artificial Intelligence by looking at language. Once you get into the problem of how people understand language, you get into the problem of what kinds of knowledge people need to use language. What do they talk about? What do they care about? How do they

think? People have the annoying habit of saying the same
thing in different ways. Consider these sentences:

Mary socked John.
Mary gave John a punch.
Mary hit John with her fist.

While they do not look alike, they mean the same thing.
One way or another we have to consider the content behind
language. The difficult part of language understanding is to
extract the content from the language. Language is like a
code. The first intellectual challenge is to figure out what
the content is by decoding.

The second intellectual challenge is to deal with what is
called the inference problem. When people say one thing,
they mean to imply other things. If we are told that John
ate dinner, we might assume that he is not hungry anymore
and that he had previously been hungry. If we are told
that John had dinner at a restaurant, we know that a
waiter or waitress probably served him. Such assumptions,
fundamental to human communication, are not logically
infallible, but they are reasonable nevertheless. Consider
the word *give* in the following uses:

John gave Mary a book.
John gave Mary a hard time.
John gave Mary a night on the town.
John gave up.
John gave no reasons for his actions.
John gave a party.

Now consider the word *hand*:

John has a hand.
John had a hand in the cookie jar.
John had a hand in a robbery.
John is an old hand.
John gave Mary a hand.
John asked Mary for her hand.

What we discover through such sentences is that the language problem is not just a problem of dictionary entry. *Give*, in some sense, means almost nothing. The meaning of *hand* varies enormously.

How is it that language has so many words that do not have any precise meaning? That is the problem I have always been interested in, and I have a long history of trying to solve it. In 1969 I directed efforts at the Stanford University Artificial Intelligence Project aimed at building natural language understanding systems. The first one that we built, MARGIE, worked with sentences like, "John paid $2.00 to the bartender for some wine." (See Schank et al. 1975.) In the course of our efforts to build algorithms that could do the analysis of such sentences, we discovered a fact that most artificial-intelligence researchers at some point run into, whatever their domain: the major problem is getting the representation right.

Paraphrases, Inferences, and Answers

If you cannot figure out how to represent knowledge, you cannot go anywhere. I devised a representation scheme called Conceptual Dependency, which is not English or any other natural language (See Schank 1972.) Instead it is an internal language designed to represent the content of natural language utterances unambiguously. Once we had translated sentences into that representation, we found that it was easy to write a program that would generate English text expressing the meaning captured by the representation. This enabled us to build a paraphrase machine that would translate from our sample English sentence into our internal representation and back again into a sentence using *paid*, or *sell*, or *buy*, or *traded*, all of which can be used to express the same meaning as the sample sentences.

At the same time we began to do inferencing. (See Rieger 1975.) As we typed in a sentence, a program would say what else might be true as a consequence of the sentence.

If John told Mary that Bill wants a book, then it might be true that John believes that Bill wants a book, or it might be true that Bill wants to read the book, or it might be true that Bill will try to get the book. Then the program tended to get carried away, producing more and more inferences. It reasoned that John and Mary may have wanted to give Bill a book and that John and Mary may have recently been together, inferring more and more things from its own inferences.

Up to this point our programs could work with language only sentence by sentence. Read a sentence; do something with it; read another sentence; do something with that. The next step was to wonder about how sentences combine. Note what happens when one sentence is placed with another:

John went into a restaurant. An hour later he walked out.

Compare that to:

John went into a building. An hour later he waved from a window.

In the first pair we have a sense of what happened. In the second we do not. In the first pair we have an ability to guess, to read between the lines, to understand what else might have been going on. Now consider these:

Mary went to a restaurant. She asked what the special of the day was.

Mary went to a store. She asked what the latest news from Iran was.

These pairs are very different in terms of the amount of implicit information they convey despite the fact that they are syntactically quite similar.

John went to a restaurant. He had some fish. He left a small tip.

What do we conclude? That he told the person in the restaurant which horse to bet on in the fifth race at Belmont?

Certainly not. We do not think about that meaning, and we do not note the ambiguity. In the early days of language-understanding work, researchers wrote programs that would note such ambiguities, and for a time there were unspoken competitions to see whose program could note the most. Some terrific examples were devised.

I wanted to write programs that see only the meaning that suits the context. Such programs must have the ability to use the different meanings of the word *tip* but to see only the right one. To do that, we had to build in a sensitivity to context. Language considered in context is much less ambiguous than sentences considered out of context.

After relating that story about John and the fish, I could ask a variety of questions: What did John eat? Who served him? What was the meal? What was the tip for? Although none of the answers was explicitly given in the sentence, we could still answer such questions. Once again the context is the key. Because we understand that the entire episode took place inside a restaurant, we can use our knowledge about restaurants to help us to infer the answers.

Summarizing News

How did we get a computer to do as well? We worked out another representation, called a script, a sequence of conceptual-dependency representations that describe everything that normally happens in a given context. Thus our program was given a script for restaurant dining, which it could use to understand a story like the example. SAM, the program that was built on scripts, was completed in about 1975. (Cullingford 1978.) This story is taken from the *New Haven Register*:

> Friday evening a car swerved off Route 69. The vehicle struck a tree. The passenger, a New Jersey man, was killed. David Hall, 27, was pronounced dead at the scene by Dr. Dana Blauchard, medical

> examiner. Frank Miller, 32, of 593 Foxon Rd.,
> the driver, was taken to Milford Hospital by
> Flanagan Ambulance. He was treated and released.
> No charges were made. Patrolman Robert Onofrio
> investigated the accident.

The program can read this story and make English-language summaries by generating from its representation of the meaning of the story. This is an example of the English-language summary:

> An automobile hit a tree near Highway 69 four days
> ago. David Hall, age 27, residence in New Jersey,
> the passenger, died. Frank Miller, age 32, residence
> at 593 Foxon Road in New Haven, Connecticut, the
> driver, was slightly injured. The Police Department
> did not file charges.

To show its power, we have used the program to generate summaries in Spanish, Chinese, Russian, and other languages.

The program can also answer questions about things that are not stated explicitly. For example, if we ask, "Was anyone hurt?" The program says, "Yes, Frank Miller was slightly injured." How does it know that? The story says that Frank Miller was taken to the hospital and was treated and released. The program infers that he was not badly hurt, just as a person would.

The problem in language-understanding work is doing that kind of reasoning. If we cannot do that, we cannot do anything more than play with words. We must forget about the words. What we have to do is to get at the ideas; the words themselves are to be gotten around.

The program that read car accident stories from the *New Haven Register* did a very good job but took sixteen minutes of computer time to read that story. There may have been a use for such programs, but they would have to be faster than sixteen minutes per story. Partly because of this problem, we began a project called FRUMP (Fast Reading and Understanding Memory Program). (See DeJong 1979.) We convinced UPI to give us the UPI wire for free so we could have news stories in machin-readable form.

Most artificial-intelligence programs work only on particular examples, and few programs handle examples that their authors had not explicitly anticipated. Our goal was to write a program that could read news stories we had not seen before, limited only to a prescribed knowledge area. We gave our program knowledge about earthquakes, diplomatic crises, invasions, oil spills, and airplane crashes. Here is an example, having to do with diplomatic relations, that FRUMP was able to handle.

> The State Department announced today the suspension of diplomatic relations with Equatorial Guinea. The announcement came five days after the Department received a message from the foreign minister of the West African country saying that his government had declared two United States diplomats *persona non grata.*
>
> The two are Ambassador Herbert J. Spiro and Consul William C. Mithoefer, Jr., both stationed in neighboring Cameroon but also accredited to Equatorial Guinea.
>
> Robert L. Funseth, State Department spokesman, said Mr. Spiro and Mr. Mithoefer spent five days in Equatorial Guinea earlier this month and were given a "warm reception."
>
> But at the conclusion of their visit, Mr. Funseth said, Equatorial Guinea's acting Chief of Protocol handed them a five-page letter that cast "unwarranted and insulting slurs" on both diplomats.

FRUMP did not read every word because we decided to increase its speed by having it skim for content, looking for certain things. It is a key-concept analyzer, not a key-word analyzer.

Once it understood what was going on, FRUMP looked for concepts that filled in its picture. The computer time was reduced to two seconds, a large improvement. Thus FRUMP involved two separate processes: the first determined the kind of story, and the second filled in the holes associated with that kind of story. Once FRUMP knew it was dealing with a story about broken diplomatic relations, it knew someone must have broken relations with somebody else; there must have been a reason; there must have been a time; and there must have been a place. The program, since it produces language-independent internal meaning representations, could translate the summaries it made into any language, given that we had a graduate student who spoke that language. Here are FRUMP's summaries for the story:

Selected Sketchy Script

CPU time for understanding: 2515 milliseconds

English summary: The United States State Department and Guinea have broken diplomatic relations.

French summary: Le Department d'Etat des Etats-Unis et la Guinee ont coupe leurs relations diplomatiques.

Chinese summary: Meeigwo gwowuhyuann gen jiinahyah duannjyuele wayjiau guanshih.

Market Research

We now had a program that could read stories straight off the UPI wire and produce representations of their content. This intrigued me because it presented the possibility of constructing a system I was interested in having. At the time I had been following two news stories in the papers: the Patty Hearst kidnapping and the New York Giants' search

for a new head coach. Almost every day there were stories
in the papers about these situations, but usually the stories
merely summarized the events up to the present time and
added nothing new of interest. What I would have liked
would be to read only about new developments, but I had
to slog through entire articles of old news to see if any new
facts were revealed.

I realized that using the FRUMP program we might
be able to build a system that would monitor the UPI
wire and inform people when events they were interested
in were reported in stories coming over the wire. We
built a prototype system that would mail people FRUMP's
summaries of stories about things they were interested in
when it found them.

But when I thought that alerting system might be a
product, I was naive. I thought that the world was such that
if you made something, someone would want it. Luckily I did
not lose any money discovering that I was wrong. I talked to
people who knew money and knew products. I asked them,
"Would you finance a company to make one of these? Would
you want one?" They would not, and they did not. This
was 1977, and the necessary computing horsepower cost
one million dollars. I would have had to become a service
bureau, but it was not clear there was a real market for
doing alerting in the service bureau mode.

Then I discovered market research. For the next three or
four years, without investing anyone's money or much of
my time, I talked to people about what they wanted. This
made me more frustrated because all my life I had built
programs on the assumption that someday people would
want to talk to them in English. I realized that people do
not really want to talk to computer programs in English.

Danger of Being Popular

I became obsessed with making a product, which is one reason
I have a company today. Another reason is that Artificial

Intelligence has received increasing publicity. We in the field began to worry about the dangers of rising expectations for our research. At that time we had not produced much of practical importance. Furthermore artificial-intelligence researchers were—and remain—flaky people, as a group, not necessarily dedicated to producing practical products. On top of that there are not very many of us.

When I started my company, everyone seemed to want to start an industrial artificial-intelligence laboratory. But where were the people going to come from? If the news is that Artificial Intelligence is great and is going to produce wonderful things, and if five years later there are no wonderful things, the reporters who wrote the science fiction turn into reporters ready to write exposés.

If this were to happen, at least I would prefer to have it happen because of my own failures rather than someone else's. I decided that I would do what I could to bring about the production of useful products employing artificial-intelligence technology.

Minuses of Front-End Systems

Around this time, a company asked us to build an English-language front end to their program. Their program was powerful, but had a complicated query language in front of it that no one could use. I said, "Fine, I will put a company together, get some people, and start building." After a few months our interface solved their problem.

We began to talk to people about the English-language front-end business. There is such a business, though I am not convinced I want to be in it. But let us briefly discuss what an English-language front end is.

One example is a toy front end we built for the Compustat data base, which contains information about stocks. The reason it is a toy is that we can put in information about only ten stocks. For example, we can ask:

```
What was the PE for IBM last year?
```

and since we work with context, we can also ask:

```
How about the last five years?
```

and since our program still knows we are talking about IBM, it produces the desired answer. We can also ask more complicated questions:

```
Which of Exxon's liabilities, as of 1981,
come due in a year?

Show me the current total assets divided by the PE ratio.
```

That is not the only way we can ask for what we want. There is no one way to say anything. We supply our users with manuals that are one-page long. The main thing the manuals say, in big print, is, "Type period at the end of sentence, then press return." Now look at a few more samples:

```
How are widget 1 and widget 2 doing?

Show each market for those products.
Do it in dollars.
Try thousands of dollars.

Show me your report in hundreds of dollars
for the large widget.  Give averages for
the last month.
```

Note that there is no irritating need to type everything over and over again. We can do things that are a little more fuzzy:

```
List each growing product this month.

Show me a report over the last six months on
medium widgets from New York, giving averages
in thousands of dollars.  Use trend data.  Show
only growing products.
```

In these examples, though the word *growing* is ambiguous, the meaning in context is not.

Although there is a business for such front-end interfaces, I do not find that business interesting. First, you have to build up new knowledge—for example, information about oil, or about stocks, or about sales—a difficult and time-consuming task. Worse yet data bases tend to be on the wrong machines. A powerful artificial-intelligence program with knowledge and content would be difficult to implement in the environment provided by most corporate computer centers. I do not recommend trying.

Plusses of Advisory Systems

My company has planned for the little machine market. We now can run on $15,000 or $20,000 machines. But now that such machines exist, the question is, "What do we want to do with them?" I do not think current data bases are very good, and I would hate to add 1980s technology to 1960s technology to get a product.

The right thing to do with these new machines is to create what I call advisory systems. I do not call them expert systems because I am not sure I believe in expert systems. I certainly do not believe in current expert-systems technology. Moreover the systems I am talking about are not that expert. An adviser is someone who has a certain amount of expertise, but it is not that grand—a travel agent, for example. A travel agent knows things, but he does not know things the way the best geologist in the world knows things or the way a very sophisticated doctor knows things.

I am suggesting that an English-language conversation with a program that is an adviser, but not necessarily a true expert can be valuable. In my company we are making deals with insurance companies, banks, and brokerage houses to provide the information they provide in a better way than they provide it. Rather than having a stock broker out in Iowa, who may not be that good, giving advice, we will arrange for each company's hotshot in New York to give the advice. Before that hotshot could not be cloned. Now he can be.

We set about cloning by doing extensive videotaping and interviewing. We find out what the expert has to say. Then we build a program that can answer questions as if they were giving that expert's advice. We build these systems with partners. It makes no sense to build one alone; you have to have a bank to build a bank assistant. We listen to what the bankers say about the skill they are interested in, and then we build what they need. Eventually we will be able to walk into a branch office in Iowa, ask questions about what we should do about IRAs, and get answers from a computer.

Building a Financial Consultant

What I envision is something like this. Some of the programs required to effect this scenario exist, but most do not.

```
Tell me your income.
```

```
50,000/year.
```

```
How much do you have in the bank?
```

```
25,000 in savings; 5,000 in checking.
```

```
What types of savings account is it?
```

```
1,500 in a one-year CD, the rest in a passbook.
```

```
Do you own a house?
```

```
Yes, a four-bedroom house, worth 100,000, with
30,000 left to pay on the mortgage.
```

You can do this now with menu systems. But menu systems constrain too much. They cannot permit the user the following sort of luxury:

```
Do you have any other investments?
```

```
No, mainly because I do not know what to invest in.
Can you give me any advice?
```

Another product we have a demonstration version of is something that I call The Ideal Business System, (TIBS). When finished, it will make business computers worthwhile. Many small businesses would spend $20,000 on a computer if they could work with it. But people are afraid of computers. One of the advantages of English is that it makes people less afraid. We are looking toward something like this:

```
Do we have ten dozen King Classic Tennis rackets
we can distribute to the XMART Department Stores?

No, we only have two dozen on hand.

How many are due to arrive in the future?

Another six dozen is due in a week.

Is there any other model we can substitute?
```

The businessperson wants something that knows about inventory, knows about accounts receivable, knows about bookkeeping, and can give general advice about particular business problems. That is the kind of system TIBS will be.

So what do we do in my company, Cognitive Systems? We are looking for joint venturers rather than customers. We are in the product design stage. It is very hard to build a product. Why do I think I can do it and other people cannot? Because ultimately the hard part of Artificial Intelligence is having qualified people to work for you. There are not very many. Fortunately I know a few.

Company X Should Forget It

When company X says it ought to have an artificial-intelligence group, I say, "Forget it. You cannot find any more people. You can raid the same places only so many times. There are not enough people out there." In the most optimistic view of the world, there are ten universities that grant PhDs in Artificial Intelligence. With the most optimistic counting, those universities produce two or three PhDs a year.

Yale gets a representatively good sample of new graduate students, the kind that had all A's from Ivy League schools; 50 percent of those students fail, never getting PhDs, because the work is too hard. It requires a mind they do not have, a certain level of imprecision, and an ability to retain a tremendous amount of knowlege. Students work on massive projects that take two or three years to complete. Adding resources does not help. If you put ten people on the same project, it does not go ten times faster. It may go ten times slower.

I think Cognitive Systems will succeed because our people were all trained by me. They have been working with me for years. They are a well-oiled team. We know how to build these things. Can we grow wildly and expand? I do not know. I just started hiring second-generation people, people trained by my students who are now professors. Our expertise is not in building a marketing organization, so I do not intend to build one. It is the roles of our partners to market the product.

For More Information

Cullingford, Richard E., "Script Appication: Computer Understanding of Newspaper Stories," PhD Thesis, Yale University, New Haven, CT, 1978.

DeJong, Gerald F., "Skimming Stories in Real Time: An Experiment in Integrated Understanding," PhD Thesis, Yale University, New Haven, CT, 1979.

Rieger, Charles J. "Conceptual Memory ⌐nd Inference," in *Conceptual Information Processing*, edited by Roger C. Schank, North Holland, Amsterdam, 1975.

Schank, Roger C., "Conceptual Dependency: A Theory of Natural Language Understanding," *Cognitive Psychology*, 1972, 3(4), 552-631.

Schank, Roger C., *Dynamic Memory*, Cambridge University Press, Cambridge, England, 1982.

Schank, R. C., N. Goldman, C. Rieger, and C. Riesbeck, "Inference and Paraphrase by Computer," *Journal of the ACM*, vol. 20, no. 1, 1975.

12
Natural Language
Front Ends

Larry R. Harris
President
Artificial Intelligence Corporation

Dr. Harris is an internationally recognized authority on natural language analysis and data base systems. His work in natural language began with doctoral research on parsing techniques and continued while he was a professor of Computer Science at Dartmouth College. He founded the Artificial Intelligence Corporation in order to develop a commercial product, INTELLECT, based on his research. Dr. Harris's early contributions to the company were primarily technical. As the company and the product evolved, Dr. Harris began to address financial and marketing issues, and in 1981 he became president. Dr. Harris has been a consultant for a number of companies and a visiting professor at MIT. Dr. Harris received the PhD from Cornell University.

The natural language interface business is exciting and explosive. Thousands of people want to access data stored in their computers and are frustrated by the existing level of technology for getting at those data. Consequently we at Artificial Intelligence Corporation have a mission: to deliver a specific technology based on artificial-intelligence natural language-processing techniques to enable nontechnical people to access the information in their computers. My goal is to give you a feeling for our INTELLECT product—what it does, how we got to where we are, and how this particular technology will affect data processing.

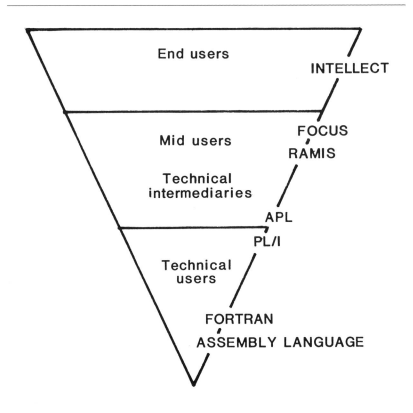

Figure 1. Market for natural language.

Figure 1 positions the product with respect to other existing tools. The inverted triangle is intended to give a feeling for the number of people in each category. At the bottom are highly trained technical users who know assembly language, for example. At the top there are broader and broader categories of people. In the middle are people who can use higher-level languages like PL/1 or APL, or the fourth generation of computer languages, like FOCUS and RAMUS.

Proliferating Technology

The layer that Artificial Intelligence Corporation addresses is the technically unsophisticated—this layer contains people who do not know and do not want to know formal computer languages but still want to be able to get information out of their machines. Our goal is to deliver that capability to them by exploiting their knowledge of English.

Here is an example of what would typically be referred to as an easy-to-use, English-like, user-friendly computer language:

```
PRINT LNAME, 82 -JUL-ACT-SALES, 82-JUL-EST-SALES,
   82-JUL-ACT-SALES - 82-JUL-EST-SALES,
   (82-JUL-ACT-SALES - 82-JUL-EST-SALES)
        / 82-JUL-ACT-SALES,
IF REGION='NEW ENGLAND' AND
   82-YTD-ACT-SALES < 82-QUOTA
```

The same question, asked through INTELLECT, together with the response, is:

```
I WONDER HOW ACTUAL SALES FOR LAST MONTH COMPARE TO
THE FORECAST FOR PEOPLE UNDER QUOTA IN NEW ENGLAND.

PRINT A COMPARISON OF LAST NAME, 82-JUL-ACT-SALES AND
82-JUL-EST-SALES OF ALL SALES PEOPLE WITH REGION =
NORTHEAST & 82-YTD-ACT-% QUOTA <100.00.

THE NUMBER OF RECORDS TO BE SEARCHED IS 40
```

	1982	1982		
	JULY	JULY		
LAST	JULY	ESTIMATED		
NAME	SALES	SALES	CHANGE	% CHANGE
SMITH	54,474	52,868	1,606	2.95
ALEXANDER	54,833	52,936	1,897	3.46
ADKINS	76,072	75,631	441	0.58
ASIN	42,144	38,214	3,930	9.33

The system derives the answer to that question and reports. The contrast between non-English and English attracts people to using a natural language system.

There is a limit to the expectations that we should have in the near term. Still, we are more advanced than most people think. Artificial Intelligence Corporation is the

foremost supplier of natural language technology. So far
we have installed over one hundred systems, at an average
retail price just under $70,000.

The Fortune 500 companies we deal with use INTELLECT
in applications ranging from personnel to commercial loans.
Some of those companies use INTELLECT with temporary
data bases for areas like budgeting, for which the data-base
lifetime may be only two months.

In addition to direct sales through end users, we have also
successfully established a number of OEM relationships with
some of the leading vendors in particular market segments—
for example, Cullinane Data Base Systems, now known as
Cullinet, sells the product as on-line English, interfaced
to their data-base system, IDMS. We have a relationship
with Information Sciences Corporation, the leading vendor
of human resources packages; it calls this system GRS
Executive. Management Decision Systems, the company
that sells the Rolls Royce of financial modeling systems,
known as Express, calls our system English Language
Interface.

Our goal is to proliferate this technology throughout the
existing framework of distribution channels. Rather than
await a new era of hardware and software, we embed the
technology in today's data-processing world.

Package versus Custom

We strive to have a package that can be sold over and
over again without varying the code. Obviously there has
to be some customization in order for INTELLECT to be
useful for a specific data base, but that customization need
not involve writing new code. Instead customizations need
involve only dictionary definitions. That was a driving force
behind the design of the product because we felt it would
not be commercially feasible otherwise. Customization has
to be such that ordinary technicians can do the job and do
it quickly.

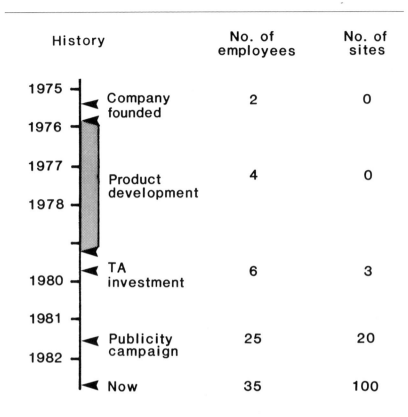

History		No. of employees	No. of sites
1975	Company founded	2	0
1976			
1977	Product development	4	0
1978			
1980	TA investment	6	3
1981			
1982	Publicity campaign	25	20
	Now	35	100

Figure 2. History of Artificial Intelligence Corporation.

Getting There

How did we get where we are? As figure 2 shows, we started in 1975, forming a company based on a research prototype that I produced while I was a professor at Dartmouth College. At that time I felt that the technology had reached the point where we could join it to the powerful data base management system technology maturing at that time.

We went through a three to five-year development process, or productization process, of putting together the basic research ideas and getting them to work in the commercial area. By 1979 we had three beta sites that produced the user feedback we needed. In some cases it took us as long as a year to get the capabilities and the fluency of the product up to a level where it was accepted and put into daily use. At that point we sought the venture capital money necessary to proceed.

In those days our product was not as powerful as it is today. We had put in the capability to deal with questions like, "Give me a breakdown of salaries by department." The word *breakdown* set up an expectation that a category definition would occur later in the sentence that would help determine how to do the processing. It turned out there was a bug in the system: if that expectation was not met, the system went off on a tangent. We got a call from a user who had typed *break down* to the machine. He asked the classic question, "Is it a bug or is it a feature?" Thinking fast, I said, "Well, actually, that is the breakdown command; we just haven't gotten around to documenting that yet." What other business could you be in where a user could actually not be sure whether a total abort was intended?

INTELLECT in Action

Our goal is not to deliver the ultimate in artificial-intelligence capability but to deliver the ultimate in user capability within the context of the existing commercial marketplace. Consider this interaction:

```
GIVE ME THE NAMES OF THE WOMEN IN THE WESTERN REGION
WHO ARE OVER QUOTA.

PRINT THE LAST NAME AND 82-YTD-ACT-% QUOTA
OF ALL SALES PEOPLE WITH SEX = FEMALE & REGION = WEST &
82-YTD-ACT-% QUOTA>  100.00.

THE NUMBER OF RECORDS TO BE SEARCHED IS 24
                         1982
LAST                      YTD
NAME            % OF QUOTA

ACORD               158.20
ARBOGAST            146.37
CENTOR              145.55
CHAMPION            147.26
```

The system's echo is a formalized restatement of what was intended. This provides a feedback mechanism so the user knows what INTELLECT thinks the user means. If it is not correct, the user can take appropriate action. There was a problem understanding this question but INTELLECT answers it anyway. The whole point to a natural language system, as opposed to a formal query language system, is that no matter how the user asks the question, he is right.

Here is another example of how the same information can be extracted with different wordings:

```
WESTERN WOMEN OVER QUOTA.

PRINT THE LAST NAME AND 82-YTD-ACT-% QUOTA OF ALL
SALES PEOPLE WITH REGION = WEST & SEX = FEMALE &
82-YTD-ACT-% QUOTA > 100.00.

THE NUMBER OF RECORDS TO BE SEARCHED IS 24
                          1982
LAST                       YTD
NAME              % OF QUOTA

ACORD                  158.20
ARBOGAST               146.37
CENTOR                 145.55
CHAMPION               147.26
```

Many people think natural language requires people to be verbose. We find the opposite is true. Consider the difference between the user's English and the echo, which is closer to what you would have to type in a formal query language. In this case, the user's English is considerably shorter.

The next question illustrates how ambiguity is handled:

```
LIST THE SALESMEN IN NEW YORK WHO ARE UNDER QUOTA.

YOUR REQUEST IS AMBIGUOUS TO ME.  DO YOU WANT:
 (1): CITY = NEW YORK.
 (2): STATE  = NEW YORK.
PLEASE ENTER THE NUMBER OF THE INTERPRETATION YOU INTENDED.
```

2

```
PRINT THE LAST NAME AND 82-YTD-ACT-% QUOTA OF ALL
SALES PEOPLE WITH STATE = NEW YORK & 82-YTD-ACT-%
QUOTA < 100.00.

THE NUMBER OF RECORDS TO BE SEARCHED IS 60
                        1982
LAST                    YTD
NAME            % OF QUOTA

BAHN               96.24
DYKES              96.10
ELEY               96.60
GRAYSON            97.42
```

INTELLECT, by definitions in its lexicon, knows that *New York* can refer to both the city and the state. The system cannot resolve the ambiguity. Therefore it asks the user if New York City or New York State is meant. Given the inherent ambiguity of natural language, it is essential that a system be able to ask the user for clarification.

The next example shows the level of inference the system will do to avoid asking for clarification:

WHICH OF THE NEW YORK EMPLOYEES LIVE IN BUFFALO?

```
PRINT THE LAST NAME OF ALL SALES PEOPLE WITH
STATE = NEW YORK & CITY = BUFFALO.

THE NUMBER OF RECORDS TO RETRIEVE IS 15
    LAST
    NAME

    BERGER
    ALEXANDER
    ALFONTE
    BAHN
```

It is important that INTELLECT not ask for clarification every time New York is used in a sentence. When we look at this sentence, how do we know that New York has to be New York State? Clearly we resolve the ambiguity by way of something that we know about Buffalo.

This illustrates the use of the inverted indexes in the data base. Buffalo is not a word in INTELLECT's own lexicon, yet we are able to determine that it is a city. Combining that knowledge with the two interpretations for New York enables INTELLECT to rule out the city interpretation for New York in favor of the one shown. Thus INTELLECT is able to make an inference and proceed much as a person would.

Next we get to a level beyond just raw retrieval of information in the data base:

SHOW PERCENTAGES FOR TOTAL SALES BY STATE.

PRINT A PERCENTAGE OF THE TOTAL 82-ACT-YTD SALES
IN EACH STATE OF ALL SALES PEOPLE.

THE NUMBER OF RECORDS TO RETRIEVE IS 300

STATE	1982 YTD SALES	PERCENT
ARIZONA	3,960,221	2.78
CALIFORNIA	28,073,666	19.74
COLORADO	4,155,372	2.92
FLORIDA	5,444,594	3.83

On one level problems can be solved simply by retrieving and displaying the data. On another level problems require information that can be derived from the data. It is important to be able to perform the necessary analysis on demand by the natural language interaction.

In other systems, to arrange for the percentages column is a two-pass process. The programs first compute the grand total and then compute the percentages. The user is forced to be aware of the actual procedural approach involved in solving the problem.

Suppose we ask, "Who are the top seven salesmen in terms of quota achievement?" An enormous amount of processing is required by this question. First, quota achievement has to be computed from what is out in the data base. Next, the system has to sort the salesmen and select the top seven so that further questions can be answered without recomputation. The INTELLECT natural language interface covers up all the underlying detail of the computation.

Natural Language Interface as Ringmaster

In building and delivering natural language capability, we have found that the artificial-intelligence component is not the only component of the problem. Creating the natural language capability is but one part of a total solution to the problem of getting nontechnical people to use computers.

The other three parts have to do with problems caused by the user's conceptual viewpoint. First, we have to convert the user's way of thinking about the data to correspond to how the data are actually stored. Second, we have to be able to answer the question at the level at which the user asks it. For example, if he wants information that is not really in the data base, we have to be able to compute it.

Third, there is a navigational problem because realistic data bases are stored in multiple files. This means we must develop ways to put information together on a file-by-file basis to derive answers. Formal languages force users to specify exactly how they want things to be done. That is something most users do not know how to do because they do not know the underlying structure of the data base.

This third point bears emphasis. There soon will be a need to interface to multiple software systems. The capabilities the user wants are not necessarily satisfied by a single data base management system, nor are they necessarily satisfied by a graphics system, nor are they are necessarily satisfied by a financial modeling tool. At various times the user may need all or many systems to work together.

To buy the best data base system, the best graphics system, and the best modeling system means to buy a system designed and supported by different vendors. The user interfaces will have nothing in common. Similarly the representation of data in the various systems will be different. It would be impossible for a nontechnical user to use the systems because he would have to learn three or four formal languages and write programs to pass data from one system to another. Writing programs is something we assume nontechnical users cannot do.

In the future natural language systems will do more than just interface to data base systems. They will also play important new roles within the information center itself, interfacing to a variety of software tools. In a sense the natural language system will become the supervisor of the information center.

Figure 3 shows INTELLECT at the very center of things, interfacing to a data base management system, to graphics systems, like IBM's presentation graphics feature, to modeling systems, such as Express, and perhaps linked with human-resource applications systems like the package offered by InSci. The user's only direct point of contact with the system is the natural language component.

The user types in a request. The natural language system analyzes it, partitions the work among the various software tools, and dispatches each of them to carry out their particular expertise to help solve the problem. Then the natural language system ties the overall solution together in a way that gets the problem solved. The goal is to avoid forcing the user to learn programming languages. Instead the system passes information back and forth.

For example, we might ask INTELLECT to produce a bar chart of actual and estimated year-to-date sales in each region. INTELLECT parses the question, retrieves data from the data base, and summarizes the data to the level necessary to do a bar graph. Then INTELLECT passes the data to the graphics package, in this case IBM's presentation graphics feature—causing the display to appear. This example illustrates the benefit that can come from tying together two very powerful software tools in such

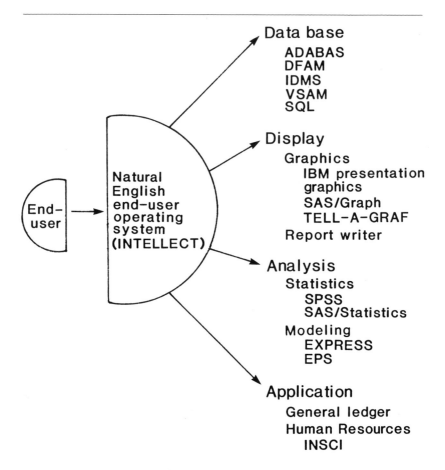

Figure 3. INTELLECT in the center of the information center.

a way that the user need know nothing about the underlying details of either one.

The Mighty Micro

Another direction where I see the tremendous growth is the microcomputer area. I will not try to argue that the only mechanism by which people should interact with microcomputers is by natural language. But in certain specific areas, other kinds of communication break down, and natural language can play a very important role.

When using data base systems that use mice or cursors, answering questions can take twenty or thirty interactions. The approach of telling the machine what to do step-by-step breaks down because of the number of steps that have to be made in just the right sequence. Typing in four or five English words is an attractive alternative.

From Prototype to Successful Package

A long lead time is required to make a research prototype into a commercial product. That is true in developing ordinary data-processing products; it is even more true when there is a heavy artificial-intelligence component. The effort to make a package product, rather than a custom product, is great. Today's expert systems are all custom expert systems. Good business sense dictates developing and selling a package product that enables buyers to develop their own applications without doing artificial-intelligence research.

For More Information

Harris, Larry R., "A High Performance Natural Language Processor for Data Base Query," *ACM SIGART Newsletter*, vol. 61, 1977.

13
Work and Play:
A Discussion

Rich

Mr. Finegold, you say your company has been influenced by Artificial Intelligence, but you avoid saying that Daisy Systems is an artificial-intelligence company. Could you point to particular people or work in Artificial Intelligence that were fundamental to your jump on the rest of the market? Could you comment on how you were influenced? Do you read the journals? Do you visit the laboratories? Do you send your people to tutorials? How do you maintain this flow of ideas that are important to your company?

Finegold

The company was founded by two engineering managers of Intel Corporation, a leader in technology in the VLSI industry. We had a problem. It used to be that the technology cycle was two years and the engineering cycle was two years. When the technology started to run faster, the marketing people began to get tired and frustrated.

When we formed the company, we were well aware of the problem. We looked for a solution in the technology. We approached Dr. Benin, consultant for Xerox PARC. The first thing that he showed us was that the technology we needed was the notion of the apprentice. We use the notion of apprentice internally. In the hardware the role of apprentice was very well defined. Some of the hardest people to find are development technicians, people who are almost engineers but hopefully will never make it.

We did not develop the technology. We visited Stanford University and looked at work done at the Massachusetts Institute of Technology. Daisy put it all together and made it into a product. We harvested what people in the universities worked on.

We are not ashamed about it. We give you all our respect. We do not claim we created the market; we just productized it. We spent time looking at what other people were doing. We keep in touch continuing to look at what university researchers are doing, and we try to influence researchers in universities.

Winston

It strikes me that it is good you did not come to this seminar three years ago because Professor Schank might have convinced you that forming such a company was impossible, with his remark that there are no people out there who would have the artificial-intelligence skills that you would need. Evidently you built your company, which is influenced by Artificial Intelligence, around people who came from outside the field. Is that correct?

Finegold

Now we are going back to the definition of Artificial Intelligence. Inside the company, using the term *Artificial Intelligence* was taboo. Whenever we bring in someone with an artificial-intelligence background to work on a project, I tell them, "You are working on advanced software. Don't say Artificial Intelligence. Say Advanced Software." Too many people use Artificial Intelligence as a reason for not delivering.

But at the same time, let's be realistic and look at what is there. It is unfair to the artificial-intelligence community. The job of people doing research at universities is to be at the forefront of things that you study, whether they are physical or not. Your business is not to make products. You are constantly losing because the definition of Artificial Intelligence is constantly changing. When I was at Intel, we hired people with artificial-intelligence backgrounds because placement and routing was Artificial Intelligence then. It is no longer because companies sell products that do placement and routing.

Rich

When it works it is not Artificial Intelligence.

Finegold

If you go with that definition, then we have nothing to do with Artificial Intelligence. But if you look at the people we brought in, you see people who were experts in placement and routing. So you say it is no longer Artificial Intelligence. We will continue to hire people who are no longer Artificial Intelligence.

Rich

Dr. Kay, where is SMALLTALK now? What happened to it? Why don't we hear more about it?

Kay

My former group at Xerox finished a book about SMALL-TALK. They beta-tested all of the implementation information in the book at a number of companies. Basically Xerox is releasing SMALLTALK to the world as a system that anybody who buys the book can implement. You can also get the system for a licensing fee. I talked to someone from Xerox who told me that a number of applications systems are now being written in SMALLTALK by companies like the New York Times.

Programming languages have a long gestation period. The first couple of versions of a programming language are not cost-effective in any reasonable way and take about three years to turn around. SMALLTALK beats the heck out of professional programming languages like BASIC and PASCAL.

But from the standpoint of what the user actually needs in the context of the things we are talking about, I do not think SMALLTALK is a solution to the problem of the universal personal computer at all.

Winston

Professor Schank, in some of the advertising that your company, Cognitive Systems, does, you use words to the effect that your products will enable users to interact with machines in unrestricted natural language. This has irritated everyone I know who does natural language research. I wonder if you feel that your use of terms like that is legitimate and, if not, why the company's advertising uses them?

Schank

It is legitimate.

Winston

Then should we conclude that natural language research should stop because the problems are solved?

Schank

That depends on just what is meant by *natural language research*. I think, for example, that research on syntax should have stopped fifteen years ago.

In some sense, Yale University's laboratory does not spend much time on natural language anymore. My *natural language project* is in reality almost entirely a memory-and-learning project. This is because the hard part of natural language is not the language, but the knowledge behind the language and the learning techniques. Those are the key and hard problems. They do not have to do with language specifically. They have to do with things like understanding intentionality. The language problem is not a problem that is separable in and of itself. But to the extent that you can nail down the semantics of the domain under discussion – that is, to the extent that the knowledge base is an oil company data base and you can write all there is to know about that data base – we can build a program that can answer your questions about it.

Of course, if you ask it about George Washington, it will not know who George Washington is, and it will not be able to answer. If you ask it about something in the data base, though, it will answer. It does not matter how you ask it. Ungrammaticality is fine with us.

I think that you are getting the same reaction I have always gotten. As soon as I say to people whose life work is syntax that syntax is not worth working on, they understandably get upset.

Rich

I have a practical question for both Dr. Harris and Professor Schank, which I think might help focus this technology. Suppose just for the purpose of discussion that I would like to hook up a natural language front end or interface to my Programmer's Apprentice. Could you estimate the amount of effort, in terms of man-years or minimum elapsed time or level of expertise or dollar cost, that it would require to create a natural language interface for something like the Programmer's Apprentice?

Schank

I do not know enough about the Programmer's Apprentice to tell you. I would need to know the whole range of questions you might want to ask. On the one hand, in many domains a natural language project would be impossible. It can be impossible if the knowledge is not sufficiently codifiable. My guess is that your domain is in this category.

On the other hand, some domains are relatively easy, because you may have something which has a range of one hundred or two hundred or five hundred kinds of things you want to say – not sentences, but kinds of things. If that is the case and if the knowledge is understandable, then it frequently takes no more than six months to build a customized system like that.

Harris

To get any kind of estimate, you have to look at the details underlying what is going on. In particular you must understand the semantics of the environment. Our whole approach has not been to build custom systems and improve the ability with which we customize language analysis at a level of building the code but to deal within a restricted semantic domain in our case, primarily the data base and data-manipulation domain. Within the sort of meta semantics that that defines, we put together a system where you could define specific domains very quickly and very easily, depending on what was in the data base. We are not at all geared up to take INTELLECT as it stands and apply it to something totally different, in context, in intent, and in use, than what we see going on in the data-base query-information center environment. It is probably something we would not be interested in doing because of marketing issues. From a technical viewpoint that is not the dimension we try to put effort into.

Rich

Professor Schank, what is it about my application that might make it unsuitable for your kind of natural language interface? What kinds of questions would you ask me? What kind of answer would I have to give that would signal to you that what I was doing was beyond what your techniques currently approach?

Schank

Ultimately the problem comes down to how well you understand the domain. Our system is a knowledge-based, content-based system. That is, we have to understand the domain to understand questions in it. The reason we can handle unrestricted English is that in the middle of a sentence we are able to do something you are doing right now, which is to guess what is coming next. Our parsing techniques are based on understanding what has been said so far and being able to figure out what else might be going on. That means we need to have a good sense of what is going on in the domain. If everything inside the Programmer's Apprentice is content driven, then we are in business. But if much of the knowledge is procedurally encoded, or implicit, as is the case in most complex artificial-intelligence programs we would be forced to try to write our system without access to all the knowledge in the domain, and we would be in trouble. In fact we are exactly on the other end of the spectrum from Dr. Harris's product; where his thing is specialized toward not knowing the content, ours is specialized toward knowing the content. Thus, although it may look as if we have similar products, they are radically different. The reason is that we have to understand the world we are talking about in order to provide the power of unrestricted language. If the programmer wants to design something and I do not know what that thing is, I can get into trouble when he tells me what it is he wants to design.

I think automatic programming in general is very hard and one of the last places you will ever see natural language processing. It also may be a place where you never want to see natural language processing because it is not necessarily the best way to talk to a machine. English is a good way to talk to a machine for people who do not know how to program. Programmers know how to program.

Harris

I want to respond to one comment Professor Schank made about the level of semantics needed. I think it is highly inaccurate to describe our approach as having no semantic information. Our goal is to work on the problem from both ends, working with the natural language analysis techniques to reduce the amount of specific semantic information needed as much as possible – to lower the requirement from the top down and to approach the problem from the bottom up. The goal is to get the critical semantic information that everybody needs dynamically from the data base systems rather than have the semantic definitions entered in by hand.

Winston

Before we leave our natural-language-oriented panelists alone, I would like to ask both of them a question that came about because of some of the remarks by Dr. Kay. How up to date is the technology that you are trying to commercialize at this moment? Is it brand new? Or has it been developing over a period of years?

Schank

The first parser we built was completed in. 1973. It was based on meaning-driven techniques, a well-known part of the MARGIE system. We modified it later, in principle, to work inside a couple of systems, most notably the POLITICS system, where it is driven by the expectations of the system based on the goals and plans of the speaker. It was rearranged in the BORIS system to be capable of understanding very large and complex paragraphs. The BORIS system was started in 1979 and was completed in 1982. The parser we use is derived from that one. It is a program whose concept has been evolving for ten years, but the technology really just got into place. So, the answer is, "Almost brand new."

Harris

I think we rely much more heavily on syntax than Professor Schank does. Research in syntax came to a head in 1972 when a number of very powerful techniques were established. The real key is not the syntactic analysis; it is how you merge or develop that information with the semantics. That is something that continues to evolve over a period of time. I think we had the basic essence of the approach down in 1975 or 1976.

Winston

Mr. Finegold and Dr. Kay talked about particularizations of a wonderful dream where people work a total design environment. Dr. Rich talked about the same sort of thing in still another domain. Do you see an explosive growth in this business of creating total design environments, a growth that would reach out and extend to the automobile industry or the more traditional industries? Or is there something fundamentally easier about your industries that have made them the first target of this total design environment kind of idea?

Finegold

The problem of the design cycle made the electronic industry a target for a total design environment. It used to be that an innovative company with an edge in technology could manipulate it and be very, very successful. After it came up with the first microprocessor, Intel had three years before competition threatened. Today that technology edge is very narrow, generally one year at most. That edge also pushes the expectation of price versus performance. New products become archaic quickly. The market needs a solution for shortening the design cycle, and it needs a solution for cost versus performance, which means how to design LSI.

Winston

Are there any technical reasons, such as the fact that the problems are inherently two-dimensional, which would make this an easier world to deal with?

Rich

It is important to emphasize the kinds of domains you can approach with Artificial Intelligence in general and with the assistant metaphor in particular. Whenever a field is well established, with existing textbooks and courses, people have already done the initial groundwork. You are in much better shape to begin an artificial-intelligence automation effort. For example, you can lay Electrical Engineering, programming, and VLSI along a kind of spectrum in terms of the maturity of the field. Electrical Engineering is an extremely mature field. There are good textbooks, and the concepts are well defined. The role of a technician is well worked out. Electrical Engineering is in much better shape than VLSI, which is still somewhat of a black art. Programming is somewhere in the middle. It is not as mature as Electrical Engineering, but there are a lot more expert programmers than there are expert VLSI designers.

Kay

The role of the programming language designers is to do exactly the opposite. The stuff that happened at Xerox happened from motivations exactly opposite from what we talked about so far. It goes back to this noble failure of the Flex Machine I mentioned earlier. Suppose you had to design a system for people at the Institute for Advanced Study at Princeton as I did in 1966 when I started working on the Flex Machine. I realized that if I was going to design a good system for them, I would not be able to anticipate very many of their needs at all. What I really wanted was a kind of kit that they could use to tailor their own information resources and tools. In fact that is one way of thinking about what a programming language is.

There are two kinds of programming languages: ones that are basically accretions of features like PL/1 and ADA, that are never finished being defined, and ones that are basically crystallizations of styles, like SMALLTALK. Pick a good style for doing something, and make that into a language. People will tend to do things in the style that the language encourages. A programming language of that kind is very close to a kit. But the problem with a kit is that in order to make certain things easy, you prevent other things from being done at all. VISICALC, practically the only good piece of software that has ever been put on a micro, is an example of a kit. You see immediately what it is. You can do worthwhile things immediately, but there is much that you cannot do within VISICALC's framework. A good programming language is an example of something that can be evaluated not by how it does when its features are working but how it does when it has no features for you.

That is the true dilemma of personal computing: the user

is unknown and has many needs, most of which cannot be anticipated in any specific way. I am much more on the side of the natural languages here, although I agree with Professor Schank that natural language is not the interesting part. It is really the knowledge base that you have to get to one way or another that really counts. So the Xerox PARC stuff naturally developed into a terrific environment simply because it was designed to be able to handle unanticipated needs by naive users. If you have something like that, it is going to be able to handle anticipated needs by expert users easily.

Remember there is no robot harder to do than the robot in the home. You can weld up a car with no trouble at all, but try making one that will sort laundry or do the dishes and you've got a robot problem. Computing in the home will take many more cycles per second than computing in the office or in industry, which is why it is taking so long to arrive in a strong fashion.

Winston

Dr. Kay, two languages have been conspicuously absent from both your good-guy lists and your bad-guy lists. Could you say a word or two about where you see the roles of LISP and PROLOG in the future development of the field?

Kay

LISP is one of my favorite languages. I believe it is one of the two great language designs of the 1960s, the other one being SIMULA. LISP is hard to define, as the DARPA people find out periodically when they try to get the LISP programmers to define a standard LISP. They always discover there is no such thing because LISP is a kind of building material that is a tribute to its inventor. It is the longest-standing good programming language precisely because it can be molded into so many different things. The one thing it has going against it is that it is not a crystallization of style. The people who use it must have a great deal of personal style themselves. But I think if you can have one language on your system, of the ones that have been around for a while, it should be LISP.

I have exactly opposite opinions about PROLOG. To be sure, it is an example of a crystallization of a style, but I believe it is the perfect example of how not to do it for the following reason. PROLOG, during the first half an hour or couple of hours that you are a novice, does absolutely magic things. It does just what you want it to do most of the time. But it is doing these things without your having had to understand anything about what is going on inside PROLOG. Then, suddenly, in order to do something real, you have to understand everything about PROLOG. In fact the transition from where you were to where you have to be in order to make things happen is a shock even for professional programmers. It is the worst kind of thing. We called SMALLTALK SMALLTALK so that nobody would expect anything from it.

If you name a system after a Greek god, you expect it to do something. Or you can name it after Pascal. Pascal was the guy who said, "Please forgive the length of this letter. I didn't have the time to make it shorter." That is a very classy statement. There is no element of that class in the language PASCAL.

Ada was the first programmer. She said the analytical engine weaves algebraic patterns just as the jacquard loom weaves flowers and leaves. That is a very classy statement. You find none of that class in ADA.

We called it SMALLTALK so in case we ever did anything good, peoplé would be remarkably surprised. The same is true of user interfaces. We have a user interface that has a very strong feature and a lot of weak ones. It is much worse than having one that is much more mediocre all the way through or only occasionally does something nice for you. User expectations are very important for designing any kind of user interface. That is where their unhappiness comes from. It has nothing to do with whether the system is doing anything good for them. If it is doing what they expect, and occasionally a little better, they are happy.

Part III

Robotics

14
Intelligent Robots:
Connecting Perception to Action

J. Michael Brady
Senior Research Scientist
Artificial Intelligence Laboratory
Massachusetts Institute of Technology

Dr. Brady's research is concentrated in the areas of robotics and computer vision. He received the BS and MS in Mathematics from the University of Manchester (England) and the PhD in Mathematics from the Australian National University.

Robotics concerns systems that interact with the real world with little or no human assistance. In robotics we work with mechanical equipment, and we work with signal processing. The robotics part of Artificial Intelligence is distinctive because of its need to interact with the real world. Moreover robotics involves a great deal of Mathematics, as well as Electrical Engineering and Mechanical Engineering. That makes it different from much of the work in expert systems, which is largely Computer Science done by people largely within Computer Science.

What Is Robotics?

Several definitions have been proposed for robotics. The following is typical: A robot is a reprogrammable, multifunctional, manipulator designed to move material, parts, tools, or other specialized devices through various programmed motions for the performance of a variety of tasks.

The force of such a definition is to exclude certain machines that are not robots, such as dishwashers and parts-transfer machinery. But the definition never mentions sensing, ruling out inspection, parts location, and identification. It also rules out machines that move autonomously, such as tracked or legged vehicles. Robotics, like Artificial Intelligence and Physics, is an evolving discipline. A definition summarizes only what somebody believes is important in what has evolved to date.

The best definition of a robot that I ever heard is one that David Grossman of IBM gave: A robot is a surprisingly animate machine.

Past and Future Generations

Instead of definitions some people like to talk about generations of robots, much like the generations assigned to computers, robot generations make as little sense as do computer generations. Commercial robots are typically grouped into three generations.

A first-generation robot is programmed by setting fixed stops. First-generation robots are used for pick-and-place applications, typically in heavy engineering industries. The Unimation 2000 is a good example of a first-generation robot. The main drawback of such robots is that they are limited to a small number of moves. First-generation robots predominate in U.S. industry.

A second-generation robot is programmed using a button box. A sequence of robot configurations is taught (there is an unfortunate tendency to use anthropomorphic names, suggesting power, flexibility, breadth of application, and intelligence) by recording them on magnetic tape. The tape is then played back, continually cycling the robot through the stored configurations. Second-generation robots have made their marks in spot welding and spray painting, largely in the automobile industry. These applications currently account for the overwhelming majority of second-generation robots. A second-generation robot is not programmable in the ordinary sense of the word. There is no conditional execution, for example. Typical examples of second-generation robots are Cincinnati Milacron's T3 (The Tomorrow Tool), the Asea IRB60, paint-spraying robots developed by Trallfa, the German KUKA robots, and the Japanese Hitachi robots.

Third-generation robots are programmable robots, robots attached to computers. They have been commercially available for about three years, although university artificial-intelligence laboratories had developed prototypes five to eight years earlier. Unimation was first in the field with the PUMA robot, programmed using VAL. Recently IBM marketed the 7535 and 7565 robots, programmed using AML. Robots from Automatix are programmed in RAIL.

One of the main drawbacks of third-generation robots is their limited ability to sense the world. Another is that the robot is programmed in the robot's view of the world, with impenetrable coordinate systems, rather than in terms of objects such as brackets and fasteners.

Future-generation robots will combine end effectors, such as arms, legs, jigs, and feeders; sensors, to discover when the robot contacts something, to find out exactly where something is, and to cope with uncertainty in the world; computers, to do conditional execution based on sensory data, to control adaptively various kinds of effectors, to interact with data bases for managing information systems and for computer-aided design, and to plan their own actions based on high-level goals. Prototype systems like the one shown in figure 1 are now the object of intensive research.

These future-generation robots will be introduced more slowly than they should be for two reasons. The first reason is that people in the industry are too sparing with computation. For years vision research and development languished because it was considered to require too much computation. Hardware costs have tumbled and powerful 32-bit microprocessors are available, but vision systems are not in place to take advantage. The second reason is that people in the industry continue to underestimate

Figure 1. Dr. Philippe Brou working on prototype vision system at the MIT Artificial Intelligence Laboratory.

the expertise available. Robot-programming languages were pushed by only a small number of companies because conventional wisdom scoffed at the idea that assembly line workers could program computers. That was before home computers showed that programming was not mysterious and before user-friendly interfaces unleashed a large pool of programming talent.

What Roboticists Do

Some artificial-intelligence roboticists are concerned primarily with mechanical issues. They worry about robot structures, end effectors, and whether a robot should be perfectly still like a tree or whether it should wander around its environment. Other artificial-intelligence roboticists work on controllers. Robots, like other complex equipment, need to be controlled to overcome disturbances that cause discrepancies between desired and actual states. Most artificial-intelligence

Mechanical structures

Arms		Kinematics
End effectors	}	Dynamics
Locomotion		Actuation

Control

Software systems

Planning and reasoning
Geometric modeling
Trajectory planning

Sensing

Vision
Tactile and force sensing
Proximity sensing

Figure 2. Parts of robotics research.

roboticists work on the incorporation of software, the incorporation of sensors, and the incorporation of compliant, sensor-based trajectories into robot motion.

In discussing each of the areas shown in the figure 2, I will describe the current industrial practice, the contribution to the area that I believe Artificial Intelligence should make, and the work going on in the various research laboratories.

Mechanical Structures

The first area of robotics concerns mechanical structures—for example, the geometry, construction, and actuation of different types of linkage. Some robot joints are rotary; some slide. What are the advantages of each? How many degrees of freedom should a robot have? The number of degrees of freedom of robots doing important work in industry varies widely, from two degrees of freedom, which is basically a turntable with a little lever that goes in and out, to six degrees of freedom, three degrees to specify points in space and three to specify orientation in space. Pick-and-place robots often have few degrees of freedom, robots specialized for spray painting and spot welding have at least five, and assembly robots usually have at least six.

What are the issues in choosing between electrical and hydraulic actuators? Hydraulics have greater power, speed, and acceleration, but they are typically less stiff and more difficult to control. Electric motors are typically less powerful, implying smaller payloads, in the region of 5 kilograms. With appropriate transmission, such as gear trains, belts, or ball screws, electric robots can be very stiff but have large backlash. This prevents them being torque controlled.

Then there is kinematics, the transformation from the variables that the robot would like to think in, the position, velocity, and (occasionally) acceleration of its joints, into the real-space variables that a programmer or applications engineer would like to believe in. These are, for example, Cartesian x, y, and z, and three angles determining attitude, such as roll, pitch, and yaw. In general the transformation from joint angles to real space coordinates is straightforward, but the inverse transformation is complex.

The inverse problem may not have a closed form solution if the arm is poorly designed. The IBM 7565 is an example of a good design that finesses the whole issue by having sliding joints that move the arm in the x, y, and z directions. Another idea is to design the manipulator so that the last three axes intersect at a single point, similar to the human hand and wrist. Such spherical wrists render the inverse kinematics easily solvable.

What is going on in the universities right now? One of the most interesting things is the design of innovative types of actuators. One experimental idea is to attach the rotor

Figure 3. Asada's latest direct-drive arm.

of a very powerful electric motor directly to a manipulator link without gears, as shown in figure 3. This gives low friction and low backlash. Professor Haruhiko Asada, now of MIT, built a prototype direct-drive arm at Carnegie-Mellon University and is building a second version here at MIT. The arm appears to be capable of carrying up to 10 kilograms, at 10 meters per second, accelerating at 5 G. These are remarkable specifications compared to current industrial robots. Most industrial arms typically move on the order of 1 meter per second. The full commercial exploitation of direct-drive arms is probably five years away.

Edinburgh, Ohio State, Toulouse, and MIT have developed fast algorithms for computing robot kinematics and inverse kinematics. These are ripe for technology transfer.

One of the reasons that current industrial arms move slowly is that they do not contain an adequate model of the inverse plant of the robot. Fast robots need better dynamic models giving better inputs to feedback controllers. Recently several university laboratories, including Purdue, Ohio State, and MIT, developed fast algorithms for iteratively computing robot dynamics. The algorithms are well suited for implementation in VLSI and for pipelined computation. A side effect of doing this would be to simplify the wiring inside a robot since every joint is currently controlled from a central computer. This should improve reliability. Probably the five-year frame for transfer is realistic.

Universities are also trying to make workspace design less ad hoc, not just in terms of how the manipulator is designed but by taking the definition of the task to be performed, perhaps with computer-aided design models, and laying out the required fixtures and jigs in a way that optimizes performance. One approach is to work in that part of the robot's work space where errors do not propagate badly. This research is in its infancy, but early spinoffs are ripe for transfer already. Japanese research has already led to trajectory planning using these techniques.

Universities, taking a cue from nature, have investigated the use and implementation of tendons. Two tendons, called the agonist and antagonist, act in opposition to make muscles act like tunable springs that can be highly compliant or very stiff.

Consider the human hand. The power plant is in the lower arm, above the wrist. This maximizes the work space of the hand, since large, heavy muscles do not get in the way of useful work. Similarly powerful motors are heavy; moving them away from the end effector reduces inertial loading, making the end effector more nimble and responsive. This research is in its early stages. Because the dynamics and kinematic problems and opportunities are poorly understood, technology transfer in ten years may be optimistic.

End Effectors

Structures exist to transport end effectors. This raises several issues: how to design end effectors, how to determine a set of grasp algorithms for using that end effector, and how to incorporate sensors directly into end effectors.

Industry mostly offers single-degree-of-freedom end effectors with at most simple binary sensors such as contact switches or LEDs. Forging applications, for example, typically use parallel jaw grippers. To pick up fabrics, sticky fingers or vacuum cups are used. To carry liquid, a ladle is used. In spot welding, the end effector is the welding tong. They are all single-degree-of-freedom effectors, and they are restricted in the tasks that they perform. Several applications require end effectors that can perform a variety of functions. Surface finishing is a good example, as is automatic assembly. In surface finishing there are two main approaches: the robot can have interchangeable end effectors, each specialized to one aspect of the task and mounted as the arm visits stations in turn; alternatively a single end effector with multiple capabilities can be used. Often the latter approach is preferred because multiple capabilities in an end effector are useful in assembly.

The more functions a hand has, the more complex the grasping algorithms need to be and the more sensory information is required. The IBM 7565 has several strain gauges built into the gripper shown in figure 4. This enables force-sensing strategies to be programmed. The algorithms used for grasping generally are adapted from work done in the universities over a decade ago.

The universities have developed ways of interchanging special-purpose end effectors quickly and reliably; this work is ripe for transfer. At the MIT Artificial Intelligence Laboratory, we investigate designs for multifingered hands capable of the same range of prehension as a human hand. We are studying two prototypes, a three-fingered hand, developed in collaboration with Stanford University,

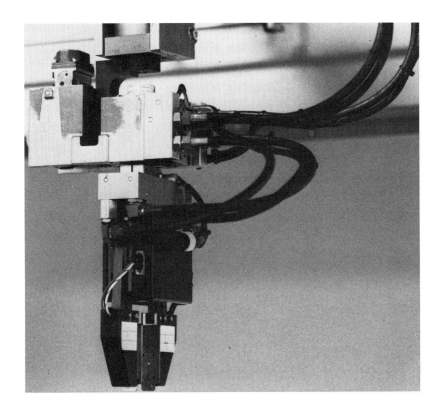

Figure 4. IBM 7565 gripper.

shown in figure 5, and a four-fingered hand, developed in collaboration with the University of Utah, shown in figure 6. I do not expect to see such dextrous hands on industrial robots for many years, but that is only one aspect of the work.

As a necessary side effect of working on multifingered hands, we are developing theories of grasping, of how a gripper of a particular design is useful in a particular cluttered environment on a particular range of surface shapes. That is what we are really after, and that is what is of potential nearer-term application in industry.

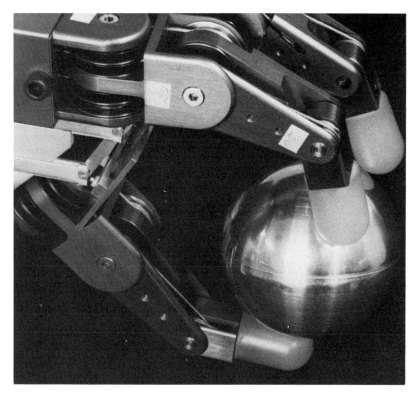

Figure 5. Salisbury's multifingered hand.

Control

Most of the control work that is being done did not come from Artificial Intelligence or robotics. Since about 1960 control theory has been concerned primarily with controlling multiple degrees of freedom in devices such as rockets, airplanes, and steam plants. These multiple degrees of freedom often interact in strange ways. Key problems concern friction, vibration, and inexact models. Robots pose new control problems largely because of their kinematic structure.

Many industrial robots are operated open-loop. The most common control regime is linear, independent joint control, in which a linear control law is closed around each joint

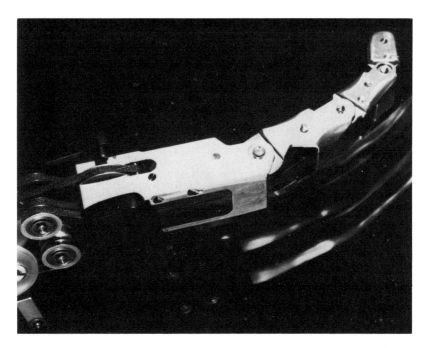

Figure 6. One finger of Wood's and Jacobsen's multifingered hand.

independently of all other joints. There are major problems with this technique. The dynamics of a typical industrial robot arm can be represented as six (or however many degrees of freedom the robot has) coupled second-order differential equations. The equation for the torque at the elbow, for example, includes a reaction torque from the wrist. Reaction torques are ignored in the independent joint formulation and treated as disturbances.

Current university work in control ranges from straightforward development to innovative research. The Germans and the Japanese have put an enormous amount of effort into nonlinear control. Another approach is model-reference control developed by Professor Steven Dubowsky of MIT in collaboration with Cincinnati Milacron. Cheap microprocessors have led to a number of projects involving distributed control. Multiple robots, the fingers of a hand, or the legs of a locomotion system, for example, call for hierarchical control, with loops within loops. Compliance calls for hybrid control of force, or other sensory modality, and position. As with work space analysis, some fruits of this research are ready for technology transfer, a steady stream of contributions can be expected over the next few years. Dr. J. Kenneth Salisbury of MIT has developed a force sensor and a technique for controlling stiffness that uses it. The technique has been implemented for one of the fingers of his three-fingered robot hand.

Software Is the Key

There is more to software for robotics than programming languages. Increasingly one needs to be concerned with entire systems, sometimes called the factory of the future. Many of the key technologies, such as distributed systems, multilayered networks, and interactive programming systems, for the factory of the future were developed originally in artificial-intelligence laboratories.

History shows a steady progression of programming languages moving from the universities into industry. In 1971 researchers at Stanford University implemented the function MOVE to tell the robot to move from here to there—quite a triumph. MOVE is one of the most important instructions ever given a robot or implemented in a programming language. The Stanford team implemented homogeneous transformations as a way of saying what *here* and *there* meant. The resulting programming language was called WAVE. It was later modified by Victor Scheinmann and immersed in a BASIC-like interactive programming system. In 1979, eight years after WAVE, Unimation introduced the first commercially available programmable robot, the PUMA. The language VAL was a reimplementation of Scheinmann's version of WAVE.

The eight- to ten-year transfer time, far too long in my opinion, has continued to hold today, and the sophisticated programming languages under development in the university centers still lead by about the same length of time. AML, the programming language for the IBM 7565, the commercially available robot that I believe is easiest to program, was much influenced by IBM people who studied at Stanford University in the 1970s. Two of them participated in the development of AL, to which AML bears considerable resemblance. The influence of LISP, the language of Artificial Intelligence, on AML is strong. AL was designed in 1972; AML became available in 1980.

Programming languages are the repository of what we know about robots. A lot of people, especially David Grossman of the Yorktown IBM group, have argued that we need a whole programming language base. The Yorktown IBM group also realized that we need to provide for users with widely varying and increasing abilities, from the naive user through the applications and systems programmers. One of the keys to providing for multiple levels of user sophistication is very rich interactive computing systems, using joysticks, mice, and window systems. Techniques for building user-friendly systems are already provided in the AML system.

Geometric Reasoning

Geometric reasoning is an important research issue because robots should understand the task and work space in ways that are more comfortable for an applications engineer. Consider figure 7, where the task is to move the block from its initial position to the final position without crashing into other work space objects. Although solving such problems is trivial for human beings, making robots do the same is extraordinarily difficult. It is one of the major problems prohibiting the linking of CAD models with robot programming systems to do flexible automatic programming for robot systems. Fortunately there has been some recent progress on these kinds of issues. Figure 8

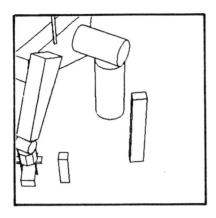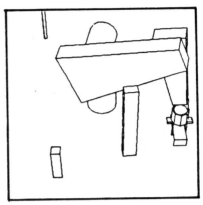

Figure 7. A task for a planning system. The block must be moved from the intial position to the final position without any contact with the cluttered environment.

shows the intermediate steps found by a geometric reasoning program of Professor Rodney Brooks of Stanford University.

Another issue we are concerned with is under what circumstances we can guarantee that a program will meet specifications. Consider figure 9, where the task is to get the palsied robot to insert the screws into the lid. The problem is that the joint angles of the robot are not guaranteed to be exact; also the orientations of the held screwdriver and the screw are not known completely accurately. The position and orientation of the box are subject to error, as are those of the lid on the box. We would be lucky to get the screw into a bucket. What if we use shorter screws or a shorter screwdriver? How does the position of the box in the work space alter our ability to meet specifications? How can we use the slightly uncertain information delivered by a sensor? Brooks has done pioneering work on this class of problems.

Sensing

There are two broad types of sensing: contact and non-contact. Contact sensing includes force, touch, and slip.

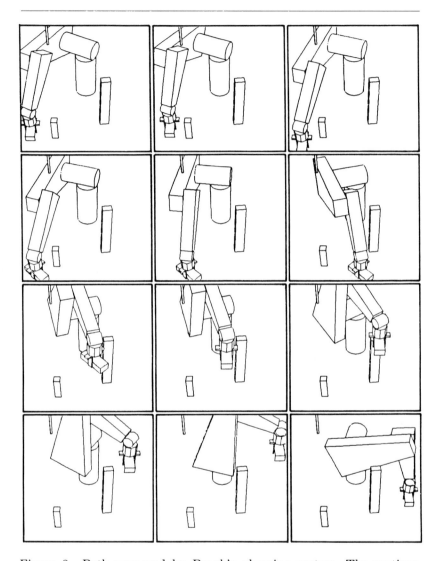

Figure 8. Path proposed by Brook's planning system. The motions are designed such that none of the arm parts bumps into the obstacles.

Noncontact sensing primarily means vision. Intermediate is proximity sensing. A variety of proximity sensors have been developed by Tokuji Okada recently in collaboration with Takeo Kanade at Carnegie-Mellon University. They are ready for transfer to industry. Noncontact sensing is

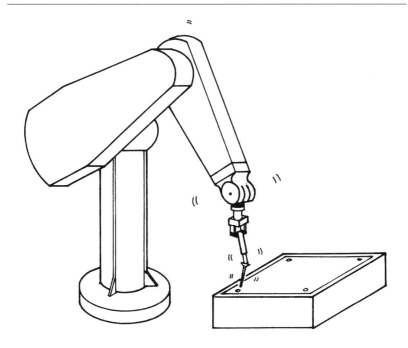

Figure 9. Intelligent reasoning systems can guarantee mating even with inaccurate manipulators.

unobtrusive and reduces positional uncertainty. With non-contact sensing a robot can adaptively change the position of an arm to match the position of an object coming down a conveyor belt.

The purpose of contact sensing can be explained by considering scribing on a complex curved surface. The path to scribe is defined in the tangent plane of the surface; the depth of cutting is defined normal to the surface. Since the curved surface cannot be known accurately ahead of time, one wants to sense forces normal to the surface—easing up if the force exceeds that desired and pressing harder if it becomes too small. Again consider inserting a peg into a tight tolerance hole as a paradigm of assembly. It is hard to do by pure position control. If the robot is made very stiff, slight inaccuracies can cause elastic deformation called wedging and jamming. An example is closing one drawer of a chest of drawers. A better approach is to take account of forces and use them to alter the trajectory of the peg. Tactile sensors enable one to recognize objects by feeling them. There are many applications awaiting the development of good tactile sensors and good algorithms for interpreting tactile sense data.

Currently available tactile sensors are subject to wear and hysteresis, do not scale well, and do not give good responses. Sensor technology is an issue of major concern right now in all of the robotics research laboratories, and there is good work going on in a number of corporations, such as the Lord, General Electric, and Bell Laboratories. Poor-quality sensors are inhibiting the development of sophisticated interpretation algorithms, just as poor TV cameras hindered the development of vision in the 1960s. One exciting approach to tactile sensor design incorporates sensors directly into VLSI processing chips, like the one shown in figure 10. By processing the sense information on the sensors, the bandwidth of communication between sensor and central processor can be significantly reduced. Most early processing of sense data is amenable to local parallel processing, well suited to VLSI implementation.

Developing sensing algorithms is hard. It does not seem to be a good idea simply to copy algorithms developed in pattern recognition and vision. Industrial robots have either poor sensors for touch or none at all. They have good sensors for force, ranging from about one-tenth of an ounce to about ten pounds. There are simple algorithms for picking objects up and simple algorithms for force trajectory. University research laboratories have some good ideas about sensor design, although most are too fragile for industry. The algorithms are much more promising. There is good work going on now, although it is likely to be at least five years before it is ready for technology transfer.

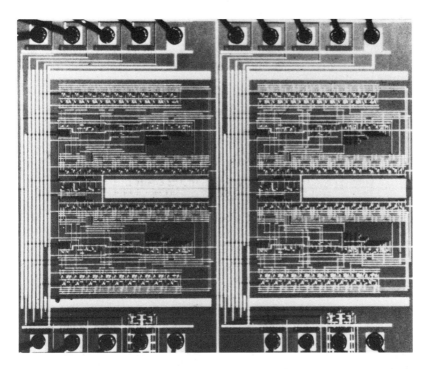

Figure 10. Raibert's touch-sensor chip with onboard processing. (Photograph reprinted from *International Journal of Robotics Research*, vol. 1, no. 3, with permission of The MIT Press.)

Vision is by far the best noncontact sensor because we understand the basic physics of vision a lot better than we understand the basic physics of the other kinds of sensors. Moreover, very reliable vision sensors are available right now, unlike those available for touch and force.

In vision, industry is using techniques that were invented in the university research laboratories about ten years ago. The basis of the vision systems used by Machine Intelligence Corporation, Octek, General Electric, and Automatix is a system developed at SRI in the early 1970s. Most of these are limited to 2-D vision, while many of the potential applications—for example surface inspection—call for 3-D vision.

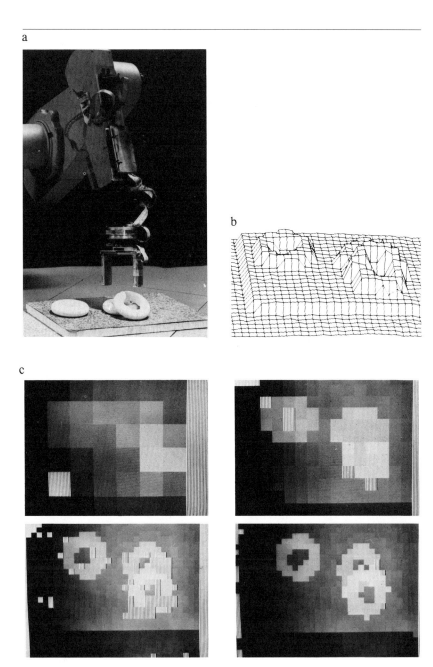

Figure 11. Part a shows a collection of doughnut-shaped objects illuminated with a random-dot pattern. Part b shows a perspective view of the final result of stereo processing. Part c shows how stereo processing moves through multiple resolution analysis. Courtesy H. Keith Nishihara.

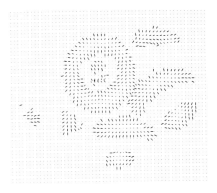

Figure 12. A pile of doughnut-shaped objects and the surface normals produced from them using shading information. Surface normals are sufficient for object identification and spatial localization. Courtesy Katsu Ikeuchi.

3-D vision is the most exciting development in vision. This research deals with understanding how we see stereoscopically (figure 11), how we determine the shape of an object from shading (figure 12), how we determine the shape of an object from a projection of its contour (figure 13), and how we perceive structure from motion and parallax.

Moreover, there is other good work going on that links vision systems directly to computer-aided design systems. The idea is to recognize images and the viewpoint from which the image was taken on the basis of stored models.

Unlike touch and force sensing, whose transfer is probably at least five years away, many vision techniques are ready now, particularly those involving structured light, inasmuch as surface data like those shown in figure 14 are now produced daily in the laboratory. They may be ready, of course, but the ten years it took for binary vision to become accepted makes me pessimistic.

Compliance

Compliance is the solution to the problem of getting robots to bring parts in contact with other parts nondestructively.

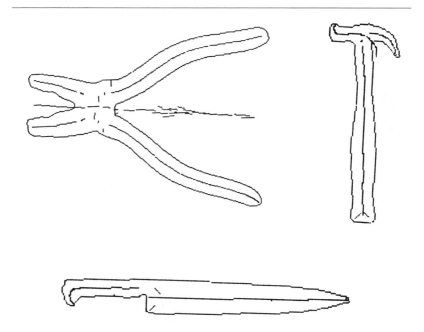

Figure 13. Axes produced from image contours using Brady's theory of smoothed local symmetries. The implemented system is insensitive to the noise produced while extracting the contours from images.

When trying to do things with very tight tolerances, we have to contend with the fact that most robots are designed for accurate and repeatable position-to-position control. Belt such a robot with a hammer, and it will not move. That is marvelous, until we want to put a screw blade in a screw, or do a bayonet insertion, or scribe on a surface.

For compliance we want a robot that is controllably stiff in various dimensions. The problem is that different tasks impose different stiffness requirements and different geometries. Earlier I discussed scribing on a surface. We want to control position tangential to the surface, and we want to control force normal to the surface. This naturally calls for a hybrid force and position controller. The problem is that the constraints are not independent. A small correction in position generates a force, leading to a disturbance in force, leading to a correction in force, leading to a disturbance

Figure 14. Surface reconstructed from laser range data using software written by Philippe Brou. Courtesy Philippe Brou.

in position, and so on. It is hard to implement hybrid controllers that are stable yet enjoy all the properties we have come to expect of pure position controllers.

The Draper Laboratory has implemented a device, Remote Center Compliance, to do peg-in-hole insertion, but it has not been exploited as much as it should have been. There has been software for doing so-called active compliance since 1976, but no one has implemented it apart from the AL system at Stanford. There have also been experimental hybrid controllers, but there is a need for much more work. Compliance is vital for assembly. Small advances can be exploited. The RCC, for example, is used daily in industry.

Slow Reality of Artificial Intelligence

What is the reality of Artificial Intelligence? Contributions to current industrial practice span arms, languages, vision, software tools, and interactive systems. There is a great deal more ready for exploitation, including various kinds of newer arms, grippers, programming systems, 3-D vision, touch sensors, control ideas, and compliant systems. There will be a steady stream of exploitable ideas and devices across the entire range of robotics in the foreseeable future. History suggests, however, that transfer will be slower than it ought to be.

For More Information

Ballard, Dana H., and Christopher Brown, *Computer Vision*, Prentice-Hall, Englewood Cliffs, NJ, 1982.

Brady, J. Michael (editor), *Computer Vision*, North-Holland, Amsterdam, 1981.

Brady, J. Michael, John M. Hollerbach, Timothy L. Johnson, Tomás Lozano-Pérez, and Matthew T. Mason (editors), *Robot Motion: Planning and Control*, MIT Press, Cambridge, MA, 1982.

Hillis, W. Daniel, "A High Resolution Imaging Touch Sensor," *International Journal of Robotics Research*, vol. 1, no. 2, 1982. Based on a MS thesis, Massachusetts Institute of Technology, Cambridge, MA, 1981.

Lozano-Pérez, Tomás, "Robot Programming," Report AIM-698, Artificial Intelligence Laboratory, Massachusetts Institute of Technology, Cambridge, MA, 1982.

Mason, Matthew T., "Compliance and Force Control for Computer Controlled Manipulators," *IEEE Transactions on Systems, Man, and Cybernetics*, vol. SCM-11, no. 6, 1981. Based on a MS thesis, Massachusetts Institute of Technology, Cambridge, MA, 1979.

Paul, Richard P., *Robot Manipulators: Mathematics, Programming, and Control*, MIT Press, Cambridge, MA, 1981.

Raibert, Marc H., and Ivan Sutherland, "Machines That Walk," *Scientific American*, vol. 248, no. 1, 1983.

Salisbury, J. Kenneth, Jr., and John J. Craig, "Articulated Hands: Force Control and Kinematic Issues," *International Journal of Robotics Research*, vol. 1, no. 1, 1982.

15
Intelligent Robots:
Moving toward Megassembly

Philippe Villers
President
Automatix, Incorporated

Mr. Villers is cofounder and president of Automatix, Incorporated, which develops, produces, markets, and services industrial robotic systems. Prior to 1980 Mr. Villers was senior vice-president of Computervision Corporation, which he also cofounded. He has been manager of advanced products at Concord Control, Incorporated, program manager at Singer Link Division, and program engineer at Perkin Elmer and at Barnes Engineering. He is a member of ASME, IEEE, SME, ACM, and RIA. Mr. Villers is a member of three MIT Visiting Committees: the Department of Mechanical Engineering, the Department of Electrical Engineering and Computer Science, and the Laboratory for Manufacturing and Productivity. He is also a member of the National Bureau of Standards Evaluation Panel for Manufacturing Engineering. Mr. Villers received the BA from Harvard and the MS from MIT.

The most exciting part of the future is that which deals with applied Artificial Intelligence. Sophisticated vision systems, initially developed by people in Artificial Intelligence, are beginning to be important, making the field of robotics the first major commercial use of Artificial Intelligence.

In part a robot is a substitute for the human brain. In part a robot is a substitute for the human arm that can handle tools or parts. And in part, in the more modern systems, a robot is a substitute for the human eye.

Complexity

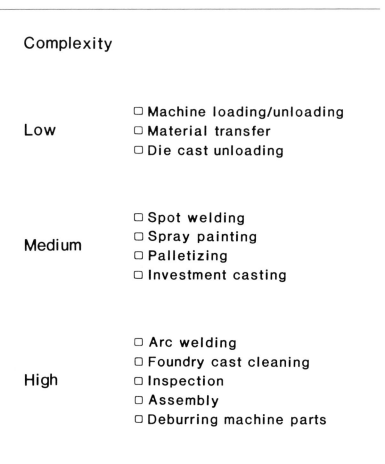

Low
- ☐ Machine loading/unloading
- ☐ Material transfer
- ☐ Die cast unloading

Medium
- ☐ Spot welding
- ☐ Spray painting
- ☐ Palletizing
- ☐ Investment casting

High
- ☐ Arc welding
- ☐ Foundry cast cleaning
- ☐ Inspection
- ☐ Assembly
- ☐ Deburring machine parts

Figure 1. Spectrum of robot applications.

Disturbing Trends

Let us also review the size of the commercial field that exists today, as shown in figure 1. These are the principal applications currently used in the United States and elsewhere. Most of today's robots fall in the middle category, with spot welding consuming the largest single number. But intelligent robotics systems form the most exciting and highest growth category.

Figure 2 shows a curve that people in industry need to be very conscious of. It shows absolute productivity in leading industrial nations. The great interest in robotics is based

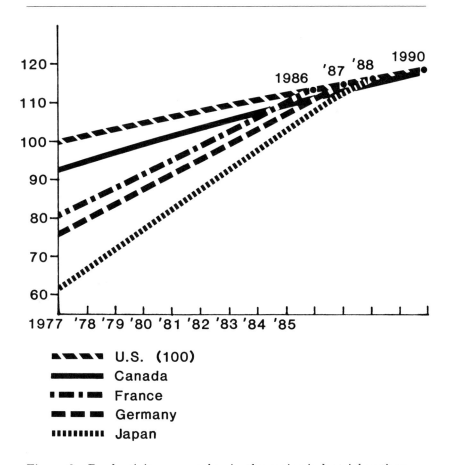

Figure 2. Productivity per worker in the major industrial nations.

on the realization that the old formula of winning markets through superior product design and marketing is no longer good enough. We have to win on the factory floor. Imagine a world in which the United States would have a few thousand token robots and the Japanese would have 50,000 to 100,000. The result would be that we would become one of Japan's new sources of low-cost labor.

Robot sales in the United States passed the $200 million mark last year and by the end of the decade should pass $2 billion. On a world scale, however, we are far from leading. Figure 3 shows the comparative view as of December 1981.

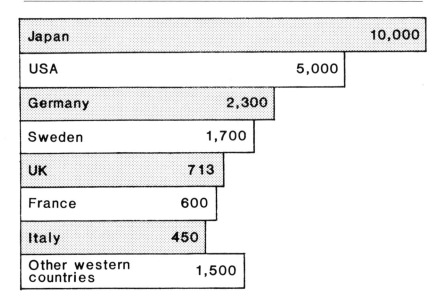

Japan	10,000
USA	5,000
Germany	2,300
Sweden	1,700
UK	713
France	600
Italy	450
Other western countries	1,500

Figure 3. World robot population. Adapted from *Robot News International*, March 1982.

Since then the gap has widened, particularly in the most advanced areas such as the area of assembly. Consider arc welding. The Japanese produced about 2,000 arc-welding robots. We produced or installed about 150. In the area of assembly, destined to become the main area for robotic applications, Japan produced 1,500 robots in 1982, almost all for domestic production. In the United States the total number built or installed is estimated to be 100 in the same year.

Vision

Artificial vision was the first of the widespread uses of Artificial Intelligence on the factory floor. The number of artificial vision installations is now estimated to be in the low hundreds and growing rapidly, covering more than a dozen industries and an increasing variety of highly diverse applications.

Figure 4. General Motors CONSIGHT vision system in action.

Figure 4 illustrates the widely publicized General Motors CONSIGHT, now in production in Canada. It is used for sorting castings in a hostile environment in a foundry with vision providing guidance for the robot.

Figure 5 shows bin picking. For those who thought bin picking had been solved only in the laboratory, Ford in Germany is doing it in production. What Ford has done, of course, is cheat a little. This is semi-ordered bin picking. Castings have been put down in rows in approximately the right position at a negligible increase in cost, making the bin-picking problem easier to solve.

Figure 6 shows the Automatix work horse, AUTOVISION[R] II, based largely on SRI technology and some work in structured lighting done at the National Bureau of Standards and at General Motors. It uses the most powerful microprocessor currently available, the Motorola 68000, which allows million-word memories, and the RAIL[R] language, our own proprietary language designed for use by nonprogrammers.

Figure 5. Bin picking in a German Ford plant.

Figure 7 depicts an application at General Motors involving automobile front ends. This illustration shows the front end of a Chevrolet pickup truck. Ninety holes must be inspected in the two seconds available. Before our system was installed, if there was any breakage or wear, as many as 1,200 bad Chevrolet front ends could be left before the next once-hourly inspection. But with our system the problem is noted immediately. A part that is bad is sprayed red. When three parts in a row are bad, the press is stopped.

Figure 8 illustrates a process-control application. An instrument cluster is undergoing automatic inspection using simulated inputs. Both analog and digital outputs are involved.

This next application, shown in figure 9, is a precursor of many to come because it involves several concepts: statistical process, control, and sophisticated multicamera vision. The idea is to inspect the gaps, such as between the car body and its hood, to do real-time statistical analysis, and to inform

Figure 6. Automatix AUTOVISION^R II vision system.

Figure 7. Inspecting a truck front end for correct hole punching.

Figure 8. Visual inspection of instrument clusters.

the upstream stations on the assembly line where hoods are being put on. The result is that corrective action can be taken before errors creep out of the permissible tolerance band, so no bad cars go down the line.

Vision Plus Manipulation

Our view is that robot systems are really just computer systems in which some of the terminals happen to be robots. We therefore stress a computer-centered approach to producing intelligent robots.

Our AI-32 controller, the controller for all our robots, uses the Motorola 68000 microprocessor and the RAIL[R] language. It controls our AID 800 arc-welding robot, our AID 600 assembly robot, our AID 900 long-reach robot, as well as our artificial vision system, which can be used with all the other products. We will introduce several other arms, all running on our universal robot controller with a

Figure 9. Using vision to monitor quality. A vision system checks for proper gaps between car body and hood.

Figure 10. Welding chair frames.

single unified language, regardless of robot geometry and other characteristics.

Figure 10 shows arc welding at Steelcase Furniture, where chairs are turned out at the rate of one every thirty-two seconds. Integrated with the system is a turntable so that a person can load and unload while the robot welds.

Figure 11 shows our seam tracker, the result of a marriage of artificial vision and welding currently undergoing field tests by a major customer. In this application our vision system is augmented with a laser beam to provide correction for the actual path of the seam, as distinguished from the nominal path. Our system works in the presence of the arc due to very special filtering techniques.

In roughly 30 percent of the cases the seam position cannot be determined with sufficient accuracy in advance. For example, visual seam tracking is often necessary when working with the thinner metals, where distortion takes place for thermal reasons during the welding process.

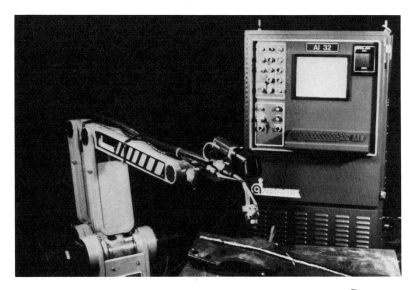

Figure 11.   Guiding a robot arc welder with AUTOVISION[R] II seam tracker.

A related problem occurs when the position of the part in space is not known with sufficient accuracy even though there is no warping or path uncertainty. For this problem we have developed a way of using the same system without the laser beam, called the Partracker^{TM}. In the Partracker^{TM}, the vision camera merely does a rectification, provides the information to the intelligent robot controller, and the standard program is executed with a coordinate system transformation.

Assembly

The third area of application for intelligent turnkey robotic systems is assembly. The robotic assembly field, still in its infancy, is clearly destined to be a giant. The example in figure 12 is from an application at Texas Instruments, now several years old. I include it among assembly examples, although it involves testing, because one of the characteristics

Figure 12.   Texas Instruments robot aids in calculator testing.

of robotics is that the traditional separation of assembly, inspection, and testing no longer exists. The main historical reason for the separation is objectivity, a problem there is no need to worry about when using robots.

You see the calculator going down a moving line underneath cameras in the ceiling. The robot picks up the calculator and puts it in a test stand, where it is tested. The robot then picks it up and puts it back on a belt. Another robot works the keys while a vision system watches the read-out to make sure that the calculation is correct. At the end of the line another vision-equipped robot identifies the calculator, its orientation, and its position so that a robot can pick it up and put it in the correct carrying case. Texas Instruments is among the companies that have done the most advanced work for in-house purposes.

Figure 13. Stuffing PC boards. A vision system verifies correct identification and proper orientation.

Now let us look at single-station assembly systems, the stuffing of PC boards with nonstandard components, shown in figure 13. Here is the end of the AID 600 arm, which has a heavy payload capability. That is important because it can handle a great deal of tooling, thereby speeding up the operation. The lampshade arrangement is used to illuminate the part properly so that the component can be identified, verifying that it is correct and not in backward.

Figure 14 shows one of the more advanced applications, one involving key caps. At the first station the key caps are put into long tubes under vision control, and each key cap is inspected for correct legend and good quality. At the next station the battery of tubes is handled by a twenty-two-fingered robot, which does the entire keyboard in batches in less than one minute, eight times faster than manually. The system uses parallel processing to make up for its lack of dexterity and speed compared to a nimble human.

Figure 14. Robot assembly of keycaps on keyboards.

Figure 15 shows a large assembly task involving an automobile car door. A number of bolts are used to adjust the window roll-up assembly. They are in slots because of assembly tolerances so the robot does not know where to find the bolt head. Two important advances are involved. First, a CAD/CAM system, made by Computervision, was used to define the assembly task and feed the information to the robot. But to execute the task, the robot needs correction for part-to-part variation of the location of the bolt head in its slot. The well-known Westinghouse APAS system, built mainly for demonstration purposes, is a single assembly system that can do mixed production, building a whole family of electric motors on the same line under software control without tooling change.

Megassembly

Since the Westinghouse system was completed, the Japanese have gone much further. We have coined the term *megas-*

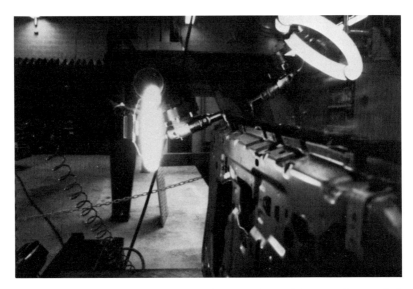

Figure 15. Bolting together car doors using vision to locate bolt
heads.

sembly for advanced assembly systems, those that involve
multistation, multiproduct, progressive assembly using ten
or more robots. In Japan there are systems with fifty to
two hundred stations, of which typically at least a third
are robotic. Many of the rest are hard automation of conventional design, and occasionally there will be four or five
stations that are manually operated, although the Japanese
are somewhat apologetic about them. This is revolutionary
because they are used for mixed production. Up to thirty
models go down the same line with just software-controlled
changes.

Videocassette recorders are made on megassembly systems
at Panasonic, JVC, and Hitachi. The Sony Walkman is made
on a megassembly system. All this has happened in the last
two years, moving the technology from the laboratory to
the production line. In the United States we must decide if
we will choose to lag in the introduction of similar systems
by three or four years, as we have in the case of arc welding.

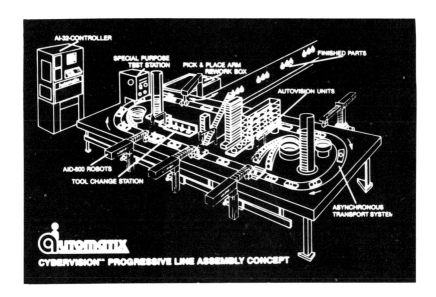

Figure 16. Megassembly system of the future.

Automatix is very much interested in Megassembly. We are talking to perspective partners in developing domestic Megassembly systems. I believe it is a very important trend, with advanced sensors destined to play a major role, even though the early megassembly systems in Japan have few advanced sensors and do not use vision.

The Future

Figure 16 shows an artist's conception of a simple megassembly system. More complex ones, with twenty or fifty stations, are typically linear, with asynchronous systems feeding the parts from station to station and providing buffer storage. There are very few of these systems in the United States; I hope that the number will increase rapidly because it already is growing rapidly in Japan.

For More Information

Gleason, Gerald J. and Gerald J. Agin, "A Modular System for Sensor-controlled Manipulation and Inspection," *Proceedings of the 9th International Symposium on Industrial Robots*, Washington, D.C., published by Society of Manufacturing Engineers, Dearborn, Michigan, March 1979.

Ohashi, T., S. Miyakawa, Y. Arai, S. Inoshita, and A. Yamada, "The Development of Automatic Assembly Line for VTR Mechanisms," presented at CIRP Conference on Assembly Automation, Amherst, MA, June 1983.

VanderBrug, G. J., D. Wilt, and J. Davis, "Robotic Assembly of Keycaps to Keyboard Arrays," *Robots 7*, Dearborn, Michigan, April 1983.

Villers, Philippe, "Megassembly: The Sleeping Giant of Robotics," in *Decade of Robotics*, IFS Publications, 1983.

Villers, Philippe, "Present Industrial Use of Vision Sensors for Robot Guidance," *Proceedings of the 12th International Symposium on Industrial Robots*, Paris, France, June, 1982.

Villers, Philippe, "The Role of Vision in Industrial Robotic Systems and Inspections," Proceedings of Electro 83, New York, New York, April 1983.

16
Intelligent Robots:
Myth or Reality

Paul M. Russo
General Manager
Microelectronics Center
General Electric Company

Dr. Russo directs major research efforts in CAD/CAM, graphics, advanced controls, robotics, factory communications, system architecture, and software technology. Prior to 1980 he was head of microsystems research at RCA Laboratories, actively involved in the development of the RCA 1802 microprocessor and a host of microprocessor-based consumer and manufacturing systems. Dr. Russo holds five patents. He has been awarded the RCA Laboratories' Outstanding Achievement Award twice and the Meritorious Award of the IEEE Industrial Electronics Society. He is a fellow of the IEEE, vice-president of the IES, and an AdCom member of the IEEE CAS Society. Dr. Russo received the Bachelor of Engineering Physics from McGill University and the MS and PhD in Electrical Engineering and Computer Science from the University of California at Berkeley, where he also served on the faculty.

The current approach to Artificial Intelligence is dominated by the clever use of brute force. We use lower-cost, more powerful computers to do things we could not do ten years ago, but we have not seen any major breakthroughs in the way things are done. To me, the *A* part of Artificial Intelligence is certainly a reality; the *I* part is a myth.

Factory automation depends upon looking at the factory as a whole, thinking in terms of the information in figure 1. We cannot look at robotics in isolation because robotics is

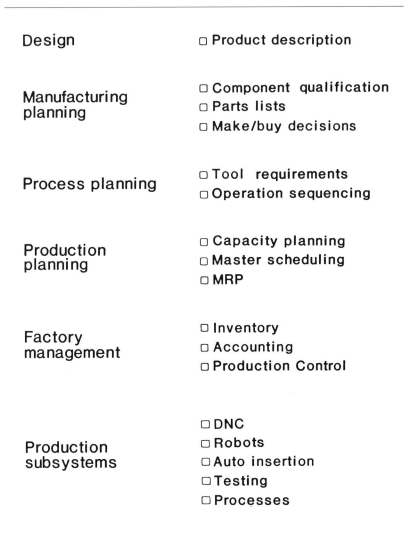

Design	□ Product description
Manufacturing planning	□ Component qualification □ Parts lists □ Make/buy decisions
Process planning	□ Tool requirements □ Operation sequencing
Production planning	□ Capacity planning □ Master scheduling □ MRP
Factory management	□ Inventory □ Accounting □ Production Control
Production subsystems	□ DNC □ Robots □ Auto insertion □ Testing □ Processes

Figure 1. Many facets of factory automation.

only a small piece of the solution. Instead we have to think about systems for design, manufacturing planning, process planning, production planning, factory management, and the actual intelligent systems themselves.

All of these systems interact, and they all share data. The sharing of data is probably the most fundamental issue to be faced if we are to learn how to build integrated factory systems. Machines already replace human muscle. Factory intelligence centers will replace human brains to gather information and make decisions. How much of that is really going on?

Factory intelligence implies a knowledge base; it implies a need for information collection, sensors, and communication; and it implies the ability to adapt to changing environments.

An intelligent factory system must have these attributes. It must have a good model of the world and good information-gathering capabilities. It must operate with incomplete data. It must be able to handle exceptions so that it can tolerate occasional failures; a factory system must not come to a halt because one piece fails. Finally, an intelligent factory system should learn, but that is a long-term dream more than anything else.

So the reality is that total factory intelligence is a myth. All we have are limited solutions, achieved through brute force computation.

Artificial versus Natural Intelligence

Let me give some examples of limited roles where artificial-intelligence concepts are being employed.

Expert systems can leverage human intelligence. Expert systems are real, they are important, and their use will increase, especially in areas having to do with the diagnosis, repair, and maintenance of equipment.

Computers can help with process planning, describing how to make a part within a given factory architecture. That kind of help is on the rise. Systems with that kind of capability are installed at between fifty and one hundred locations worldwide.

Computers can be part of smart sensors, permitting adaptive control. Smart sensors allow machines to be less accurate, to be more tolerant to changes, and to respond to the real-world environment.

Finally, computers can replace humans in routine tasks, but humans must handle many exceptions. Moreover, humans must make the strategic decisions, like those concerning what equipment to buy and what processes to put in. Computers cannot handle the really big problems.

The Japanese

Figure 2 shows the various technologies fundamental to robotics. They include mechanical design, controls, sensors, software, the technology of robot manufacture, and the applications of robots. The three in the middle are those that I believe are most subject to influence by Artificial Intelligence. According to my own assessment, the United States leads today in all three categories, however, we must be very careful about the Japanese fifth-generation computer project. U.S. leadership may change in the future.

The current robot market is dominated by manipulators. In that area Japan is clearly the leader, and the impact of Artificial Intelligence is low. But the market is evolving from selling manipulators to selling what we call focused-application systems such as welding systems and assembly systems. The market for such systems is increasing, and therefore the importance of Artificial Intelligence is increasing.

The Future

In the longer term robots will be just one element in integrated manufacturing systems that link numerical controls, programmable controls, CAD/CAM, and communications. Here the leader, especially in CAD/CAM, is the United States. As shown in figure 3, the importance of Artificial Intelligence is high, and the market today is almost nonexistent.

Robots are going to get smarter in the future. The difficult problems of today, like bin picking, will be routine in the

Technology	United States	Japan
Mechanical design	Lead	Lag
Servos/drives	Equal	Equal
Controls	Lead	Lag
Sensors	Lead	Lag
Software	Lead	Lag
Manufacturing of robots	Lag	Lag
Application of robots	Lead	Lead

   Impact of Artificial Intelligence

Figure 2. Some comparisions between the United States and Japan in key robotics technologies.

Business	Leader	Importance of A.I.	Current market
Manipulators	Japan	Low	High
Focused applications	U.S., Japan	Increasing	Increasing
One element of automation systems	U.S.	High	Low

Figure 3. Evolution of the robotics business.

future. We are going to have higher performance robots with lighter structures. Today a robot can pick up only about 5 percent of its own weight because the robot's structure must remain rigid. It cannot tolerate any motion or any flexing. In the future, smart sensors will enable robots to compensate for flexing, enabling much higher performance.

Increasingly robots will be parts of systems. Companies will sell total solutions, not just robots.

Factory automation and flexible manufacturing will allow companies to respond to changing market demands quickly. Reprogrammable factories will become reprogrammable islands of automation through the increasing use of manufacturing cells and group-technology concepts.

Finally, the importance of information management and communications will grow. Information handling and computer control will be the major obstacles to tying factories together into integrated systems in the future.

No Breakthroughs

As for Artificial Intelligence, I see more of the same until there is a major breakthrough in our understanding of how humans deal with incomplete data, make decisions quickly, and react smoothly to unforeseen circumstances.

Computers are becoming less expensive, making the computational costs of more applications reasonable. I do not see any major breakthroughs on the horizon right now in Artificial Intelligence.

General Electric plans to be a major participant in factory automation. We are bullish on intelligent robots and intelligent sensors. But as far as making money in Artificial Intelligence, I think the best way is to hold meetings with paid attendance, such as this one.

Winston

I have an uneasy feeling about the relationship of robotics to Artificial Intelligence. Dr. Brady has called robotics the intelligent connection of perception to action. When phrased that way, Artificial Intelligence is a part of robotics rather than the other way around. The rooting of robotics in Artificial Intelligence is something we may raise some questions about.

Mr. Villers, you discussed some of the current applications of vision that your company is particularly eager to exploit. How important is vision?

Villers

I have observed an unusual coincidence. The opinion of the importance of vision among robotics vendors is divided into two camps. Those vendors who have vision in their product lines say that it is very important; those who do not have it in their product lines say that it is not needed.

Brady

Nevertheless most of the discussions today have been about 2-D vision. The major research push that we have seen in the university laboratories in the last seven years has been in 3-D vision. There has also been a large push in various other kinds of sensor modalities. When do you think that we will begin to see commercial exploitation of the kind of 3-D vision systems we have been developing in the university laboratories?

Villers

The first step in that direction is 2 1/2-D vision, using structured lighting. For example, we measure the height difference of a particular point as distinct from trying to do a complete reconstruction of the part in 3-D. The main thing that is holding back full 3-D systems is that none approaches being a real-time system. Having to wait twenty or thirty minutes to be able to interpret what you saw limits it to certain narrow classes of inspection applications. Some more work will be needed before that kind of time scale ceases to be representative of what is required to reconstruct a part.

Brady

I think that is absolutely right. It should be pointed out, however, that the actual kinds of computing developed for 3-D vision have been essentially those that lend themselves to parallel implementation using the kind of VLSI circuitry now being developed. It seems to me that would not be a major risk for some company that wanted to do 3-D vision on a five-year time span.

Villers

I agree that within five years we will see significant commercial use of 3-D vision. In industry a company that jumps in to what has been done in the university laboratories and tries to commercialize it usually goes out of the business, and conversely the company that does not keep up with what is going on in the universities also goes out of business, but a little later. Something in between seems to be the right policy.

Winston

That brings to mind a question concerning what seems to be excessive gloominess on the part of Americans about the issue of competition. Dr. Russo, what do you view as the right way for U.S. industry to collaborate with universities to reduce the possibility that we will be wiped out in what appears to be a highly exciting technical area?

Russo

I am not at all as gloomy as you intimated. U.S. industies tend to be ahead technologically. What I think has happened, for various reasons, is that our visible-to-the-consumer businesses, such as automobiles and consumer electronics, have not invested in automation to the extent that high-technology businesses have. It is not just a technology issue; it is a question of having the financial incentives and the reasons to implement them. We have not had good management in those areas in the past. As far as competing in those businesses, I see no reason why the United States cannot compete successfully. There is no trick to it; it is the way you win football games—blocking and tackling, getting down to basics, making quality products, using leading-edge technology, and addressing markets that need solutions.

Villers

In terms of the users of robots, I think that the fact that the Japanese lead is increasing rather than shrinking is a matter of great national concern and should be, since the kind of megassembly systems I described are ordinary techniques with which hard automation or manual labor cannot effectively compete. That should be a matter of great concern.

As far as robot manufacturers are concerned, because of the volume differences, robot arm manufacturing is already dominated by Japanese producers. GE, IBM, and Automatix use arms made abroad, in many cases in Japan. Fortunately the area where we are still very strong is the area most relevant to this particular community—Artificial Intelligence. More intelligent controllers with better software and better sensors are an area of U.S. strength. Automatix sells more artificial vision systems in Japan than any Japanese firm does.

Winston

Do you find that your sales force is still engaged in proselytizing about the usefulness of robotics, or can you confine your sales efforts to selling Automatix as opposed to selling the concept of robotics?

Villers

Let me contrast the situation with my experience twelve years ago in the CAD/CAM industry at Computervision, where we had tremendous difficulty convincing people that they should listen to us at all. In the case of robotics that is not the case. Between the Japanese and the media, few U.S. managements are dense enough not to believe that if they intend to have a future, automation and flexible automation is necessary. The convincing we have to do is that the particular job they have in mind can be done cost-effectively and, of course, that we are the most suitable vendor. The basic question of whether robotics is important never comes up.

Brady

Dr. Russo, do you consider the problems of robotics to be essentially solved and that the major challenge is the development of flexible manufacturing systems? Given the existence of hierarchical and local-area networks, what do you consider the major challenges to be? What are the costs? What are the time scales?

Russo

You need a systems approach, and robots are only one piece of the puzzle. Although there are still challenges in robotics, there are lots of challenges everywhere in the process. I feel the biggest one is the data-handling challenge, moving toward the paperless environment, linking CAD systems data bases with manufacturing data bases, being able to handle exceptions, and have the thing run as a flexible manufacturing automated environment.

Brady

To what extent do you think that some of the ideas of Artificial Intelligence could contribute to that flexibility? After all one of the key contributions of Artificial Intelligence has always been that it could develop software that responds predictably to situations that could not be described in advance.

Russo

We are now implementing automated process planning that uses artificial-intelligence concepts in one of our plants in Charlottesville. Even in the manufacturing of a standard line of numerical controls, every one is a little bit different. You want to develop a process plan to tie everything together through the flow of that factory. That is going to be done with the aid of computers that use a lot of artificial-intelligence concepts. Some of those are more difficult and more challenging than just vision or just robotics.

Villers

Earlier someone described how expert systems for medical diagnosis worked well on theoretical patients and poorly on real patients. The same thing occurs on the factory floor. A flexible manufacturing system as a theoretical process is really not intractable. In terms of real processes, Artificial Intelligence is needed in several areas but particularly in the area of self-adaptive systems that can deal with the normal occurrences and variability in manufacturing. Whether you call it megassembly, as I do in assembly, or flexible manufacturing systems, in machining, it is the same concept of having the subdivision of labor reach its ultimate limit in large, complex operations without the limit of human boredom. People are willing to be treated as robots only up to a point. But there is no equivalent problem with robots. It is just a problem of organization and adaptation.

Brady

It is tremendously difficult to capture knowledge. What you have just been raising, in fact, is the whole issue of encoding the knowledge about various kinds of processes and about parts in order to build flexible manufacturing systems. How difficult do you think that is, and what kind of time scale do you think we are talking about?

Villers

That is a very difficult problem, and yet the time scale is right away. Why the paradox? Because just as the bin-picking problem has been solved in the restricted but commercially useful case, there are flexible manufacturing problems in the restricted case that are commercially useful right away. The more difficult problems will take a lot longer.

Winston

Mr. Villers, you are seated next to two industrial giants. What do you feel the role of a relatively small company like Automatix will be in the development of robotics? Do you see lots of small companies springing up like minicomputer companies used to spring up?

Villers

It has already happened. There are over fifty companies in robotics and over thirty companies making some claim to being in some form of artificial vision. That process is taking place as it did in the minicomputer industry, and I expect the traditional shake-out will follow.

I believe that being small is, on balance, an advantage. When the industry is small, it is a question of whether you would rather be David or Goliath. If you are David you had better not carry too much armor; you had better be very nimble and run quickly. In a young industry I would rather be on the side of David than on the side of Goliath.

The history of technology shows that in the last twenty-five years, most new fields have eventually had in their leadership companies that grew up in that field and that very large companies that came in from other fields did not dominate it. IBM still does not dominate the small computer field. There is a little company started by Ken Olsen that is doing all right. The CAD field is not dominated by General Electric and IBM, which are both respected figures in it, but by my old company, Computervision, which grew up in that industry. The giants are giants, but it is difficult for a giant to operate in a tiny field.

Winston

Do you regard dreams of robots walking through the parks picking up beer cans so far out as to be dangerous science fiction, or do you see that type of robotics in the future?

Villers

When I was a graduate student here, I saw an amusing development of Ivan Sutherland, called SKETCHPAD, which was the beginning of CAD/CAM. Students have the opportunity to see here what could be commercially important years later. That is very exciting. Some students have the even more exciting experience of playing a role in making it happen. So without assuming that what is in the cartoons is going to be on the factory floor, the ability to see the beginning kernels here and then see them gradually introduced in industry is tremendously exciting.

Russo

I think there is excitement across the board in factory automation. I look at robots as very exciting; I look at CAD/CAM and graphics as very exciting. The technology is moving down into our future CAD/CAM systems, which will allow you to take objects, view them as solid models, and move them around.

Winston

The area of nuclear safety comes up from time to time. Some of my friends have told me it is already too late because we will not have any robots in time to go in to fix those things. They point out that the fusion era, if it ever comes, will be even worse because fusion plants will be even dirtier than present atomic power plants. Do you see these things as opportunities or as distractions from the main thrust of America's budding robotics industry?

Russo

You have to look at the maturity of the market. The point is that companies are primarily out to develop business. They need to make a product that will sell in large enough quantities to get returns on their investment, or the price has to be high enough per unit, a sort of a contract business where you can do special applications. With the current state of the nuclear business in this country, the volume of robots to repair the plants would not be very large.

Winston

I chose a bad example. There must be many things like coal-mining safety or repairing long-distance high-tension wires.

Brady

Are there going to be new opportunities because there are going to be new kinds of production capabilities?

Villers

The examples cited are from a neighboring and related field, the field of teleoperators, machines remotely controlled by human beings. That is true of nuclear safety, coal mining, underwater operations for a variety of purposes, and assembly operations in space. I also think it will give rise to a new breed of hybrid robot. A robot, of course, operates under program control, a teleoperator under remote human control. At the present time the field you are talking about is not generally considered part of industrial robotics, and the manufacturers of industrial robotics systems have not turned their attention to the distinct teleoperator field.

Winston

You have already brought up this subject of volumes and pointed out that volumes are of concern to you. As these volumes grow, do you see anything dramatic happening in the pricing of robots or the way they are made? Are they going to be built out of extruded plastic? What do you see as the future of that kind of business?

Russo

You will get more performance for the buck certainly. In certain technologies, like mechanical structures, progress will be slower. The big breakthrough there will be the ability to use smart sensors that will allow the use of lower-cost, flexible structures, which can be made of plastic or other materials. The controls area will follow the traditional computer price-performance curve. You will get a lot more computing power for less money as time goes on. The same is true for sensors.

Brady

Most of those little plastic robots that cost from $50 to $1,500, even those controlled by little microprocessors, typically are used for education. I wonder if we will see the development of robots out of special kinds of cheap, composite process materials, that you will be able to buy for about the same price as personal computers now, that will do a reasonably useful set of things, for example, in the kitchen.

Russo

I can't think of a reasonable set of useful things you could do in a kitchen with a robot.

One of the problems here is the law of diminishing returns. We had an internal discussion at GE where one person went to INTERSIL with a need for a custom chip—semi-custom, actually—for an application. He said, "I'm willing to pay $25 for 40,000 of the chips but I will pay you $1 if I can get a million." I was quick to figure out that you are better off selling him only 40,000 chips. I think at some point we have got to look at the total market, if the robot is going to cost $1,000$ and you are a large company with large overhead. My prediction is that those will tend to be specialties.

Brady

The big incursion of computers began when they appeared in very small companies. Do you see the same kind of trend within robotics?

Villers

I think you are going to see industrial robots used in very small companies. It is already happening in Japan. The smallest company to use an industrial robot in Japan has one employee, who also happens to be president.

Brady

Where do you think the main opportunities for new companies, new products, and venture capital activity will be in the next five years in robotics? Obviously there is a broad spread from sensing through mechanical structures through artificial-intelligence programming. Where do you think the main opportunities lie for people who want to get into this field?

Russo

If you want to restrict it to the area of robotics, I would draw an analogy with the history of numerical controls, where a large market developed in terms of programming aids for machines—either stand-alone work stations or time-shared services that would allow you to program your robot in higher-level languages, in a CAD/CAM environment, to simulate the whole function, and then post-process the information to a specific robot that you have at hand. I see a big opportunity there.

Winston

Are there really no VISICALCs in this area? Is there nothing that I can do to start my company tomorrow with a little widget that will identify objects with three fingers or inspect printed circuit boards?

Villers

There are always opportunities, but the problems in the field have to do with standardization. What made VISICALC interesting is that you could sell it for large numbers of already produced personal computers, and you could have several versions to take care of several popular lines. If you had to sell a personal computer designed to work with VISICALC with every VISICALC, I suspect the sales would not even have come within two orders of magnitude.

Winston

My guess is that is false. I think an enormous number of personal computers were sold specifically to run VISICALC. The computer was sold to go along with VISICALC, not the other way.

Villers

Even if you are right, the cost of the personal computer makes that by no means absurd. Standards are missing in robotics. For instance, it is ridiculous that every manufacturer has to design his own end effectors for every possible purpose. But as long as there are no standards on interfaces and on end effectors, there can be no ready market for small companies that would specialize in making good end effectors. Similarly in terms of interfaces of various sorts and in terms of application programs, there is no way to write an application program that will run on two manufacturers' robots. In many cases there is no way for an outside software firm to write one application program that will run on one manufacturer's robot.

Russo

From a development point of view, robotics is fairly mature now in the sense that what is now in the marketplace was developed in past years. You do not see what is going on now. If you had asked that question three or four years ago, you would have gotten a long litany of things that could have been done. Right now the problems that are unsolved are very difficult to solve. Companies like Automatix, GE, and IBM are pursuing areas that they believe they have expertise in. There will be a lot of new products coming out in the next two or three years that are currently under development. But you do have a two- to three-year development cycle, so you cannot judge the state of the art by looking at the marketplace.

Villers

In high technology one of the secrets to being an entrepreneur is getting into a new field at the right moment. Several years ago the opportunity in robotics was wide open because not a great deal had been done. There are always new fields that open up about which the same statement can be made. If I were starting today, I would not be an entrepreneur on last year's frontier or that of the year before. I would be an entrepreneur on this year's frontier or next year's frontier.

Part IV

Today and Tomorrow

18
The Problems
and the Promise

Marvin Minsky
Donner Professor of Science
Artificial Intelligence Laboratory
Massachusetts Institute of Technology

Professor Minsky has been one of the most influential leaders in the field of Artificial Intelligence, emphasizing approaches to problems of symbolic description, knowledge representation, semantics, machine perception and learning, and, recently, in psychological and physiological theories of imagery, memory, and new computational structures. He was an early contributor to the modern field of intelligence-based mechanical robotics, planning the early stages of several such projects both in and outside of MIT. Professor Minsky is a member of the National Academy of Sciences and president of the American Association of Artificial Intelligence. He is on the Board of Governors of the L-5 Society and a fellow of the Harvard Society of Fellows, the IEEE, and the AAAS. Professor Minsky received the BA in Mathematics from Harvard University and the PhD in Mathematics from Princeton University.

It is my impression that American industry does not understand the way ideas develop or how they have to be nurtured in order not to fall behind in the long run. That is a startling indictment, but in areas like automotive machinery, consumer electronics, steel, glass, and many other fields, we all know that someone goofed. The prosperity that is just around the corner for the world, I think, is quite glorious. It is questionable whether America's industry and citizens will have a reasonable share of it.

Missing Links

Most of the things you hear about are applications. It is very important in Artificial Intelligence to pick a good problem to work on. But look carefully at the applications systems: they are wonderful, they save money, and they solve problems. But are they intelligent?

The existing applications programs are smart in some sense. But I think that something is missing in all of them. For example, the expert systems now being marketed and manufactured for particular special purposes do not learn, and they do not have common sense. They are too narrow.

Why is it that artificial-intelligence systems do not learn? The answer is simple: first, only half a dozen people have worked on the problem of writing programs that learn, and, second, the problem is hard. The medical systems are wonderful, but they do not know what a person is. We have a magnificent kidney program at MIT that in its area, is probably as good as the best medical specialist, but it does not know that the kidney is in the body in any sense. Nor does it know what a body is. Nor does it know that if you yell at someone, he will get depressed and act sick.

The Well Is Running Dry

In the laboratory we regard the term *expert system* with a certain amount of scorn. Frank Lloyd Wright once said an expert is a person who does not have to think; he knows.

In a sense today's expert systems demonstrate a marvelous fact we did not know twenty-five years ago: if you write down if-then rules for a lot of situations and put them together well, the resulting system can solve problems that people think are hard. It is remarkable that much of what we think requires intelligence can be done by compiling surface behavior rules. Many people in this field are surprised at that.

Similarly twenty-five years ago we did not know that if you wrote a chess program that looked at all possible moves for about five layers ahead, it would rank at the level of a middle-ranking chess club person. There is no chess program that plays at the grand master level, but there are chess programs that play at the expert level. Curiously, the less intelligence these programs have, the better they have done. There have been some experimental programs that explored strategic concepts and tried to understand why taking someone's queen would be good. But the programs in the little chess machines now for sale say that if you lose your queen, you have lost a certain number of points. Those work pretty well.

The success of rule-based systems bodes ill for making further progress. Companies hiring people who have been trained in this area must look ahead a few years. There is no significant increase in the number of people working on the ideas that we will want to use in ten years. The number of people doing basic research in Artificial Intelligence is probably under one hundred people and maybe under fifty. The explosion in Artificial Intelligence does not resemble the explosion in Molecular Biology.

If someone discovers that a new antibody can be attached to one T cell and cause it to eat a bad T cell, then there are dozens of people, maybe hundreds or thousands, who are qualified to work on applications of that antibody. When someone makes a discovery in expert systems, there are not dozens of people to carry on. Among the most successful work that we have done in our Laboratory was making a robot that could pick up blocks and stack them. In doing that we painfully discovered many facts of common sense, such as the fact that you should put the bottom block on the table first if you are going to build a tower.

There are no programs yet that can understand simple mechanical causality. How can a program know that you can pull with a string but not push with it?

Mimi Sinclair, a psychologist in Geneva, has studied what children do with sticks, spoons, bottles, and pails. She discovered that a typical child at some time in his or her life will spend three or four weeks almost singlemindedly fussing with containers and inserting things in apertures. If you look superficially at these children, they look as if they are playing. But if you look closely at slow-motion videotapes, you will see that a child is a little scientist making hypotheses. This process is extensive, meticulous, and goes on for hours a day for several weeks. You rarely see an adult with the attention span of a child, studying something so carefully, except when you watch someone learning to shoot baskets or to play chromatic scales on the piano. Then you find adults spending hours doing microexperiments. They will not realize they are doing experiments, of course, they say it is just in their hands, not their brains.

Basic Research

My point is that there is very little basic research going on right now. The general principles of most of the expert systems being made today are very close to the specifications published in Alan Newell and Herbert Simon's *Human Problem Solving* over ten years ago. The procedures described in their book descend from ideas that appeared in Henry Ernst's robotics program in 1960.

If we do not start to encourage people to work on simple matters like telling cups from saucers and apples from bananas and people from chairs, we are going to lose out, and our software will come from Japan.

There is a frightening precedent in the way we got most of the good Englishmen about ten years ago. The British National Research Council decided that Artificial Intelligence was childish. There was a report that led to the breaking up of the groups at the critical-mass universities, particularly the University of Edinburgh.

The same sort of thing happened in the United States. John Pierce believed that computers could never understand language. In the early 1970s he became the head of a National Academy of Science committee that decided that work on Artificial Intelligence and natural language was fruitless and that the government should not support it. Fortunately the Defense Advanced Research Projects Agency paid no attention. A couple of years ago there was tremendous fear in the scientific community that the Reagan administration was going to cut basic research budgets. It changed its mind, and the basic research cuts have not happened. But the opposite has not happened either.

Many of my students do not do projects that they would like to because we cannot afford to buy enough LISP Machines. The big laboratories at the Massachusetts Institute of Technology, Carnegie-Mellon University, and Stanford University have fairly good equipment, but none has the amount of equipment per person that is needed to pursue basic research at full speed with high morale. One consequence is that the computer-starved students are more easily tempted by industry.

High salaries are another temptation, and that is a problem that I see no way to solve. I am, however, thinking of starting a private research institute to do basic research in Artificial Intelligence, feeling that something has to be created that is in between the universities and the companies. [This company, Thinking Machines, is now in business.—Ed.]

What Industry Does Not Do

I think it will be almost impossible for industry to do basic research in this field. Many industries think they are doing basic research, but nothing basic seems to come back to the field from the application. You can say you are doing research if you are making a DIPMETER ADVISOR, but I do not see new fundamental ideas for constructing such programs emerging from that research.

IBM has made a tremendous contribution in supporting research in the universities. Its efforts in basic research in its own laboratories have worked in Physics but have not worked well in Computer Science. Xerox succeeded for a while. The Xerox Palo Alto Research Center was well funded, had very good equipment, and for five or seven years was one of the few good industrial laboratories. Bolt, Beranek, and Newman did basic research on a shoestring for many years.

None of the artificial-intelligence groups in industry is doing really basic research. They do not make machines that learn. They do not work on the simplest problems of common sense. In general they are not working on the kinds of things that ten years from now could produce a new wave of intelligent systems, just as the current wave of expert systems comes from the basic research done in the mid-1960s.

Forgotten Successes

The successes that have come out of Artificial Intelligence are sometimes forgotten, along with the credit. In about 1965 we banned daytime computer-game playing in our Laboratory. We had invented a game called Spacewar that everyone loved, but it ran only on our main research computer. Spacewar, written by Model Railroad Club students and other hackers in the early 1960s, is very much like Asteroids and similar games of today.

In the early 1970s some students got some capital and tried to market such things; they went broke. Computer-based video games really started to be successful in the late 1970s, and this was because the microprocessor then cost $100 instead of $20,000. The reason that the students did not succeed was because the time was not right.

Word processing also came out of the artificial-intelligence community.

Time sharing was invented by artificial-intelligence people in around 1960 or 1962, on the first PDP1, before DEC was really a computer company. Finally, about seven or eight years later, the commercial world started to make time-sharing systems.

Moribund Software Industry

There is a language, called PROLOG, that is becoming popular because it has some automatic deduction ideas. The Japanese, in their fifth-generation project, have decided to use this ultra-hyper-modern gadget, PROLOG. The Japanese will provide their researchers with machines that are good for that.

We did this once, in 1970, with a language called PLANNER. It turned out to be uncontrollable. That might have been our fault or PLANNER's, but I do not think it was our fault. I think the Japanese will program in PROLOG for two or three years, write some very sophisticated programs, and then give up and go back to LISP. But even after a three-year waste of time, they will be ten or fifteen years ahead of Americans who are still trying to get industrial people to use languages like PASCAL.

The American software establishment is in terrible shape. The modern languages that are supposed to replace FORTRAN and COBOL are no better than their predecessors. The reason is that to make an intelligent system, you eventually want the system to be able to learn to improve itself. In order to do that, that system must write its own little programs. I defy anyone to write a PASCAL program that can write a PASCAL program or a FORTRAN program that can write a FORTRAN program.

A key feature of LISP is that you can either compile things or leave them in their source-code form. In fact, in fancy systems, if the compiled form is inconvenient, you can uncompile the program again. It seems to me that a modern language is one that can talk about itself as well as other things. My test for adequacy is whether you are programming in a language that can express things like simple programming ideas. If it cannot, failure is around the corner.

Threat Is Internal

Many marvelous things are happening, but many of them are happening because of research done ten or fifteen years ago. These things are now within the reach of practical applications because computers have become a thousand times cheaper. In 1970 memory cost a penny a bit or so or maybe five cents; now memory is a hundredth of a cent a bit. Processors are much cheaper and faster. It is odd, then, that industry is using software developed a long time ago under other conditions.

Let me return to the people problem. When I have a good student, there is no place I can send him other than a university, and the universities have stopped expanding on the whole. There is no place the good student can work for five years on a hard problem that does not have a near-term industrial payoff. There is no place a young person can work for five or ten years on a really hard problem the way all those Einsteins and Pasteurs did when they faced a hard problem.

I am not an expert on the future, and I do not know if the Japanese fifth-generation project will overtake us. They use the right words, but that does not mean they are a serious threat. Maybe they are, and maybe they are not.

The serious threat is internal—in not providing young researchers with nonindustrial environments where they can work for five or ten years with good equipment. The United States is in a state of remilitarization. When I spoke last summer at the Artificial Intelligence Association meeting, I complained that there then was a plan to build one hundred B1 bombers. As Carl Sagan said plaintively one day, maybe we can make do with ninety-nine. Just one of those machines that cost a \$1 billion would probably pay for ten years of basic research.

But there is no plan. The only agency that funds basic research on a large scale is DARPA. The National Science Foundation tries, but it is forced to divide its money up among a lot of little projects, and you cannot do well in this field unless you have five or ten people, a staff, and very good equipment.

Big Companies

I do not have a solution. I once tried to get a little research money from a wealthy company that has boasted about how large and capable its artificial-intelligence group is. This proposal to support a few students bounced back and forth for three years. Generally I am discouraged with what happens when large companies get involved. They do not seem to understand where the ideas came from and where the new ones will come from in another decade.

***

Question from the audience
How do you feel about the prospect of eventually achieving really intelligent machines?

Minsky
It is a very hard problem. I certainly believe that we are making progress and that as we learn, the machines will become more intelligent. Someday they will become smarter than people. I do not think there is anything wrong with people, but I believe that evolution creeps along and that there is no reason to think that just because we are here now, we are the end of human evolution either. Since machine evolution is only thirty years old, computers are not as

smart as a four-year-old child, but I do not see why more and more research should not help.

Let me say something about time scales and perspectives. One strange thing is that somewhere in the milieu, there arose the idea that Artificial Intelligence had reached a plateau. People ask, "Why is Artificial Intelligence on this plateau where it does not get any new ideas?" This is ridiculous. For the number of people working on the fundamental issues, the new ideas are coming along fine. Professor Winston and I work on learning in our Laboratory, and there is progress there, involving reasoning by analogy.

Elsewhere there are a lot of people interviewing experts and writing down rules for how they work, and that is a valuable part of understanding how experts work. But it is important to make machines that learn by experience, that themselves interview experts and find out how they work, and do it themselves, and read books, and embody the things that make people so smart.

We are alway in a hurry to see the fruits of our research. Nobody would invest in something with a payoff of three hundred years. Well, nobody? It was three hundred years from Newton to Einstein. There was no decade in that three hundred years when nothing was discovered. There was no plateau in the development of modern physical science. Nor has there been any in Artificial Intelligence.

Suppose there is a student with an idea. He learns the techniques. He reads. He finds out what other people have done. In about five or six years he has written a thesis. So the time between a good idea and understanding its implications and fitting it in with other ideas is generally about five years. Artificial Intelligence dates perhaps from about 1957. So you see, Artificial Intelligence is old enough for only five or six waves of ideas. The grim fact is that it always looks as if there is a plateau in the last five years because you do not know what the good ideas are yet.

The short answer to the question is that the machines we create will become more intelligent. It might be fifty years, or twenty five, before a few great ideas produce remarkable improvements in intelligence. It might be that we need one hundred more pedestrian ideas, in which case the machines will not be smarter than we are for one hundred years.

Question

Do you think LISP is outdated and should be replaced?

Minsky

LISP is about twenty-five years old. What should replace it? LISP is not static. What we want in a modern language we do not yet know. One of the things that we want in intelligent systems is the ability to solve systems of complicated constraints automatically, but I am not sure that is the kind of thing you want to put into a language. The reason why LISP has retained its popularity in Artificial Intelligence is that it is not a language so much as a language that you write your own language in. When an artificial-intelligence person wants to make a program to reason by analogy, he starts with LISP because in a week or two he can write in LISP the elements of another language that he really wants to use. In PASCAL you just do not go around writing another language that you would rather have than PASCAL because PASCAL's syntax is too rigid and the way it allocates memory is too inflexible. LISP is really the machine language of high-level languages.

For More Information

Hillis, W. Daniel, "The Connection Machine," Report AIM-646, Artificial Intelligence Laboratory, Massachusetts Institute of Technology, Cambridge, MA, 1981.

Minsky, Marvin, *The Society of Mind*, book in preparation.

Minsky, Marvin, "Plain Talk about Neurodevelopmental Epistemology," *Fifth International Joint Conference on Artificial Intelligence*, Cambridge, MA, 1977.

Newell, Allen, and Herbert A. Simon, *Human Problem Solving*, Prentice-Hall, Englewood Cliffs, NJ, 1972.

Winston, Patrick Henry, "Learning New Principles from Precedents and Exercises," *Artificial Intelligence*, vol. 19, no. 3, 1982.

19

**An Investment
Opportunity?**

Frederick R. Adler
Managing Partner
Adler & Company

*Since 1967 Mr. Adler has been a lead investor in venture
capital and other situations. He is a founder, director,
secretary, and chairman of the executive committee of Data
General Corporation, was a founder of Intersil Memory
Company (an affiliate of Intersil, Incorporated), has been a
director and member of the Executive Committee of Applied
Materials, Incorporated, a director and chairman of the
Finance Committee of Elscint Limited, is a director Sci-Tex,
Limited, is chairman and director of Lexidata Corporation, a
director of Biologicals, Incorporated, and a trustee of Teachers
Insurance and Annuity Association of America. He has also
been executive vice-president and a director of Loehmann's,
Incorporated, a director of Vita Food Products, and a founder
and director of Expediter Systems, Incorporated.*

I have heard thirty definitions of Artificial Intelligence,
all of which seem contradictory. Not only do they seem
contradictory, but I do not think I can make money out
of any of them. Artificial Intelligence has all of the surface
trappings that high-risk investors look for. It is touted as a
new frontier with great possibilities and unlimited potential.
Much of the artificial-intelligence research is going on in
universities. That is wonderful because you can steal people
who are not used to high pay.

Lots of books and articles are being written. Once in a
while, I even see someone reading one. Things are rumbling

and buzzing in the big, respectable companies like Atari, Bell, DEC, GE, HP, IBM, Schlumberger, TI, and Xerox, to name a few. The Japanese are spending their usual half-billion dollars on something. The start-ups have appeared with all the wonderful corporate names with ENTECHs, TECHs, and HYPERs. There are important well-attended conferences, perhaps the ultimate proof that the area is hot.

Fads versus Needs

It is clear that Artificial Intelligence has taken the first big steps toward venture capital respectability. Money has begun to pour in. The real question for me is whether it is a promise or reality, whether it is hype or truth. In other words, when will money not only go into it but also come out?

It is very easy to put money into a venture—you write a check. Getting money out is another problem. The company in theory has to work. So far at least, signs of that are not here.

On the other side, although there is a great deal of hype, there is enough reality in the area that I am reasonably sure that companies can be created and that those companies can make money. What is not clear is how much money and whether there are valid venture capital investments at this point. I think we know which race tracks to go to, but I am not sure which horses are going to win.

Until now there has been little profit. Arnold Kraft has described a program that configures computers, which I would call profitable even though it is in a large company environment. That program saves DEC millions of dollars a year. The same program probably could be modified and used in another company. That would have to be considered a profit-making activity.

For long-term venture capital money the words and titles are unimportant. What a sensible venture tries to do is to satisfy a need, not to fuel a fad. Ultimately each company in this area will be judged on the same basis as those in other areas: Is it profitable? Does it contribute? Does it satisfy a need? Each must have good, profit-oriented management. Being creative is not enough.

Successes and Standards

Someone recently told me that he understood my company put more money into Artificial Intelligence than any other company had. I told him I did not know what he was talking about. We have not put a dime into Artificial Intelligence.

We have been on the periphery of using common sense in some companies. We have tried to do a few things that make it easier for people to operate their companies. For example, we backed Daisy, Aryeh Finegold's company, and we remain the largest shareholders. But Daisy certainly is not in Artificial Intelligence per se. Its business is putting design rules and a variety of other things into work stations to make it easier for engineers to create VLSI designs. We will probably move down the line to the process itself, and I suspect we will be doing mask making and a variety of other things.

All of these things, however, are things that have been done for twenty or thirty years without using LISP or a LISP-like language. These things do make experts operate better, and they do include elements of expert judgment. In that sense they may be on the edges of Artificial Intelligence, but they certainly are not Artificial Intelligence.

We have a company that specializes in interpreting EKG information. Unlike most others it uses microprocessor technology to do real-time signal analysis. We use real-time algorithms to deal with signal changes and have eliminated most off-line analysis. The system is much more reliable and sensitive than competing ones, but I do not regard it as Artificial Intelligence. I regard it as a very normal progression using technology that has been unused but available for a long time.

We have done the same thing in an Israeli company, SCITEX, where we use sophisticated pattern-recognition techniques and inference algorithms to transmit high-quality pictures without transmitting the bulk of the picture. We get magazine-quality reproductions rather than newspaper-quality reproductions. Instead of putting pictures on a jet, we now send them by satellite or over telephone wires. The software fills in the holes. I never thought that was Artificial Intelligence.

We have a few robotics companies. They use image-processing techniques developed in the late 1960s. We use techniques for making machines adapt to the real world. In one of them we have managed to guide a robot's arm after synthesizing a path between two located items. If that is Artificial Intelligence, it is probably on an IQ level of about 70.

These companies do useful work. Each satisfies a need. Each makes money. Each is growing rather well. When you talk about long-term venture capital, as distinguished from venture capital focused on quick return in the stock market, companies have to be judged by those standards.

There is a good deal of money to be made in such companies, and I believe that venture capitalists are willing to finance such companies on a rational basis.

Trends and Opportunities

But in spite of the talk and excitement, the area is still undefined. The limits have not been set even by the participants. It is difficult to find companies that have goals that resonate with what we venture capitalists look for in an investment, which is essentially a company that will have sales of $50 million to $100 million after five or six years. There will be companies that will make it. But it is going to be infinitely more difficult than the people now writing about the area think.

The trend will be toward solutions in major problem areas. For example, there is much talk about Schlumberger's use of Artificial Intelligence in oil well analysis. Artificial Intelligence can be used there very effectively. Any programs that are developed will be bought quickly because the returns are so enormous that the people who develop anything of substance will make a great deal of money. The limitation will be that the people who develop them will have to work either extremely closely with the people in the industry or themselves will have to come out of that industry. The application is more the key than the technique, and the solution will depend on the total understanding of the needs of the market.

The market is potentially enormous. With the right team, funding could be obtained in a matter of weeks—maybe even faster.

But if you have developed a process-control system for a certain industry, even though the industry has many similar processes to control, your process-control system may not be a good product. Unless there is a substantial common thread, it will take a long time to develop a large, profitable company because your program will have to be tailored to the needs, company by company. You will be a consulting company, and perhaps you will do reasonably well, but I doubt if you have a reproducible general-application product of the kind we venture capitalists like.

Funding could be obtained but probably less than for companies with reproducible, general application products. Consulting companies usually have great trouble raising money at reasonable rates. The amount of money that could be raised would be based on the team and on the desperateness of the industry's need.

Now let us consider work stations, like those of Symbolics. I believe the area will be extremely competitive. The technology is moving rapidly. The work station will have to be very advanced because it is going to be a big-cost item.

An area in which I think there is some room at the moment is 3-D visual object recognition equipment. Everything currently is 2-D. The MIT Artificial Intelligence Laboratory has a prototype 3-D object recognition vision system now. If you move to a custom circuit design, it is thought that that machine could recognize objects in a quarter of a second. If it can be done in a quarter of a second now, my guess is that it can be done much faster soon. Speed is a critical element in most robotics systems. A company could be built there. Backing for that company with the right group, I suspect, could be obtained very easily.

Romance versus Profit

The artificial-intelligence area has to be assessed in the same way as any other venture capital area. Is the need large enough so it will be reproducible in volume? Can it reach the $50 million figure? Is the team good enough to do it? Is the management profit oriented? If the motive is to bring Artificial Intelligence into the 1980s, or something romantic like that, that is wonderful, but if not done at a profit, it will not happen. It is a waste of time.

Substitutes versus Advisers

Now let us consider expert systems. We have looked at a lot of expert systems companies. We have turned down seven medical deals in the last five years. These deals involved companies with programs designed to make work easier for everyone from cardiologists to pharmacologists. In each case we thought that the key element was the substitution of a program for the expertise of the expert. We are more enthusiastic about programs that are intended to be advisers and checkpoint monitors rather than substitutes. We like programs that bring expertise to users, who can then use their own expertise and their talents for recognizing symptoms, recalling history, and the like. I believe that people who develop programs like that can build rather large companies in all sorts of areas. Medicine is just one such area.

Enormous money will be made in the general artificial-intelligence-oriented software area. A few companies will last, but they are going to have to be measured by the same standards that apply to other software companies. I am chairman of Micropro, a company interested in seeing where the ideas of Artificial Intelligence will fit in on our future developments. We are putting together some user-friendly things in integrated packages. If we are looking at artificial-intelligence work, you can bet that every other microcomputer software firm is too.

Whether there will be independent artificial-intelligence software companies, however, is doubtful because all of the talents currently needed in ordinary software companies will still be needed. Without those talents, you are going to have a small-niche company, and a small-niche company is not worth building.

This area is one of enormous potential. But it is important to avoid the hype, to avoid solutions to specific small problems. This is an area where everybody seems to be looking for problems to solve. It is an area of tools that are developing rather than an area of needs that have to be satisfied. That has to change. We have to pick areas of need as DEC and Schlumberger have done. If you come up with any of those areas, my firm and others are loaded with money that we would love to give.

***

Question from the audience
Do you have any comments about the role of market research?

Adler
I use market research, but market research is not a substitute for decision making or common sense. What market research does is get a lot of facts. One of the weaknesses of the venture capital business is that we have too many geniuses. All venture capitalists are geniuses. Their instinct is to rely on their brains rather than to check their facts. That is why we lose so much money.

Question
Why do you turn down expert-systems companies? Is it because they are not adviser-oriented systems?

Adler
The systems that we turned down, in my judgment, were too brittle. They gave yes-no answers, leaving us concerned that doctors would not use them because there was no role for the doctor. I have not met a doctor yet, anymore than I have met a venture capitalist, whose ego is small enough to handle that.

20

Financing the Future

William H. Janeway
Vice-President and Director
F. Eberstadt and Company

William H. Janeway is a vice-president and director of F. Eberstadt & Company, Incorporated, a New York investment banking firm. He joined F. Eberstadt in 1971 and since 1978 has served as director of the corporate finance division. Mr. Janeway received the BA from Princeton University and the PhD in Economics from Cambridge University.

F. Eberstadt is an independent investment firm, wholly owned by active employees, all of whose business is based on investment research in technology-related industries. We provide brokerage services to financial institutions, information services to major corporations, and equity finance to growing companies. Our purpose is to identify, to evaluate, and to structure investment opportunities, principally for institutional investors, occasionally for corporate investors, and for ourselves as venture investors.

This MIT Colloquium presents a collective progress report on an intellectual revolution. Even more the Colloquium itself represents a meta-report on Artificial Intelligence's progression from intellectual revolution to something more: the introduction into society's technical-industrial base of new techniques for grasping, for structuring, for discovering, for inventing reality. To use the technical term, Artificial Intelligence is in the process of becoming transparent to a rapidly expanding, increasingly diverse population of users. Conversely Artificial Intelligence's emergence from infancy is suggested by the presence and intercourse among such a varied group of practitioners from the several segments of our industrial economy: the academic, institutional; the institutionalized, large corporate; and the small corporate, entrepreneurial.

The evidence of this Colloquium is that evaluating the reality of Artificial Intelligence is of substantially greater interest in industry than among investors. In fact the evident interest of industry may represent a leading indicator. F. Eberstadt's anticipation that this is the case underlies our role in creating this Colloquium.

My task today would seem to follow from this; for Artificial Intelligence, like Biotechnology before, seems ripe for the attentions of the capital markets and those who participate in them. Now capitalism's ultimate test of enterprise—from the creation of the East Indian Company to today's hot new issue market—resides in the financing process. Whatever is to be done first is to be financed: whether through the diversion of capital resources within an existing entity or through the external funding of a new venture. Even in the public sector our political economy is so suffused by the capitalist mode of what Marx termed expanded reproduction that analogous tests of cost-benefit, payback, and return on investment are conventionally, reflexively applied—as if the arguments of the implicit analytical equations had objectively discernible and predictable values.

Three Propositions

Consider the following propositions. To discuss financing the future of Artificial Intelligence presupposes that

Proposition 1. Between those who finance and those who are financed some measure of agreement can be reached as to what Artificial Intelligence is.

Proposition 2. Artificial Intelligence has a future.

Proposition 3. The future of Artificial Intelligence will be expressed through activities that in principle are suitable cases for financing.

Before considering each of these propositions in turn, let me summarize my own response as:

Proposition 1. Unnecessary.
Proposition 2. Misconceived, and—nonetheless—
Proposition 3. In part, yes.

Proposition 1

At the margin the financing process may depend hardly at all on mutual agreement as to the actual content of the activity being funded. Perhaps the most noteworthy of all the ventures financed in the London capital market at the time of the South Sea Bubble was one "whose purpose will be disclosed at a later time." The transaction itself may be its own reward for those who are parties to it.

Of course, these thoughts most forcefully come to mind at a time when "Greater Fool Investing" is again at a peak not seen in half a generation. Let me make two extended points. As in all exercises in diagnosis of which I am aware, a binary distinction is useful here. In a hot new issue market two generic types of buyers appear: those who buy in order to sell and those who buy in order to buy. The demand of the former depends strictly on the ability to turn the merchandise acquired for a quick gain; they have no interest in being around at that later date to learn the purpose their capital is to finance. The bubble feeds on the rationing of this demand as the characteristic, undiscriminating feeding frenzy builds its own momentum. In turn, demand from the second sort of investor is also driven by rationing yet remains by definition selective. These investors accept the imperative to pay up in order to obtain the first piece of a position to be accumulated over a substantial time and at a variety of valuations. In a hot market the excessive price paid at the offering may be deemed to include an entry fee for having enough capital at risk to justify the subsequent devotion of time and energy.

In the environment of a hot market, therefore, proposition 1 is unnecessary. Yet hot markets demonstrate conclusively how one can know *that*, without knowing any of the specific particulars which pertain to that *that*. Specifically one can know that this hot market will self-destruct, the bubble will burst, the greater fools will wise up. And then communicating each venture's purpose, educating potential investors in its technical content and market promise, learning how the identification and evaluation of market opportunities shape the conception and development of technical applications—all this will again be of interest. It will, of course, concentrate interest on proposition 2.

Proposition 2

The proposition that Artificial Intelligence has a future is trivially misconceived since it evidently has so many. There may be another sense, however, in which the collective future of Artificial Intelligence is problematic. Some two years ago we at F. Eberstadt began to acquaint ourselves with Artificial Intelligence. First, we went to the various academic centers. We rapidly got a feel for the Artificial Intelligence community, its shared language and premises, its personalities and their temperaments, its broadening objects of interests. Second, we began to search beyond this Artificial Intelligentsia for more or less practical efforts to put Artificial Intelligence to work. Beyond a small number of industrial projects and a comparable number of missionary entrepreneurs, we found widespread disdain of Artificial Intelligence and even more widely spread ignorance among a variety of people who in fact were engaged in projects recognizably similar in purpose and even in approach to artificial-intelligence programs. So, in partial response to the recurrent question, What is AI? we formulated a tentative proposition: Artificial Intelligence ceases to be Artificial Intelligence when it enters the real world, at which point it becomes something like advanced Computer Science.

Over these two years we have seen a cultural transformation. The Artificial Intelligence community has swung off the defensive. The attendance at this Colloquium is the outward and visible sign of this transformation. In parallel with the process that explains why proposition 1 is unnecessary, the third level at which proposition 2 is misconceived is this: we may now be at a point of reversal, as whatever is plausibly definable as advanced Computer Science seeks to gain recognition as Artificial Intelligence. That is to say, right now Artificial Intelligence has a rather appalling future as a slogan rationalizing the greed-driven triumph of hope over expectations.

It is precisely at this point that we in the audience become dependent more than ever on those at the podium. A certain discipline in the discipline is our best—perhaps our only—defense against excess. Again, as with proposition 1, there will be life after life. Beyond the generalized future of Artificial Intelligence, hyped as it inevitably will be, continuing education of users and investors in the multitude of specific features of Artificial Intelligence is in the enlightened self-interest of the community. This is just as much the case if, in reaction to today's hype, it again becomes fashionable to disguise genuine breakthroughs in Artificial Intelligence as mere incremental advances in Computer Science—all of which in turn suggests that proposition 3 does, after all, have some meaning.

Proposition 3

Beneath the frenzied froth of transiently self-justifying speculation, there is a discipline of finance. One concise formulation derived from this discipline is the capital asset valuation model. From purchase of a piece of equipment to purchase of a share of stock in a corporation, any investment can be modeled in these terms: the present value equals the sum of the discounted net cash flows more or less confidently expected to be received over a period of time.

The equation has four arguments: a discount rate, a set of cash flows, a degree of confidence, and a time period. Typically the first and last of these are set outside the realm of the model: the former influenced by market convention and by recognition of the progressively smaller contributions to present value of events at more distant dates. Consequently I want to focus on the two other arguments: the prediction of cash flows and the confidence factor.

The task of setting out a plausible pattern of revenues and expenses represents a formal discipline that all too often is satisfied in practice. All too often, the supply of numbers expands to meet the demand for rationalization. That is not to say that there is no purpose in rigorously relating forecast revenues both to a thorough evaluation of market opportunities and to the expenditures required to support them. However, I would make one further point in two different ways:

- Each step in constructing financial projections requires separate and honest assessment of the state and limits of relevant knowledge.

- Successful completion of the exercise results in a dangerously consistent reification of a piece of the future that threatens to presume an inappropriately confident degree of expectation.

Applied with intelligence and integrity, exercises in financial forecasting can function as a defense against excessive enthusiasm, whether emanating from technologists or marketing people. Such evaluations help explain how a backlog of technical innovation can cumulate, frustrating (if not bankrupting) entrepreneurial engineers and their venture investors alike. This is what is happening now with respect to the application of available technology to manufacturing processes: an order of magnitude improvement in productivity yields no positive present value when industry is operating at, say, 50% percent of capacity. Now, as with every other new technology, Artificial Intelligence will be implemented in a real, historically evolved macro- and micro-economic environment. Its implementation will be properly subject to such rational financial discipline as is available from time to time in a world of contingency and chance, driven by greed and fear.

As the world-weary investment banker said, "I never met a forecast that wasn't conservative." The closer to the frontier of knowledge that one is operating, the more important it is to concentrate on forecasting what needs to be learned. The more important, I would emphasize, to recognize those projects which are not reducible to the terms of the capital valuation model. When individual, institutional, and corporate investors are most fervently begging to be financially exploited in order to fund essays in commercial exploitation of new technology, then is the premium on responsible imprecision greatest. Except at the most absolutely cynical end of the spectrum, where the first transaction is intended from the start to be the last interaction and the next stop is Brazil, some respect is owed to the certainty that performance will be related to promise over time.

In this respect, let me offer a very different test to supplement conventional misapplication of the asset valuation model: namely, the ability to tell a plausible story as to how the venture or company in question can grow to support an excessive present value on a competitively fundamental basis—i.e., a market multiple times visible earnings—within a reasonable planning horizon. The dual implication is: that implausible stories and unreasonable planning horizons exist and that the mechanics of the capital asset model are no substitute for the exercise of experienced judgement as to plausibility and reasonableness.

Caveats

In the autumn of 1981 I spoke at the first MIT-F. Eberstadt collaboration, the conference on Biotechnology. I concluded then by suggesting that in the financing of any technology high enough to lie beyond the comprehension of the vast majority of potential investors, the guiding rule should be caveat vendor, let the seller beware, for it is the seller who will be called to account once the hype has ended and the manic market has come, as the English nanny always said it would, "to end in tears." Realism on the way in is likely to prove its own reward. *Caveat vendor* does not mean, given the opportunity, one ought not to take advantage of the extraordinarily attractive valuations that the market offers from time to time. It does mean that those taking advantage have good reason to convince themselves, if they can, of the plausibility and reasonableness of the story they will tell.

Many of the applications of Artificial Intelligence are likely to define ventures to be both implemented and financed within existing, large organizations, especially industrial corporations. The same is true of Biotechnology, for example. It is especially the case with respect to applications whose present value is derived from cost reduction and productivity enhancement. Selling process technology to industry subjects a new company to a double burden of risk. First, the vendor's performance is as good as the user's implementation. Second, the demand function for capacity-related goods is the second derivature of the level of final demand for the target industry's output: acceleration or deceleration for the final demand will send the derived demand from zero to infinity and back again. This means that the financing decision will often be an internal one, where the discipline on the vendors may be the more immediate as it relates to continuity of employment.

The packaging of ignorance by artifice to obtain finance distorts not only the returns actually received by investors. Distortion of research activity in order to obtain finance on such terms is both a professional and a social cost that we in this country seem ill equipped to appreciate. I find it depressing not to have been surprised when I learned the extent to which artificial-intelligence research has been funded by the Defense Department. Once again, national security offers the cover under which our society escapes from the calculus of capitalism. In Artificial Intelligence, as in all other research activities, much that is in the laboratory should stay there and be funded as a social charge whose benefits are purely, in economic terms, external—freely disseminated and unappropriated as a private return by any owner or investor. Only some pieces of the future of Artificial Intelligence should be financed as I have defined the process, and those may be the ones that by definition no longer arc Artificial Intelligence.

21
TODAY
AND TOMORROW:
A DISCUSSION

Winston

My impression is that many of us will leave this meeting thinking that Artificial Intelligence is not exactly Bioengineering yet. But why are we so gloomy? One reason may be that Artificial Intelligence is an unusual enterprise with respect to definition. It is hard to know what it is even after we have talked about it for two days. It is hard to know what it is after working on it for fifteen years. Artificial Intelligence is a field defined by its objectives rather than by its tools.

Another reason we tend to be a little gloomy is that we have been given the impression that people who can do Artificial Intelligence are difficult to find, but in fact we have seen a range of speculations on that particular issue, ranging from Professor Schank's saying that no one can do it other than himself and his students to Mr. Kraft, who did it with existing people at DEC and a little help from Carnegie-Mellon, to Mr. Finegold, who did not know he had an artificial-intelligence company until we asked him to join this seminar.

I think they are all right. Artificial Intelligence is a diverse field, and some kinds of Artificial Intelligence are accessible to any smart person with a background in Computer Science and the right book. Other kinds of Artificial Intelligence require a slow accumulation of wisdom over a period of years, including wisdom that cannot be found in books.

Dr. Brown has a well-deserved reputation for looking at what we are doing in Artificial Intelligence thoroughly and doing it with a methodology that is to be admired by all. But let me make an observation and then ask a question. I think we all believe Xerox surely must have had extraordinarily visionary management to have created a laboratory of this sort. We do not hear the same kinds of things being said about IBM or other giants in the computer industry. We always come back to Xerox and the Xerox PARC laboratory. On the other hand, I sensed that former Xerox employees feel something went wrong with this vision, and perhaps that there was some calcification. First then, do you think that something went wrong, and in particular, do you think that Xerox PARC is backing away from its previous commitments to fostering basic research? And second, how does your group feel about getting Artificial Intelligence accepted inside Xerox and about the Alto not being better exploited?

Brown

I am quite surprised that there is a belief in the community that we are doing less basic research now than we have in the past. I believe that we are doing at least as much basic research now as we previously did. I do not see the downward trend. However, I think the kinds of research we are now doing involve less playing around with technology for technology sake and more probing into the fundamental issues of computation, intelligence, and how Computer Science can be informed by serious studies of the mind.

There is always a problem if you take a company that comes from the more traditional computer-science orientation and try to get it to accept artificial-intelligence systems. Traditional Computer Science has a hard time understanding the paradigms under which we operate. It is strange, but true, that we have more success getting our ideas and knowledge-based systems into line organizations within Xerox that deal with copiers, for example, than those organizations that deal with systems. In fact Xerox has a publishing house in Boston that soon will have more of our LISP Machines than even our own research lab.

I think also there has been a belief that Xerox has made all kinds of catastrophic mistakes by not coming to market with the Alto. The Alto is, of course, a brilliant achievement, however, there is another side to it. I happen to be one of the few people who thinks that in some ways Xerox may actually have been held back by the Alto. What happened is that the research groups responsible for the Alto did a brilliant job of pushing the technology to the very extreme. But in those days that meant building a personal machine that was limited to only 64K of memory. However, many of the ideas we have been talking about here are not imaginable within the confines of such small machines.

Those early 64K machines enabled Xerox to make phenomenal advances in user interfaces, bit-map graphics, and so on. But these small memory machines tended to define and limit the kinds of functionality we were able to experiment with. Now that we have personal machines with huge virtual memories we begin to appreciate how much we counted on beautiful user interfaces to overshadow the limited functionality and extensibility of some of these early systems.

I believe a lot of things that PARC should have been experimenting with a long time ago did not happen because we cringed at the thought of cramming those ideas into that little box. The MIT Artificial Intelligence Laboratory, on the other hand, did not go the small, personal machine route. In fact it initially stayed with large mainframe machines and then in the mid-seventies developed a large-scale personal machine that enabled it to explore personal tools and systems that demanded a lot of memory. I think that caused MIT to evolve quite different views from Xerox, even in terms of the functionality one might expect in document-preparation systems. Now you notice we are bringing the two views together. The new personal LISP Machines emerging from MIT and Xerox both have beautiful interactive graphics, stemming from some of the ideas emerging out of SMALLTALK and some powerful ideas that came out of the MIT Artificial Intelligence Laboratory. For the first time we can have a cost-effective marriage of these two world views, and I think that is what is going to stimulate a wide range of exciting new activities in PARC.

Winston

I asked Dr. Brown if the executives at Xerox put pressure on him to develop products. He said, "No; as a matter of fact, they did not." He said that he found researchers at Xerox to be extraordinarily schizophrenic about the subject of product development versus basic research. One the one hand, they are angry that Xerox did not rapidly take their systems or ideas to the marketplace. On the other hand, when Xerox attempts to enlist these same researchers in transferring the technology out of PARC, they complain that management is trying to turn them into a development laboratory.

Dr. Kay, do you concur with that observation? What are your feelings with respect to how these unusual people who form the most creative cadre of people in Artificial Intelligence can in fact be harnessed to something that will have commercial possibilities?

Kay

The remark about the schizophrenia of the Xerox PARC people is absolutely right. I can think of instances that colored it. One was when Xerox management tried to raid PARC in order to save SDS as it was slowly sliding down into the water. A couple of courageous management people at PARC sacrificed five years of their careers to hold off Xerox from that. PARC was not set up to save SDS or to have anything to do with it. That feeling of invasion was something that tempered its way along.

Part of the problem has to do with management styles. One style of management is to handle things the way a colonel takes over an arbitrary battalion and leads it into battle. The idea is that the battalion already exists, and the manager has to marshal a set of resources that he may have not had a great deal to do with creating. That leads to ideas like management by objective.

We owe much of our industry right now to ARPA and NASA. ARPA's style during the 1960s was pretty wide open. It funded people rather than projects, partly because the ARPA funders were drawn out of the research community. But the funders were not only from that community but also knew that if they were not in the trenches, they really did not know as much about what was going on as the good people did, if the good people were any good at all. Their idea was to fund people rather than projects, taking lumps on the percentages and occasionally finding out that a person was not as good as previously thought.

That led to about 90 percent of the interesting inventions in Computer Science in the 1960s: time sharing, graphics, and personal computers. Thank goodness they did it. There was no one else around interested in coming up with that kind of money.

My experience in doing research is that there is no way of managing a group of people who are not first class to do first-class work. Research tends to be done in two ways. One is the commando approach where you hand pick a team by trial by fire, to work together. Then there is the genius approach, which is a pretty good one, too. Some people who are smarter than everybody else go off by themselves to work, and you take percentages on that.

As management by objectives has come in, the amount of serendipity that has been turning up in the last decade has been much smaller than it was in the 1960s. A lot of the good things that happened depended on a certain randomness in approach because people really do not know what they are doing.

My definition of Artificial Intelligence is that it is stuff that is interesting that we do not know how to do yet.

When we are exploring in that area, we have to make allowance for the random character of the terrain being explored. The geniuses and hand-picked teams make a great deal of sense. Instinct. All of those areas that are hard to rationalize are the very things that make up research.

I think this is why businesspeople and research people do not get along very well. The businesspeople want rationalizations. Research people look for something beautiful or pretty or interesting. Those kinds of words strike fear into the hearts of funders.

But that is the approach that works. So let's quit worrying about why it works and start getting more of it.

Janeway

I am occasionally pleasantly stunned to discover that some concept that has survived in economic theory for several generations actually does have some relevance. I think that what Dr. Kay has just said is a marvelous example of a concept that has been kicking around in Economics for about 150 years—namely, the concept of external economies, which are benefits, gains from private activities, from individual acts, gains that cannot be captured by the people who are doing or funding those acts.

We are dealing here with something that is very rooted. I think it is a big mistake to think about this as a matter of temperament or of style. If only those business school graduates were a little more visionary. It is not supposed to work like that. That is why you have civil society. That is why you have taxes. That is why some margin of resources is taken away from the sector in which private returns, the capturing of returns from activity, is precisely the purpose. The schizophrenia at Xerox is replicated at the microlevel throughout the system and characterizes the system as a whole. To what extent is it really a belief inside the business enterprise that has returns to achieve and present to stockholders? Is it possible to have a kind of internal tax, regardless of the external environment, regardless of what happens to profits over any conceivable future? Is it possible to carve out that kind of shelter? Or should we be lobbying for more government funds so that the National Science Foundation budget can be increased by a factor of twenty or two hundred?

Russo

Every major organization that has a central research and development center is doing just that. They use the profits to fund research and development. Are these research centers in industry doing research or are they not doing research? At General Electric I would say that the bulk of the work going on is applied research. That is, it is really advanced development looking for feasibility but aimed at specific goals. A certain percentage of the GE laboratories' funding is exploratory work.

In general I am not sure I agree with the concept. Having been in research and development centers most of my life before I came to GE, I think that research people are not necessarily against working on long-term product ideas. The biggest ego satisfier is seeing your product succeed in the marketplace. I do not buy the fact that you want to work on something just because it is beautiful.

Janeway

It is important to point out that we have been talking about the big companies. As we hear about the Fifth-Generation Japanese project and the Japanese challenge particularly to the big companies, it is important to note that this is the only political economy in the world that has evolved a structure of venture capital that largely exists to support that which the big companies have one way or another found themselves incapable of implementing successfully.

Russo

Many of the fundamental developments in technology —the light bulb, the transistor, the telephone—were made in large companies. It is the productizing of these new things that small companies tend to do well because they are able to travel new roads, following the vision of an entrepreneur. They do not have to convince an upper management that might feel that its own markets are threatened by these developments. The real key is that the small company entrepreneurs seem to productize and test market innovative products much more so than some large companies.

Janeway

How do you feel about the question of whether having a project identified as Artificial Intelligence is positive or negative, particularly when it comes to selling that project, whether inside the company or outside, for fund raising, in order to move it along?

Harris

Artificial Intelligence Corporation has been around since before it was in vogue to be an artificial-intelligence company. We used to lose a lot of points on the name of the company. People laughed and made various jokes. Now the name is viewed as an asset in many situations. I do not know how long that will last. People are looking for a particular solution to a certain problem. If Artificial Intelligence provides a better solution to that problem than other options, then the people are happy. In that sense, whatever comes out of Artificial Intelligence has to obey those basic rules of nature that all products do.

Winston

Dr. Janeway, what is your perception about what we have got going so far? Is it healthy? Will the new start-ups form the basis for explosive growth or catastrophic disaster? I am stimulated to ask this question because it has been my observation that some of the small companies that have started up seem more determined to squash each other than to make a profit, which leads me to wonder about the health of the basic entrepreneurially-oriented artificial-intelligence community.

Janeway

There is a measure here of the extent to which Artificial Intelligence is moving from the university into the industrial environment and beginning to find practical applications. There seems to be greater success inside large corporations that understand their own needs pretty well and have begun applying artificial-intelligence techniques to the solution of those needs. On the other hand the first set of new companies founded to exploit the technology should have a heavy missionary element. There clearly is that.

I think we will see that a number of companies, like Daisy, will discover after some years of corporate existence that they in fact have been becoming artificial-intelligence companies, whether or not they call themselves that.

There is one big question that is often asked by the venture people. I am inclined to feel it may be a phony question. The venture people feel that all this sounds very interesting. There clearly are some applications. But where is the reservoir of frustrated talent looking for stock options, for an equity kicker for their commitment? If the number of people actually doing serious research is between one hundred and one thousand, it is not enough to start an industry on. When Biotechnology got rolling, there were tens of thousands of molecular biologists, biochemists, and cell biologists.

Winston

You are touching one of my stimulus-response buttons, the one that has to do with technology transfer to American industry. On this particular theme, I have a certain amount of latent hostility toward the system as it exists right now. The latent hostility has to do with our reluctance to copy some of the better features of Japanese technology extraction. I think I will deal with this by describing two separate events that have occurred to me in the last year.

On one occasion we were beginning at the MIT Artificial Intelligence Laboratory a major new program in the area of robotics. We called it the Year of the Robot, although we knew it would stretch out into the Decade of the Robot. It was tremendously exciting to us because we thought that it was an area ready to be catalyzed. We thought we would be able to bring together a lot of people at MIT who had not talked to each other before and a lot of people from outside MIT who needed to talk to each other more. One of our ideas was that we would copy the Japanese technique of technology transfer that has to do with placing a top young person from a company in an academic institution. So we went forth with the idea that we would solicit this kind of interaction with some of the larger companies involved in robotics.

One of these large companies had a person we wanted very badly, so we entered into some discussions about whether that person could come. After six months we managed to convince the people in the trenches that they could part with the person for a few months. But the following six months were so occupied with legal gymnastics that I thought I was going to have to take a law degree before we were through.

The other half of the story concerns some interaction I had with people at Fujitsu who wanted to send a researcher to work at MIT. I told them we have two rules. One is that the person will have to be a person that someone at MIT wants to work with, and the other is that we will have to be convinced that MIT and the country at large will get at least as much out of the exchange as we are giving up. There was no legal battle. There was no discussion of patent rights. There was no question of taking software back to Japan. They wanted to put the person in MIT because they wanted him to absorb methodologies, points of view, attitudes, and ways of doing things that that person could take back.

There is an incredible contrast. It is only the tip of the iceberg, I think, with respect to things that we have to figure out if we are going to have realistic coupling between what is happening in the universities and what is happening in U.S. industry.

Dr. Harris, as a warning to the rest of us, as a person who emerged from a university community to start a successful small company, can you recollect what was your biggest surprise with respect to the kinds of things that you have had to worry about?

Harris

One is the issue of marketing. I feel that the differences between similar artificial-intelligence products are hard to perceive from the surface. The success of artificial-intelligence companies is going to depend on marketing as opposed to technical differences between the products.

Another is the importance of customer support. It is critical that the customer-support role is performed. But given the numbers of people capable of supporting artificial-intelligence technology, how will we be able to hire these people for customer-support roles if we can barely afford to hire them in the research laboratories? We clearly cannot have a product that depends on artificial-intelligence expertise to support it.

The fundamental techniques used to develop the product have to be such that when the product gets produced, it can be supported by technical people who do not have artificial-intelligence backgrounds. Many companies do not seem to take that into account. This, of course, was to some degree anticipated. One of the biggest surprises was the extremely long and difficult missionary-sell period where the essence of what we were trying to promote as a solution was mistrusted by the data processing establishment. I thought that people would storm our doors once we built a better mousetrap.

Kay

My favorite quote about reality is from *The Hitchiker's Guide to the Galaxy*: "Reality is frequently inaccurate."

I think what Doug Adams was trying to say is that the attempt to provide a context for what we think is going on forces it into molds determined by how we choose to see the world.

I think I would like to try to steer things back to the source of a lot of these ideas. It is a rare company like AT&T with Bell Labs that does a reasonable amount of basic research. The amount of basic research that actually makes it into the world is made by the traditional technology-transfer process of the spinoff company from either a university or a big company. But I think that the ultimate source of all of these ideas is the university. And it is time for industry to start putting money back into the universities. The kinds of research support that we were used to getting from the government have not been seen in any strong way since the Vietnam war. The amount of money has not grown at the rate proportional that it should, and the character of how the money is given and what is expected in return for it has changed greatly. The universities are one of the few places that can be looked at with pride as a negative profit center.

My belief is that the universities are the places where the new and interesting things will come from, as long as the government and industry are not going to get together to do large projects as the Japanese do. And that is starting to dry out.

I am making a plea for more support in the liberal arts. It has been my experience that it is much easier to teach somebody who still has the glint in his eyes from liberal arts how to program and about Artificial Intelligence. You can teach almost everything that is known that is worthwhile in Computer Science to somebody in a year. There is not that much of it. But if you take an engineer who really thinks of himself as a nerd-type engineer and try to get the glint in his eye, you will be in deep trouble. It is extremely difficult to get them going the other way.

In our society we have hard nerds and soft nerds. The hard nerds are the ones who used to have the slide rules at their belt; now they have calculators. The soft nerds are the ones who get violently ill whenever anybody mentions an integral sign. I think that most of the creative scientists around are people who have their feet firmly in both cultures because both cultures feed the creative process very strongly. I think one of the pleasant surprises that people find out about MIT is that the liberal arts program is very good.

Russo
I think that we are not making the distinction between the people who are doing artificial-intelligence research versus the people who can develop artificial-intelligence products. Your comment about being able to teach everyone everything in a year may not be true for doing basic research, but it may be true for developing applied artificial-intelligence products. I think that the population of people who can do artificial-intelligence product development is substantially larger than the fifty or one hundred doing artificial-intelligence research.

Janeway
With respect to the desirability of a more intimate interface between industry and universities, we must remember that business is ultimately constrained by a bottom line consideration. AT&T is bound to be more so now than when it was a quasi-public agency with quasi-taxing powers through the operating companies.

The public funding of public projects, the social underwriting of investments with demonstrable and profound external economy, meaning specifically basic research, is a problem and a task that no degree of ideological gymnastics by the David Stockmans of the world should distract us from addressing. Write your senators and congressmen. There is nothing that matters more.

22

**From the Blocks World
to the Business World**

Patrick H. Winston
Karen A. Prendergast
Artificial Intelligence Laboratory
Massachusetts Institute of Technology

The commercial world has become intensely interested in opportunities spawned by the technology of Artificial Intelligence. Unfortunately it is hard to get a real grip on what is going on because few people have real experience translating the ambitious dreams of Artificial Intelligence into money-making realities.

Consequently the purpose of the MIT Colloquium on which this book is based was to provide an opportunity for representative experts to share their experiences and their attitudes. One intended result was debate, argument, and difference of opinion, all of which we have preserved in this book.

Where We Are

The MIT Colloquium helped to define the state of the art. In the early days of Artificial Intelligence, the world of toy blocks was the most popular domain for developing and testing ideas. Now there are artificial-intelligence systems that are both rooted in artificial-intelligence research and proven in commercial use.

A closer look shows that most of the proven systems are based on technology that has been well understood for as much as fifteen years. Creators of these proven systems succeeded because they did fine jobs of connecting established technology to pressing needs, not because they were obsessed with the latest ideas of Artificial Intelligence for their own sake.

Investors must realize that today's technology is still modest. The companies that will make money in the near term will be those that are able to connect the fledgling ideas developed in the 1970s and early 1980s to the most vulnerable needs of the late 1980s. Soon, however, the ideas of the 1970s and early 1980s will be exhausted, leaving untouched commercial opportunities of immense importance.

Consequently the long-range future will depend a great deal on our current national policies and on the national policies of others, particularly Japan.

Japan and the Fifth Generation

The Fifth Generation Project is Japan's ambitious plan to seize worldwide leadership in the computing industry. The plan focuses on Artificial Intelligence, raising the possibility that Japan may reap most of the profits derived from expensive basic research done in the United States.

In their extremely influential book, *The Fifth Generation*, Edward A. Feigenbaum and Pamela McCorduck explain why we in the United States should be concerned, making the following points along the way:

Knowledge is the new wealth of nations. The old wealth had to do with material things. This new wealth has to do with acquiring and using superior knowledge to design smarter, manufacture better, market stronger, and generally outwit and outperform competition, both domestic and international. Feigenbaum and McCorduck believe that Artificial Intelligence is the key to acquiring and using superior knowledge and that Artificial Intelligence will soon become a major determinant of who is on top economically.

The second computer revolution is the one that matters. The second computer revolution is the revolution based on Artificial Intelligence. It is the one that matters because strength in Artificial Intelligence ensures strength at everything that Artificial Intelligence can help with. And that may be just about everything.

The Feigenbaum-McCorduck scenario is unsettling. Consequently there is a natural tendency to create counterscenarios. Some critics argue, for example, that there is nothing to worry about – that the Japanese cannot win – because the Fifth Generation project's concrete goals are impossibly ambitious. A contrary view is that they cannot lose, for the Fifth Generation is in reality a rapid education effort aimed at making a broad yet quick introduction of the artificial-intelligence perspective into Japanese industry. It does not matter if the public goals are reached because succeeding with the education effort is inevitable. Consequently, any viable plan for keeping the United States competitive in Artificial Intelligence must include a strong educational component.

What Should Serious Universities Do?

We are not far from the day when all freshmen in science and engineering schools will have personal computers. MIT, under the direction of Gerald L. Wilson, Dean of Engineering, recently began an ambitious project designed to revolutionize the use of computers at the university level. The project involves installing and linking together over 3,000 work stations around campus. Faculty, staff, and students will work together to develop imaginative and innovative ways to learn more and to learn better.

How will we use all those computers to learn more and to learn better? One answer lies in Seymour Papert's book, *Mindstorms*. Papert first points out that one of the best ways to learn something is to teach it to someone else. Papert then champions the idea that the student might as well be a computer.

Following Papert's lead, we argue that science and engineering schools should teach freshmen how to create programs with human-like intelligence. People who have created such programs will have a better understanding of what it means for a person to become an expert. Since much of education is devoted to making human experts, future human experts should know what is involved as soon as possible.

The student who knows about expert programs can approach his ordinary subjects expecting to learn what kind of knowledge is involved, how that knowledge should be represented, what procedures exist for working with the knowledge, how much knowledge is needed, and what exactly the knowledge is. When the student approaches, say, electrical network theory, he will be more comfortable because he will understand that Kirchoff's laws and circuit connections constitute constraint knowledge. He will see that differential equations provide useful representations for that knowledge, learn that various transform procedures exist for working with the knowledge, will be comforted by observing that there is not too much knowledge, and will note, in particular, that the sum of the currents into any node is zero.

All this can happen because we humans learn a great deal through analogies, and programs with humanlike intelligence are splendid sources of rich analogies for our own human thinking.

Even now there are plenty of illustrative systems, for there are systems that analyze circuits, sequence proteins, synthesize chemical compounds, design integrated circuits, interpret instrument signals, lay out gearbox drive trains, configure computers, and diagnose disease.

The time to begin, of course, is now, before more conservative computer-oriented subjects establish deep roots and become difficult to replace.

What Should Serious Companies Do?

In many major Japanese corporate research centers, there are a few people who speak English conspicuously better than the rest. In general these are the elite few who were selected early in their careers to spend a year in the United States to absorb ideas and attitudes.

When such people write to the MIT Artificial Intelligence Laboratory asking to visit, they never question ownership of patent rights or request financial support. When they come, they work day and night to complete projects that contribute to the reputations of their hosts. But when they leave the United States, they know what to do and how to do it, carrying abilities that no book can teach.

We need to adapt this practice to our own use, for it is the fastest way of transferring technology from the place that has it to the place that needs it. We need our own domestic visiting tradition. One approach is to develop multimonth, in-house training programs, but few companies have enough in-house expertise to have such programs. Another approach is to do what the Japanese do: most serious companies should try to send their best young technical people to a strong university research center for a year.

But domestic visiting is not our tradition, and there are objections to making it our tradition. The obvious objections have flaws.

Why shouldn't my company simply hire some bright PhDs when we need them? There are too few to go around. Besides, if your company makes widgets, you want a person passionate about widgets to make better widgets using Artificial Intelligence. It is difficult to divert a person whose passion is Artificial Intelligence into widget making.

How can my company possibly spare its best person for a year? If you do not put someone in a United States research center, your Japanese competitor will.

What about protecting my company's rights to employees' patents? The best thing to do about patents is to forget them. The point of visits is to learn for the medium and long term, not to develop instant products.

Won't another company try to recruit my company's person? Certainly someone will try. You will have to compensate your person more since he will be worth more. You have an advantage though – you have demonstated that you believe in your employee and in his future. In addition, by placing your employee in a university research community, you will have an on-site recruiter for graduating students, a powerful asset.

Won't my company's person collaborate with a competitor's person on a research project that the competitor will be able to use? Probably not. The idea is to absorb methods and views, not to invent something proprietary. But in any event, the situation is symmetric. The real losers are the companies that do not have anyone visiting university research laboratories.

How can my company get a person into an appropriate center? A company that wanted to place a person in a university artificial-intelligence center a few years ago had to place the person at MIT, Stanford, or Carnegie-Mellon. Fortunately the opportunities are expanding rapidly. Today there are twenty or so American universities with strong efforts and talented people. Enter into discussions with university researchers whose interests resonate with yours and offer to send your best person for a year. It is hard to turn down the opportunity to have a few salary-free, mature, hard-working people around.

Shouldn't my company insist its employees earn credits and work toward degrees? No. The need is to educate people who work in other fields to bring the methods of Artificial Intelligence to those fields. A degree in Artificial Intelligence at any level may be a diversion.

In the end, our inertias may be too great, and we may need to stimulate ourselves as a country to do this. There is a lot of room for legislators to be innovative: by using government money, by devising favorable tax deals, or by inventing favorable government-contractor regulations. Since the goal is to ensure the long-range economic survival of our country, there will be a lot of credit for those in Washington who lead the way.

Balancing Euphoria with Reality

Euphoria about the future of Artificial Intelligence is in the air. But we must be certain to balance that euphoria with reality. It will take time and hard work to transform the commercial potential of Artificial Intelligence into achievements.

We must encourage the rapid transfer of technologies developed in university research laboratories to industrial development and production engineering laboratories.

We must develop mechanisms for educating people. Both undergraduate students and people already working in industry must learn to use the ideas of Artificial Intelligence.

And we must provide the seed corn for our future: in our rush toward commercialization, we must find ways to keep university research centers healthy and strong. Such centers need top-notch researchers, adequate space, superior computing resources, and time for basic research. Satisfying these needs takes money. But satisfying these needs ensures the success of the imaginative projects, many with no obvious commercial potential, that will lead us into the future.

How to Learn More

We hope that this book has stimulated interest. Here are some ways to learn more:

First, there are many books that provide good introductions to the field. These include: *Artificial Intelligence, Second Edition* (Winston), *Building Expert Systems* (Hayes-Roth, Waterman, and Lenat), *Computer Vision* (Ballard and Brown), *LISP* (Winston and Horn), and *Robot Manipulators: Mathematics, Programming, and Control* (Paul), all cited in the bibliography.

Second, there are journals. Every library should subscribe to *Artificial Intelligence* (North Holland Publishing Company, Amsterdam), to *The AI Magazine* (American Association for Artificial Intelligence, Menlo Park, CA) and perhaps to a half dozen other, more specialized journals, like the *International Journal of Robotics Research* (The MIT Press, Cambridge, MA).

Third, there are many established academic research centers that offer courses and have active artificial-intelligence work. In addition there are research companies like SRI International and BBN. All publish technical memoranda and reports.

Fourth, there are professional meetings, particularly the biannual International Joint Conference on Artificial Intelligence and the annual meeting of the American Association for Artificial Intelligence (not held in years when the international conference is in North America).

And finally, there are companies in the expert-systems business that sell their expertise. Teknowledge was the first expert-systems company to be formed. Their business, and now that of others, is to build knowledge systems that have exceptionally high value and that solve problems that other technologies cannot cope with. Inference Corporation has a similar business plan. Others, with more specialized objectives, are Applied Expert Systems and Syntelligence, both of which propose to explore the applications of expert-systems technology to the financial world. Intelligenetics is oriented toward a combination of Artificial Intelligence and biomedical applications. Computer Thought works in the area of computer-aided education. Artificial Intelligence Corporation and Semantec offer products for natural language interaction, and Cognitive Systems combines work in natural language with work in expert systems. While these are representative, there are others, and the list is lengthening rapidly.

Bibliography

Abelson, Harold, and Andrea diSessa, *Turtle Geometry*, MIT Press, Cambridge, MA, 1981.

Ballard, Dana H., and Christopher Brown, *Computer Vision*, Prentice-Hall, Englewood Cliffs, NJ, 1982.

Brady, J. Michael (editor), *Computer Vision*, North-Holland, Amsterdam, 1981.

Brady, J. Michael, John M. Hollerbach, Timothy L. Johnson, Tomás Lozano-Pérez, and Matthew T. Mason (editors), *Robot Motion: Planning and Control*, MIT Press, Cambridge, MA, 1982.

Brou, Philippe, "Finding the Orientation of Objects in Vector Maps," PhD Thesis, Massachusetts Institute of Technology, Cambridge, MA, 1983.

Brown, John S., Richard R. Burton, and Johan de Kleer, "Pedagogical, Natural Language and Knowledge Engineering Techniques in SOPHIE I, II, and III," in *Intelligent Tutoring Systems*, edited by D. Sleeman and J. S. Brown, Academic Press, London, England, 1982.

Buchanan, Bruce G., and Edward H. Shortliffe, *Rule-Based Expert Programs: the MYCIN Experiments of the Stanford Heuristic Programming Project*, Addison-Wesley, Reading, MA, 1984.

Campbell, A. N., V. F. Hollister, Richard O. Duda, and Peter E. Hart, "Recognition of a Hidden Mineral Deposit by an Artificial Intelligence Program," *Science*, vol. 217, no. 3, 1982.

Clocksin, William F., and Christopher S. Mellish, *Programming in Prolog*, Springer-Verlag, New York, 1981.

Cullingford, Richard E., "Script Appication: Computer Understanding of Newspaper Stories," Ph.D. Thesis, Yale University, New Haven, CT, 1978.

Davis, Randall, "Expert Systems: Where Are We? And Where Do We Go from Here," Report AIM-665, Artificial Intelligence Laboratory, Massachusetts Institute of Technology, Cambridge, MA, 1982.

Davis, Randall, and Jonathan King, "An Overview of Production Systems," in *Machine Intelligence 8*, edited by Edward W. Elcock and Donald Michie, John Wiley and Sons, New York, 1977.

Davis, Randall, and Douglas B. Lenat, *Knowledge-Based Systems in Artificial Intelligence*, McGraw-Hill Book Company, New York, 1982.

Davis, Randall, Bruce G. Buchanan, and Edward H. Shortliffe, "Production Rules as a Representation for a Knowledge-Based Consultation Program," *Artificial Intelligence*, vol. 8, no. 1, 1977.

Davis, Randall, Howard Austin, Ingrid Carlbom, Bud Frawley, Paul Pruchnik, Rich Sneiderman, and Al Gilreath, "The Dipmeter Advisor: Interpretation of Geological Signals," *Seventh International Joint Conference on Artificial Intelligence*, Vancouver, British Columbia, Canada, 1981.

DeJong, Gerald F., "Skimming Stories in Real Time: An Experiment in Integrated Understanding," Ph.D. Thesis, Yale University, New Haven, CT, 1979.

de Kleer, Johan, and John S. Brown, "Assumptions and Ambiguities in Mechanistic Mental Models," in *Mental Models*, edited by D. Gentner and A. S. Stevens, Lawrence Erlbaum Associates, Hillsdale, NJ, 1983.

Dipmeter Interpretation: Volume I—Fundamentals, Schlumberger, 1981.

Gershman, A., "Building a Geological Expert System for Dipmeter Interpretation," *Proceedings of the European Conference on Artificial Intelligence*, July, 1982.

Gleason, Gerald J. and Gerald J. Agin, "A Modular System for Sensor-controlled Manipulation and Inspection," *Proceedings of the 9th International Symposium on Industrial Robots*, Washington, D.C., published by Society of Manufacturing Engineers, Dearborn, Michigan, March 1979.

Feigenbaum, Edward A., and Pamela McCorduck, *The Fifth Generation*, Addison-Wesley, Reading, MA, 1983.

Harris, Larry R., "A High Performance Natural Language Processor for Data Base Query," *ACM SIGART Newsletter*, vol. 61, 1977.

Hart, Peter E., Richard O. Duda, and M. T. Einaudi, "PROSPECTOR—A Computer-based Consultation System for Mineral Exploration," *Mathematical Geology*, vol. 10, no. 5, 1978.

Hayes-Roth, Frederick, Donald A. Waterman, and Douglas B. Lenat (editors), *Building Expert Systems*, Addison-Wesley, Reading, MA, 1983.

Hewitt, Carl E., and Peter de Jong, "Open Systems," Report AIM-691, Artificial Intelligence Laboratory, Massachusetts Institute of Technology, Cambridge, MA, 1982.

Hillis, W. Daniel, "The Connection Machine," Report AIM-646, Artificial Intelligence Laboratory, Massachusetts Institute of Technology, Cambridge, MA, 1981.

Hillis, W. Daniel, "A High Resolution Imaging Touch Sensor," *International Journal of Robotics Research*, vol. 1, no. 2, 1982. Based on a MS thesis, Massachusetts Institute of Technology, Cambridge, MA, 1981.

Holland, Stephen W., Lothar Rossol, and Mitchell R. Ward, "CONSIGHT-I: A Vision-controlled Robot System for Transferring Parts from Belt Conveyors," in *Computer Vision and Sensor-based Robots*, edited by George G. Dodd and Lothar Rossol, Plenum Press, New York, 1979.

Kornfeld, William A., and Carl E. Hewitt, "The Scientific Community Metaphor," *IEEE Transactions on Systems, Man, and Cybernetics*, vol. SMC-11, no. 1, 1981.

Lehnert, Wendy G., Michael G. Dyer, Peter N. Johnson, C. J. Yang, and Steve Harley, "BORIS—An Experiment in In-Depth Understanding of Narratives," *Artificial Intelligence*, vol. 20, no. 1, 1983.

Lozano-Pérez, Tomás, "Robot Programming," Report AIM-698, Artificial Intelligence Laboratory, Massachusetts Institute of Technology, Cambridge, MA, 1982.

Mason, Matthew T., "Compliance and Force Control for Computer Controlled Manipulators," *IEEE Transactions on Systems, Man, and Cybernetics*, vol. SCM-11, no. 6, 1981. Based on a MS thesis, Massachusetts Institute of Technology, Cambridge, MA, 1979.

McDermott, John, "R1: A Rule-Based Configurer of Computer Systems," *Artificial Intelligence*, vol. 19, no. 1, 1982.

McDermott, John, "R1's Formative Years," *AI Magazine*, vol. 2, no. 2, 1982.

McDermott, John, "Domain Knowledge and the Design Process," Proceedings of 18th Design Automation Conference, Nashville, TN, 1981, *Design Studies*, vol. 3, no. 1, 1982.

McDermott, John, "XSEL: A Computer Salesperson's Assistant," in Machine Intelligence, edited by J. Hayes and D. Michie, 1982.

McDermott, John and Barbara Steel, "Extending a Knowledge-Based System to Deal with Ad Hoc Constraints," *Seventh International Joint Conference on Artificial Intelligence*, Vancouver, British Columbia, Canada, 1981.

Michie, Donald (editor), *Expert Systems in the Micro-Electronic Age*, Edinburgh University Press, Edinburgh, Scotland, 1979.

Minsky, Marvin, *The Society of Mind*, book in preparation.

Minsky, Marvin, "Plain Talk about Neurodevelopmental Epistemology," *Fifth International Joint Conference on Artificial Intelligence*, Cambridge, MA, 1977.

Minsky, Marvin, "K-lines: A Theory of Memory," *Cognitive Science*, vol. 4, no. 1, 1980.

Newell, Allen, and Herbert A. Simon, *Human Problem Solving*, Prentice-Hall, Englewood Cliffs, NJ, 1972.

Ohashi, T., S. Miyakawa, Y. Arai, S. Inoshita, and A. Yamada, "The Development of Automatic Assembly Line for VTR Mechanisms," presented at CIRP Conference on Assembly Automation, Amherst, MA, June 1983.

Papert, Seymour, *Mindstorms*, Basic Books, New York, 1981.

Paul, Richard P., *Robot Manipulators: Mathematics, Programming, and Control*, MIT Press, Cambridge, MA, 1981.

Pople, Harry E., Jr., "On the Mechanization of Abductive Logic," *Third International Joint Conference on Artificial Intelligence*, Stanford, CA, 1973.

Pople, Harry E., Jr., "Heuristic Methods for Imposing Structure on Ill-Structured Problems: The Structuring of Medical Diagnostics," in *Artificial Intelligence in Medicine*, edited by Peter Szolovits, Westview Press, Boulder, CO, 1982.

Raibert, Marc H., and Ivan Sutherland, "Machines That Walk," *Scientific American*, vol. 248, no. 1, 1983.

Rich, Charles, and Howard E. Shrobe, "Initial Report on a LISP Programmer's Apprentice," *IEEE Transactions on Software Engineering*, vol. SE-4, no. 6, 1978.

Rieger, Charles J. "Conceptual Memory and Inference," in *Conceptual Information Processing*, edited by Roger C. Schank, North Holland, Amsterdam, 1975.

Salisbury, J. Kenneth, Jr., and John J. Craig, "Articulated Hands: Force Control and Kinematic Issues," *International Journal of Robotics Research*, vol. 1, no. 1, 1982.

Salisbury, J. Kenneth, Jr., and B. Roth, "Kinematic and force Analysis of Articulated Mechanical Hands," *Journal of Mechanisms, Transmissions, and Automation in Design*, vol. 105, 1983.

Schank, Roger C., "Conceptual Dependency: A Theory of Natural Language Understanding," *Cognitive Psychology*, 1972, 3(4), 552-631.

Schank, Roger C., *Dynamic Memory*, Cambridge University Press, Cambridge, England, 1982.

Schank, R. C., N. Goldman, C. Rieger, and C. Riesbeck, "Inference and Paraphrase by Computer," *Journal of the ACM*, vol. 20, no. 1, 1975., pp. 309-328.

Sheil, Beau, "Power Tools for Programmers," *Datamation*, February, 1983.

Shortliffe, Edward H., *MYCIN: Computer-based Medical Consultations*, Elsevier, New York, 1976. Based on a PhD thesis, Stanford University, Stanford, CA, 1974.

Shortliffe, Edward H., and Bruce G. Buchanan, "A Model of Inexact Reasoning in Medicine," *Mathematical Biosciences*, vol. 23, 1975.

Smith, Brian C. "Reflection and Semantics in LISP," *Proceedings of the 1984 Principles of Programming Languages Conference of the ACM (POPL)*, February, 1984.

Smith, Reid, G. and James D. Baker, "The DIPMETER ADVISOR System, A Case Study in Commerical Expert System Development," *Schlumberger Doll Research Technical Report*.

Stallman, Richard M., and Gerald J. Sussman, "Forward Reasoning and Dependency-directed Backtracking in a System for Computer-aided Circuit Analysis," *Artificial Intelligence*, vol. 9, no. 2, 1977.

Stevens, Albert L., R. Bruce Roberts, Larry S. Stead, Kenneth D. Forbus, Cindy Steinberg, and Brian C. Smith, "Steamer: Advanced Computer Aided Instruction in Propulsion Engineering," Report 4702, Bolt, Beranek and Newman, Cambridge, MA, 1981.

Sussman, Gerald J., and Richard M. Stallman, "Heuristic Techniques in Computer Aided Circuit Analysis," *IEEE Transactions on Circuits and Systems*, vol. CAS-22, no. 11, 1975.

Szolovits, Peter (editor), *Artificial Intelligence in Medicine*, Westview Press, Boulder, CO, 1982.

Szolovits, Peter, Lowell B. Hawkinson, and William A. Martin, "An Overview of OWL, a Language for Knowledge Representation," Report TM-86, Laboratory of Computer Science, Massachusetts Institute of Technology, Cambridge, MA, 1977.

VanderBrug, G. J., D. Wilt, and J. Davis, "Robotic Assembly of Keycaps to Keyboard Arrays," *Robots 7*, Dearborn, Michigan, April 1983.

Villers, Philippe, "Megassembly: The Sleeping Giant of Robotics," in *Decade of Robotics*, IFS Publications, 1983.

Villers, Philippe, "Present Industrial Use of Vision Sensors for Robot Guidance," *Proceedings of the 12th International Symposium on Industrial Robots*, Paris, France, June, 1982.

Villers, Philippe, "The Role of Vision in Industrial Robotic Systems and Inspections," Proceedings of Electro 83, New York, New York, April 1983.

Waters, Richard C., "The Programmer's Apprentice: Knowledge Based Program Editing," *IEEE Transactions on Software Engineering*, vol. SE-8, no. 1, 1982.

Williams, Michael D., James Hollan, and Albert L. Stevens, "An Overview of STEAMER: An Advanced Computer Assisted Instructional System for Propulsion Engineering," *Behavior Research Methods and Instrumentation*, vol. 2, no. 13, 1981.

Winston, Patrick Henry, *Artificial Intelligence, Second Edition*, Addison-Wesley, Reading, MA, 1984.

Winston, Patrick Henry, "Learning New Principles from Precedents and Exercises," *Artificial Intelligence*, vol. 19, no. 3, 1982.

Winston, Patrick Henry and Richard Henry Brown (editors), *Artificial Intelligence: An MIT Perspective, vol. 1*, MIT Press, Cambridge, MA, 1979.

Winston, Patrick Henry, and Richard Henry Brown (editors), *Artificial Intelligence: An MIT Perspective, vol. 2*, MIT Press, Cambridge, MA, 1979.

Winston, Patrick Henry, and Berthold K. P. Horn, *LISP*, Addison-Wesley, Reading, MA, 1981.

Winston, Patrick Henry, Thomas O. Binford, Boris Katz, and Michael R. Lowry, "Learning Physical Descriptions from Functional Definitions, Examples, and Precedents," *National Conference on Artificial Intelligence*, Washington, D. C., 1983.

Glossary

ABEL

Experimental medical system for diagnosing acid/base electrolyte disorders.

Actor

Procedure that does its work by generating new actors and by sending messages to other actors.

ADA

General-purpose computer programming language intended to be the primary language used in U.S. defense applications.

Advisory systems

Expert system that interacts with a person in the style of giving advice rather than in the style of dictating commands. Generally advisory systems have mechanisms for explaining their advice and for allowing their users to interact at a detail level comfortable to the user.

ALGOL

Early post-FORTRAN, general-purpose, high-level programming language. In the United States ALGOL has mostly given way to PASCAL, a descendant, which is more powerful and easier to use.

AL

Experimental robot programming language on which AML is based in part.

AML

Modern manipulator-oriented programming language for robot programming. AML is a product of International Business Machines.

APL

Acronym for a programming language. APL is popular because of its ability to do certain mathematical calculations extremely compactly.

Artificial Intelligence

Science of making machines intelligent in order to make them more useful and to understand intelligence.

AUTOVISION^R II

Vision system for robot applications. AUTOVISION^R II is a product of Automatix, Incorporated, of Billerica, Massachusetts.

Backward chaining

That problem-solving technique characterized by working backward from hypothesized conclusions toward known facts.

BASIC

Simple, easy-to-learn programming language introduced at Dartmouth College.

Bit-map display

Display consisting of a large array of tiny, individually controllable dots. Advanced types may have a million or more dots, each of which may be more or less bright, in color, or both.

BORIS

Experimental, narrative-understanding natural language system developed by Roger Schank and his students.

C

Popular programming language, especially for systems programming.

CAD

Acronym for computer-aided design.

CAD/CAM

Acronym for computer-aided design and computer-aided manufacturing.

CADUCEUS

Diagnosis system for internal medicine under development by Harry E. Pople, Jr., and Jack D. Myers, M.D., at the University of Pittsburgh. Formerly called INTERNIST.

CALISTO

Experimental system for modeling and monitoring large projects.

CASNET

Experimental system for dealing with disease processes. Usually associated with a specific application focusing on glaucoma. Also the acronym for causal-associative network.

Causal model

Model in which the causal relations among various actions and events are represented explicitly.

CommonLISP

Popular dialect of LISP that is likely to become a sort of standard.

Configure

To specify how the various parts of a computer system are to be arranged.

CONSIGHT

Industrial object-recognition system, developed by General Motors, that uses special lighting to produce silhouette-like images.

CPU

Acronym for $\underline{c}$entral $\underline{p}$rocessing $\underline{u}$nit, that part of a computer that does the computing. Other key parts are the memory modules and the input-output modules.

Cursor

Prominent, easily seen, user-controlled symbol that identifies a location on a terminal's screen.

DARPA

Acronym for the $\underline{D}$efense $\underline{A}$dvanced $\underline{R}$esearch $\underline{P}$rojects $\underline{A}$gency of the U.S. Defense Department.

DENDRAL

Early rule-based expert system that helps determine organic-compound structure using data from mass spectrometers and nuclear magnetic resonance machines.

DIPMETER ADVISOR

Expert system that helps analyze dipmeter data. The dipmeter is an important tool used in the oil industry to determine subsurface tilt. The dipmeter produces tilt and tilt-direction data as it moves through an oil well bore hole.

Dynabook

Early specification for a book-sized computer for education and entertainment proposed by Alan Kay. The Dynabook concept was a motivating banner when Kay was at the Xerox's Palo Alto Research Laboratory.

EMYCIN

Nonspecific part of MYCIN consisting of what is left when the rules are removed. EMYCIN becomes a new problem solver by adding rules for a different problem domain.

End effector

Robot's hand or gripper.

Ethernet

Local network for sending messages between computers by way of a single coaxial cable that snakes through all of the computers to be connected. A coaxial cable is a cable consisting of a central wire surrounded by a grounded cylindrical shielding sheath.

Expert system

System that performs a task that normally takes humans a long time to acquire. Most expert systems are rule-based systems. Most are able to solve simple problems quickly and to explain their own reasoning, but few are able to break their own rules, to run simulations, to take a different perspective, or to learn.

EXPRESS

Sophisticated financial modeling system. EXPRESS is a product of Management Decision Systems.

Fifth generation

Label used by the Japanese for their ambitious program to achieve supremacy in the computer business. Separated from previous generations by higher speed and by employment of Artificial Intelligence.

Flex Machine

Early personal computer designed by Alan Kay. In his words, "a noble failure."

FOCUS

Modern, sophisticated language for data-base interaction.

FORTRAN

Early programming language that still dominates scientific computing by virtue of the massive amount of accumulated software that has been written using it. FORTRAN is the acronym for formula translator.

Forward chaining

Problem-solving technique characterized by working forward from known facts toward conclusions.

FRUMP

Acronym for fast reading and understanding memory program. FRUMP is experimental language understanding system developed by Gerald F. DeJong to scan the UPI newswire, locating and summarizing stories belonging to certain classes.

Gate-array technology

Approach to integrated circuit design. Rather than starting over with a blank slate each time, the circuit designer adds specializing detail to a partially wired array of basic circuit elements.

Hacker

Person devoted to intricate computer programming, particularly that programming done for its own sake. A good hacker is an expert programmer. A bad hacker is a poor programmer.

Hardware debugging

Process of finding and fixing malfunctioning electronic equipment, particularly digital equipment.

HARPY

Simple experimental speech-understanding system intended to show what can be done without resorting to sophisticated techniques.

HEARSAY II

Sophisticated experimental speech-understanding system stressing the importance of multiple specialized procedures and complicated techniques for procedure interaction.

Heuristic

Anything that helps to guide problem solving. Use is generally restricted to those things that are not guaranteed to be successful.

IC

Acronym for integrated circuit, an electronic circuit consisting of a chunk of semiconducting material on which many electronic devices have been simultaneously fabricated. Modern techniques make it possible for individual ICs to contain tens of thousands of transistors.

INTELLECT

First commercially successful natural language interface. INTELLECT is sold by Artificial Intelligence, Incorporated, of Waltham, Massachusetts.

Intelligent Robot

Rrobot backed by powerful reasoning software for things like sensing, recognition, mating, trajectory planning, and error recovery.

InterLISP D

Dialect of LISP championed particularly by Xerox.

INTERNIST

Former name of a diagnosis system for internal medicine. See CADUCEUS.

Knowledge Engineer

One who designs and builds expert systems.

Knowledge Representation

A vocabulary of symbols and some conventions for arranging them so as to describe things.

LED

Acronym for light-emitting diode.

Link

Early personal computer, perhaps the first.

LISP

Popular programming language for use in Artificial Intelligence. LISP is the acronym for list processing language. LISP was the first language to concentrate on working with symbols instead of numbers. Although introduced by John McCarthy in the early 1960s, continuous development has enabled LISP to remain dominant in Artificial Intelligence. Lately LISP has proved to be an outstanding language for systems programming as well.

LOGO

Education-oriented programming language conceived by Seymour Papert and his associates. LOGO is intended to help people learn about powerful ideas, such as feedback, by seeing those ideas at work in programs. LOGO is suitable for children as well as for adults.

LSI

See VLSI.

MACSYMA

Large computer system with procedures for helping people do complicated applied mathematics developed by Joel Moses and his colleagues at the Massachusetts Institute of Technology.

Manipulator-oriented language

Programming language for describing exactly where a robot's arm and gripper should go and when. To be contrasted with task-oriented languages for describing what the effect of robot action should be.

MARGIE

Early experimental language-understanding and paraphrase-generating system developed by Roger Schank and his students. A principal purpose was to show that language can be understood without attention to details of syntax.

Megassembly systems

Multistation, multiproduct assembly systems containing at least ten robots.

META-DENDRAL

Learning system designed to generate rules for DENDRAL automatically.

Mouse

Hand-held device that is rolled about on a table to move a terminal's cursor.

MYCIN

Early rule-based expert system, developed by Edward H. Shortliffe, M.D., that helps to determine the exact identity of an infection of the blood and that helps to prescribe the appropriate antibiotic.

Nand

Basic logical circuit used in designing digital hardware. The acronym for not and.

Nor

Basic logical circuit used in designing digital hardware. The acronym for not or.

Object-oriented language

In robotics a synonym for task-oriented language. In general use a programming language in which procedures for doing things are accessed through descriptions of the things to be worked on.

PASCAL

Popular general-purpose, high-level programming language, descendant from ALGOL.

PC

Acronym for personal computer, a computer that is powerful enough to be user friendly and inexpensive enough to be nonshared.

Personal computer

See PC.

PERT

Technique for charting project plans that exposes the dependency of each task on prior tasks. A principal use is in identifying a project's critical path, that is, that set of tasks for which any completion delay ensures delay of the entire project.

ΦNIX

Automatic program synthesizer, developed by Schlumberger, specialized to helping oil experts working with rock models and bore-hole log data. ΦNIX generates rock-constituent computing FORTRAN programs from equations representing hypothesized geology.

Pixel

Acronym for picture element. Inside a computer, an image is represented as an array of pixel values representing the brightness at various points on whatever retina-like sensor is used.

PLANNER

Extinct experimental programming language similar in many respects to modern PROLOG.

PL/1

Popular general-purpose programming language.

POLITICS

Experimental narrative-understanding natural language system developed by Roger Schank and his students. Successor to MARGIE, predecessor of BORIS.

Programmer's apprentice

System that helps programmers program by keeping track of decisions, recalling program skeletons, automatically testing revised programs, supporting natural language interaction, and translating to and from various program representations.

Power tool

Any powerful programming device that dramatically increases programmer productivity.

PROLOG

Programming language based on formal logic. PROLOG is the language the Japanese have adopted as the main language for their Fifth Generation Computer Project.

PROSPECTOR

Experimental expert system intended to help geologists interpret mineral data and predict the location of mineral deposits. In one landmark experiment PROSPECTOR correctly pointed to a major unknown extension of a known molybdenum deposit.

PUFF

Expert system developed for aiding in the diagnosis of respiratory diseases.

QUIP

Experimental work station, under development by Schlumberger, for geologists oriented toward enabling rapid testing of geological and rock models.

R1

An alias. See XCON.

RAIL[R]

Modern programming language for robot programming. A product of Automatix, Incorporated, of Billerica, Massachusetts.

RAMUS

Modern, sophisticated language for data-base interaction.

RCC

Acronym for remote center compliance device, a mechanical arrangement of linkages that easily inserts peglike objects into tight-fitting holes. The RCC has a promising but largely neglected future in automated assembly.

Robotics science

Science of connecting perception to action through intelligent programs.

Rule-based system

System in which knowledge is stored in the form of simple if-then or condition-action rules.

SIMULA

One of the first object-oriented programming languages. Originally intended for simulation work.

SKETCHPAD

Early experimental system for computer-aided design.

SMALLTALK

Programming language developed at Xerox's Palo Alto Research Laboratory. SMALLTALK has popularized a style of programming according to which procedures communicate by sending each other messages. SMALLTALK is considered especially good for graphics-oriented programming.

SOPHIE

Experimental instruction system, developed by John Seely Brown, that taught students how to debug electronic circuits.

STEAMER

Experimental instruction system that teaches propulsion engineering. Features sophisticated procedures for graphics-oriented simulation and for qualitative reasoning.

Stiction

Static friction, the force that tends to keep two mated surfaces from moving relative to one another.

Task-oriented language

Programming language for describing what the effect of robot action should be. To be contrasted with manipulator-oriented languages for describing exactly where a robot's arm and gripper should go and when.

TEIRESIAS
Experimental system developed by Randall Davis for helping human experts formulate rules for rule-based expert systems.

VAL
Manipulator-oriented programming language for robot programming. A product of Unimation, Incorporated, of Danbury, Connecticut.

VAX
Line of powerful computers manufactured by Digital Equipment Corporation.

VISICALC
First of the electronic-worksheet personal computer software products.

VLSI
Acronym for very-large-scale integration, the process of producing integrated circuits containing tens of thousands of electronic devices.

VMS
Widely-used operating system developed by Digital Equipment Corporation for its line of computers.

UNIX
Popular operating system developed and licensed by Bell Telephone Laboratories.

WAVE
Early experimental robot programming language on which VAL was based in part.

Window system
A system that divides a terminal's screen into pieces as when various-sized pieces of paper are arranged on a desk.

Work station
Computer system that acts as a partner to a person, in work or play, greatly facilitating productivity.

XCON

Hugely successful expert system developed to configure computers—that is, to specify how all the components should be placed and how they should be connected. XCON, sometimes called R1, was jointly developed by Digital Equipment Corporation and Carnegie-Mellon University.

XSEL

Expert system for assisting computer salespeople.

XSITE

Expert system for helping to ensure that a site can handle the necessary power, air conditioning, and space for a computer installation.

Index

DATE DUE

GAYLORD			PRINTED IN U.S.A.